D0383750

Mover
of
Men
and
Mountains

MOVER OF MEN AND MOUNTAINS

THE AUTOBIOGRAPHY OF

R. G. LeTourneau

MOODY PUBLISHERS
CHICAGO

© 1960, 1967 by Prentice-Hall, Inc.
Reprinted by Special Arrangement
MOODY PRESS EDITION 1967, 1972

Cover design: Ragont Design
Illustration: Ron Mazellan

Library of Congress Catalog Card Number
60-8319

ISBN-13: 978-0-8024-3818-8

We hope you enjoy this book from Moody Publishers.
Our goal is to provide high-quality, thought-provoking
books and products that connect truth to your real needs and
challenges. For more information on other books and products written and produced from a biblical perspective, go to
www.moodypublishers.com or write to:

Moody Publishers
820 N. LaSalle Boulevard
Chicago, IL 60610

53

With deep love and appreciation, I dedicate this book to my beloved partner and wife, Evelyn, who for over four decades has always been by my side to give me love, cooperation, and understanding when others doubted. Through the years she has joined me in mutual devotion and prayer to our Heavenly Father and has helped me keep faith when the vision of others was limited—truly a helpmate given by God.

1

For 25 years or more, I've been traveling this land of ours and a few foreign countries trying to teach and preach by word of mouth and example, that a Christian businessman owes as much to God as a preacher does. The rest of the time I build machinery, almost any kind of machinery as long as it is big, and powerful, and can move around to do things no other machine could do before. Some people think I'm all mixed up—that you can't serve the Lord and business, too, but that's just the point. God needs businessmen as partners as well as preachers. When He created the world and everything in it, He didn't mean for us to stop there and say, "God, You've done it all. There's nothing left for us to build." He wanted us to take off from there and really build for His greater glory.

I speak in churches and auditoriums large and small across the land, usually about six times a week, and most often I start out by saying, "I am just a mechanic whom the Lord has blessed." I'll let that serve as a starter here. As a mechanic, I like my machinery because I learned early that man is worth what man produces, and good machines help him produce more. Had I been born 100 years earlier, I would have been a good blacksmith, as men like me had been since the Bronze Age. But the Lord chose to put me here when electric motors and gasoline engines were just starting to turn, and with His blessings I have been able to take part in and contribute to the development of those great, heavy-construction machines that have helped produce our twentieth century.

Recently I built an eight-wheeled digger that out-produces the work of thousands of men at the time I was born. Instead of pushing a 100-pound wheelbarrow, the operator pushes a button and picks up the loads of 1,500 wheelbarrows, rolling off with them at 15 mph instead of two. Its rubber-tired wheels are eight feet high by over three feet wide, and inside the hub of each wheel is an electric motor that delivers more power than the giant steam engines of my youth. When it dips its twin buckets into the ground, it scoops up 150 tons of dirt in two minutes, and then lopes off to dump its load at the push of another button. Distance for distance it moves for eight cents a cubic yard what cost a dollar when I started out in business, and dollars were about three times their present size then.

I find a great deal of satisfaction in watching that brute in action, and more in the challenge of finding some better way of getting it to move 200 tons even more efficiently. In my talks, along with the statement that I am just a mechanic whom the Lord has blessed, I frequently add that He uses the weak to confound the mighty. There is no logical explanation in the world to account for my development of that digger. It combines two huge mobile Diesel engines with AC generators and DC generators, and it pours enough electricity to light a small town into a score of AC and DC motors. Yet I never got past the seventh grade in school. At the age of 30 my garage had failed and I was $5,000 in debt. At the age of 44

I lost so heavily on contracts that my employees, with more faith in me than I had in myself, took up a collection to get me back on my feet. That was me, working on my own.

If there is no logical explanation of my development of the digger, there is a theological one, available to all of us, including the weakest. By accepting God as your partner, no limit can be placed on what can be achieved. But God is no remote partner, satisfied if you go to church on Sunday and drop some religious money—the small change that goes to church—on the platter. He isn't overwhelmed if you read the Bible once in a while and obey the Golden Rule. That isn't active Christianity, but just a half-hearted way of getting along. When you go into partnership with God, you've got a Partner closer and more active than any human partner you can ever get. He participates fully in everything you let Him do, and when you start putting on airs, and thinking you're doing it with your own head of steam, He can set you down quicker and harder than a thunderbolt. There's nothing dull about being in partnership with God.

God has set me down with some terrific jolts from time to time, but when my attitude has improved, and He has seen genuine repentance, He is the only Partner Who can supply total forgiveness. Not that He is easily fooled. As one preacher put it, "God will forgive your sins, all right, but I wouldn't make a policy of going to Heaven raising Hell on the way."

But to get back to the weak confounding the mighty, in spite of my limited education, I became, with the help of the Lord, what is known in the heavy-duty equipment field as an industrialist. Among my competitors are such giants as Caterpillar, General Motors, International Harvester, Allis Chalmers and some eight others, all big corporations with high-powered executive staffs and engineering departments. In their midst I am the hick from the backwoods of Duluth, but during World War II it was our organization that built over fifty per cent of the earth-moving equipment used in combat. According to reports, what with the building of highways like

3

the Alcan and the Ledo Road in Burma, the building of airports and artillery emplacements all over the world, and the plowing away of rubble in demolished cities, more earth had to be moved during World War II than during all the combined wars of history.

We are proud of that record, naturally, but we wouldn't be human if we didn't find a satisfaction of another sort. The machines that did the job were what my competitors had declared to be some of "that crazy LeTourneau stuff" right up to the outbreak of hostilities. Now, nineteen years later, they are all turning out the same equipment with only minor changes. Maybe we don't confound them. They seem to be prospering. But we keep them confused. That new digger of mine can lose their biggest load in the rear end of its rear bucket.

When I have talked about this long before an audience, I've been known to apologize and say, "I didn't come here to preach a sermon. Give me time and I'll say something."

What I want to say is that what I've done, anyone can do with the help of God. Reporters have often asked me, "Did you start from scratch?" My answer to that is, "Every time." I've been financially broke so often and in debt so long that it was a big day for us when my wife and I could move out of a cook shack and into a brand new tent. Spiritually, too, I was a bankrupt even before I lost my first dollar. Yes, I started from scratch, all right, and was still starting from scratch at the age of forty-four. And the One who picked me up and started me over with my strength and ambition fully restored is the same Lord and Savior available to all for the asking.

I could have learned that early in life, as my seven brothers and sisters did. We come from a long line of ministers and missionaries on both sides of our family. My grandfather, Jean LeTourneau, was a Huguenot minister, sent with his bride, Marie Louise, from Lyons, France, to the Grande Ligne Mission in Quebec in the 1840s. From all accounts, he and his

4

wife had a rough time. The Protestant Huguenots were no longer subjected to the fanatical persecutions of the eighteenth century, but neither were they made especially welcome. Added to that was the primitive housing of the mission and the long, fierce Canadian winters. For a young couple from southern France, the winters must have been pretty grim, but they stuck it out until after my father was born on January 12, 1857, in St. Sebastian, Quebec. Then, both broken in health, they moved to Richford, Vermont, only five miles from the Canadian line.

"That's a French Canadian for you," my father once said. "When he crosses the border, he thinks he's as far south as he can get."

Grandfather LeTourneau set up a boarding school in Richford, with Grandmother doing the cooking for about twenty students while taking care of her own sons, Joshua, Caleb, and Joseph, and daughter Rachelle. In his spare time and on Sundays, Grandfather continued to serve as minister among the Protestant French Canadians who made up the bulk of the population.

I never really knew my grandparents; my one recollection of my grandmother when she visited us in Duluth is that she was small and spoke only in French. But I have a great admiration for them. In Richford, to serve both God and humanity, they drove themselves night and day until once more they collapsed from the strain. Ordered by their doctor to give up teaching and the ministry, and live an outdoor life, they bought a farm north of town, and then because there was a stream tumbling through the farm that Grandfather didn't want to waste, they built a saw mill. There may be harder jobs than trying to farm in the rock of Vermont and run a saw mill, but I've never found them in heavy construction work or iron foundries.

By tradition, the eldest son, Joshua, known to us as Uncle J., was to run the farm and the mill, and my father was to be trained for the ministry. Neither my uncle nor my father ever spoke about the accident that changed the plans, but as a mechanic I can see what happened. The crude water-powered mill of the 1870s, wet stone floors made greasy with sawdust, no safety precautions, and a young boy straining at logs too big for him. Uncle J. lost his arm in that accident, and it was my father, much too young, who had to take over the farm and the mill.

I think Uncle J. regarded his lost arm as more of a chance for escape than a handicap. Although no one had ever heard of a one-armed type-setter, he became one, and then a news-paper reporter, publisher, and successful printer in Duluth. My father settled down to his responsibilities as he had been trained to do, but the evidence is that he didn't like it.

In 1880 a town like Richford did not go in heavily for Youth Entertainment Centers or recreation of any kind. You had your Sundays off for church where you were taught more the fear of God than the love of God. It might even have been heresy to think of God intimately enough to call Him Partner. I know from long talks with my father, after we got over feuding, that his only recreation was going to the Richford Blacksmith Shop to watch his young friend, Robert Gilmour, learn how to shoe horses and shape red-hot iron. And young Gilmour got his recreation by coming out to the farm to watch my father saw lumber.

What made Richford endurable for Caleb Thucydides was the arrival in 1880 of a new school teacher named Elizabeth Johnston Lorimer. According to the Martin Genealogy book, of which my brother Bill has a copy, she was an eighth-generation Martin on her mother's side, the original Samuel Martin having arrived in New Haven, Connecticut, around 1645. The Lorimers were Scotch, and had arrived in the vil-lage of Beebe Plains, Quebec, in 1830. Like the Martins, the Lorimers ran strongly to ministers, three of Elizabeth's four brothers being reverends.

I have it on the good authority of my Uncle Albert Lorimer that his family had strong objections to one Caleb Thucydides

6

LeTourneau when he began squiring Elizabeth Lorimer around to the church suppers. They had high respect for his Huguenot parents, but they didn't think he was the last word in rock-bound, New England stability.

"My sister Belle warned her that he wouldn't stay put, that he'd carry her off, and we'd never see her again," Uncle Albert told me.

My own idea, based on some frank opinions of my mother, is that being carried off was the least of her worries. As she moved from Richford to Beebe Plains to Duluth to Portland, Stockton, Long Beach, and Uplands, with minor stops in between, her favorite quotation was, "Whatsoever state I am in, therewith I'll be content." And she certainly was. One December in Uplands she came in with a bouquet of flowers from the garden, and looked at the clock with immense satisfaction. It was 5:00 p.m. and the sunshine was pouring down. "It's eight o'clock in Richford," she said. "And cold, son! It's so cold I can hear it crack from here."

Father and Mother were married on Christmas Day, 1881, and moved into the big, comfortable, two-story-plus-attic farmhouse. They were a long time in getting away. Harold was born there on June 1, 1883. William was next, born on June 24, 1885. Then my sister Mattie, born on January 22, 1887. I was born on November 30, 1888, and named after my father's best friend, Robert Gilmour.

Apparently I was the straw that broke the camel's back. Within weeks of my arrival father shipped us up to our Lorimer grandparents in Beebe Plains, and then he and Robert Gilmour headed south.

"That was the year after the big winter of 1888," my father told me, "so Bob and I decided we had spent our last winter shoveling snow. We took a train to California, and then went all the way down into Baja California, a couple of hundred miles south of San Diego. Nobody had ever heard of frost down there so we put our money down on a couple of farms, and started back for you folks."

They never did see those farms in Mexico again. Returning to Vermont, they made a detour by way of Duluth to see my Uncle J., then running a big printing plant there. Uncle J. was getting ready to build a fine house up on the hill, overlooking Lake Superior, and knowing Dad and "Uncle Bob" were excellent craftsmen, he offered them the job, "cash on the barrel-head." They figured they'd have time to build the house and get back to their farms in Mexico just in time to catch the next rainy season. But when that house was finished, other buyers admired the workmanship, and ordered more. By the time we were all reunited in Duluth in 1890, Dad was well on his way to becoming a successful building contractor. Robert Gilmour had a growing blacksmith shop and he took in Uncle Emanuel Richards (Aunt Rachelle's husband) as partner. Forgotten were all thoughts of farming in Mexico.

2

To hear my mother tell it in later years, as a boy I was restless, inquisitive, energetic, determined, and ambitious. In the less-biased opinions of my brothers, I was restless, destructive, wilful, stubborn, and fanatically determined to amount to nothing. My father's opinion of me during my first fourteen years was usually expressed in a wide selection of Bible verses aimed at describing the fate of rebellious boys like me.

I don't know what there was in our temperaments that made Dad and me clash so during my boyhood. My older brothers Harold and Bill could work happily with him all day, but let me appear on the scene, and sooner or later the sparks would fly. I know he prayed often to God for help in guiding me, and I know he worked on me harder than on all my brothers and sisters combined. That only served to make me think I was the only one he picked on, and my back got stiffer than ever.

Like the serious row I had with him over carrying drinking

9

water from our spring-fed well, about three blocks from the house.

"It's Bill's turn," I argued. I was about ten, and I was keeping close track of when it was Bill's turn or mine, a few incidents of late leading me to suspect Bill was slipping a few extra turns my way.

"Well," said my father abruptly, "it won't break your back to help your brother once in a while. Get the bucket."

I got the bucket and hiked over to the well, furious at what I considered an unjust order. It was a small, bricked-up well topped with a cistern pump, and when filled to overflowing by a little spring, it held about a dozen barrels. I started pumping and emptying the bucket into the overflow gully. I worked my back into a knot pumping the well empty. Then I marched back and told my mother I couldn't get any water because the well was dry.

When Dad was informed of this at lunchtime, he was flabbergasted. "But that well was full this morning. It can't be dry."

"If Bob says it's dry, it's dry," said my mother. "You know he wouldn't lie about it."

Not until the next day, with the well once more filled and overflowing did Dad solve the mystery. And as can be expected, when he discovered the work I had done to avoid carrying out his order without resorting to falsehood, he was not exactly filled with fatherly good will.

Then there was the time he ordered me to chop some wood, and I cut up some choice fence posts he had brought home. And the time I nearly killed the family cow trying to ride it bareback. And on and on.

I can't say I had a wretched childhood, but it could have been a lot happier if I had let it. The home Dad had built for us was up on the northeast side of Duluth in what is now the beautiful residential section called Lester Park. It was large enough and comfortable even when our family grew to include five boys and three girls, and in the 1890s it was a paradise for children. A few clearings for farms on both sides, the wilderness behind, and a view of Lake Superior in the front. Fishing, swimming, and hunting all around as long as the snow was gone, which was not for very long in Duluth.

My folks belonged to the small church group known as the Plymouth Brethren, a closely knit group intensely loyal to the church and each other. Probably its most unique feature was that women had no voice in the conduct of the services, nor were they allowed to talk in church. But they talked afterwards.

I attended regularly—I had no escape—and heard a lot about God without learning a thing. School was worse. From nine to four, endurable in the fall and spring when we could run outside during recesses and lunch, but impossible during the bitter winter days. Then the teacher had the older boys keep the wood stove at red heat and the classroom at about 90 degrees while we roasted there in heavy winter clothes and long woolen underwear. No matter that we semi-rural kids had walked a mile or more—blizzards were no excuse—and that even the town kids had outside chores. Our principal didn't want any of us to get "the pneumonia" during the school hours. The result was that all of us had runny noses from the first frost until spring when we got soaked in the rivulets of melting snow and came down with mumps, measles, scarlet fever, diphtheria and everything else in the book.

I had one odd experience when I was in the fifth grade. Before that I had always had just enough black marks to overcome the red ones and get me "passed" from one grade to the next. In my fifth year I suddenly discovered arithmetic made sense. Geography was not just some pink, green, and yellow areas on a map, but real places, perhaps with palm trees instead of snow. And reading—if you read from one paragraph to the next instead of spelling out one word at a time, you could get a lot of fascinating information from books. I was so amazed at this sudden awakening that I read

11

through all the books in the fifth grade and most of the sixth grade's books too.

My teacher was delighted, my folks were stunned, and on this great wave of enlightenment I was skipped over the sixth grade and into the seventh. What a mistake that was for me. The seventh-graders had put in a long, earnest year on the subjects I had skimmed over so swiftly, and when it came to reciting, I wasn't in their league. Maybe with time and understanding, I might have caught up, but pampering is one thing a promising student didn't get then. Instead, he was usually pounded to a pulp as a sissy, a fate from which I was spared because I was already approaching six feet, and was the biggest hulk in the class. That only made it harder on me. I was not only the biggest in the class, but also the dumbest. We call what I had an inferiority complex today, and I was crawling with it. I quit trying entirely, and came to hate school with an almost physical violence. I wanted to break windows and kick out walls.

I wasn't doing any better outside of school. For years my brother Harold and then my brother Bill had carried papers for a circulation man named Pinky, on a route that, for a quarter-of-a-cent a paper, returned twelve cents a day, six days a week, or nearly $3 a month. Now it was my turn, and I muffed it.

If it was a cold and snowy day, I'd be LeTourneau of the Yukon, running a trap line, and when I'd reach the end of the route, I'd find myself with five or six extra papers and no idea of what houses I'd skipped. Or if it was a fine day, I'd get to day-dreaming on almost any subject but customers. The first time Pinky fired me for too many complaints, Bill was able to intercede, but when my improvement lasted only a few days, I was fired with complete finality.

The disgrace of it all. I couldn't hold a job for eight months that my brothers had held for years. Worse, I had lost the family claim to the route for my brother Louis, next in line of succession.

"Boy, you'll cut wood for this," said my father.

"How much wood?" I demanded defiantly.

"One chunk for every paper."

"And if I cut more than that?"

"If you cut more than that, Bob, I'll believe it when I see it. But if you do, I'll pay the same per stick as you got per paper. Birch wood, of course."

I made enough out of that to buy a .22 rifle, and had to quit only when the woodshed was full. And Dad never again offered to pay me on a piece-work basis for manual labor. I could close my mind to physical drudgery and go day-dreaming off on a score of wild ideas like becoming a lumberjack and riding white pine logs down the St. Croix River to Stillwater, or running a steam shovel in the iron mines at Hibbing, or running a trap line up near International Falls. As long as I thought Dad would have to pay for it, I was ready to work my body to a frazzle.

I built my first piece of what might be called earth-moving equipment when I was twelve. It was a heifer-pulled snow plow designed to get me out of several hours of work opening paths with a shovel. It was a V-shaped affair with curving sides to thrust the snow up and to both sides, and it might have worked. The heifer kicked it and me to flinders before I could find out, curing me forever of any regard for animal power of any kind.

That summer Dad had Harold and Bill working with him on building contracts, leaving me around the house as general chore boy. Harold was getting ready to go to the University of Minnesota to study engineering—he became an executive engineer for Standard Oil of New Jersey—and Bill was preparing himself for a general business course—he was a natural born merchandiser and was my sales manager in 1938 before opening his own successful hardware business. I simply didn't have enough to do. I chopped the wood, hauled the water, and hoed the garden all before noon and then ran wild through the woods and along the lake shore. I didn't know how wild I was myself until I started showing off for some friends.

We were down at the lakeshore, and I pointed to a large rock, thrust up like an island about 100 yards out in deep water. I might add that the temperature of Lake Superior rarely reaches 50 degrees even after a long hot spell. "Race you to the rock," I said, and with that I stripped and plunged in. The other kids were still testing the water with their toes, a little dubiously, when I climbed up on the rock. Finally a couple did jump in and swim out to join me. But after we sat around in the sun a while, the icy swim back didn't look so inviting.

"There's only one way to do it," I said, "that's to plunge right in." One of the fellows was standing at the edge of the rock, some ten feet above the water. "Is it all clear down there?" I asked. "Looks like it," he said. I took two steps, and made a flying leap over the edge. In mid-air I saw the vague outline of a rock about three feet below the surface. Now that I am bald, you can see the exact configuration of that rock on my skull. Sixteen stitches were required to close the scalping I got that day.

I came up stunned and started to call for help. Then the cold water acted like a restorative and away I went, beating my rescuers to shore by 20 yards. I ran home before collapsing, saved by the first of many miracles in my life.

I know Dad was scared to death when he saw the condition of my head, and he and Mother prayed long that night for me to come out of the state of shock I had dropped into after the doctor's needlework. But the next day, when I was as sound as ever, he concealed his vast relief by remarking, "Only fools jump in where angels fear to tread." For some reason that hurt me more than the dent in my head.

Being confined to bed until the doctor returned to check me out, I found plenty of time to feel sorry for myself. I felt that I was unloved and unwanted. I decided there was only one thing for me to do. I would run away.

You can be sure if you want an excuse to do something

wrong, the Devil will give you a good one. Shortly after that, with the approach of cold weather, I was ordered to chop some wood and made the mistake of cutting up Dad's fence posts as I mentioned earlier. He was furious. I couldn't see my offense as that serious, and offered to cut some new posts to make good his loss. As usual, when I argued with him, I didn't soothe him any. His final remark was that if I hadn't done it on purpose, I was too dumb to know a good fence post when I saw one.

That was it. I waited until dark, and then ran away, taking with me only the clothes on my back. It was one of those pitch-black nights with a biting north wind that marks the coming of winter to the North-country, and I wasn't running very fast in the rutted, rocky road. In the timbered stretches of the road I thought I saw more wolves than any 13-year-old kid should face, but I couldn't quit. I think if there had been any real wolves, I'd have let them tear me apart rather than return home in defeat. I saw a hole blacker than most in the darkness and knew it to be a ravine in which we had often played, so I felt my way into it to a ledge sheltered from the wind. There I spent the night, wondering what my father would say when they found me there, frozen stiff.

Hunger drove me out at daybreak, but I had an answer for that. I knew that I was not far from the small farm of Mrs. Spagmo, a kind-hearted Swedish widow for whom I had done a lot of chores. I figured that if I milked her cow for her, she'd give me a breakfast that would carry me all the way to Two Harbors where I would be sure to get a job as cabin boy on an ore boat.

I figured correctly, and while I was deep in pancakes, Mrs. Spagmo asked if I couldn't delay my nautical career long enough to let her run in to Duluth on a few errands. She'd pay me a dollar for hitching up the horse, feeding the chickens, and digging up the potatoes in her small patch.

With offers of such wealth at the very start of my career, I couldn't resist. Then she was late in returning, so I had to milk the cow to earn my supper, and milk it again in the morning to earn my breakfast. The upshot of it all was that I had run a mile away from home, and there I stayed as Mrs. Spagmo's hired "man."

I know now, of course, that Mrs. Spagmo had talked it over with my parents, and that they were agreed it might do me a world of good to stay with her, if she could put up with me.

I soon found myself fenced in with all sorts of restrictions. Back home, as the fourth of what were now eight children, I was kept fed, clothed and washed with systematic regularity. Here, as the sole charge of a lonely widow, I was washed until I thought my skin was wearing out. My personal program was arranged from pre-dawn milking to hauling in the last load of wood to carry the stove through the night. School, too, and now I had a mile farther to walk. "There were no dumb Swedes in my family," Mrs. Spagmo said, "and I won't have one now, even if he does have a French name."

She meant well, but I was fighting a stubborn battle. Every school day I walked by the family house without glancing to left or right, and walked by it the same way in the evening. The snows kept getting deeper and the days shorter, but I wouldn't give up. In class I resisted teachers with the same single-minded stubbornness. I was definitely on the road to Hell, and working hard to stay there.

My Aunt Rachelle and Uncle Emanuel Richards were having the annual Thanksgiving gathering of LeTourneau families and other Vermont friends at their house on the west side of Duluth that year, so I got word at school from my sister Mattie that Mother wanted me to be there. "And if you aren't there, and people ask about you, Mother is going to feel pretty bad trying to explain the silly situation you've worked yourself into."

I didn't want that to happen, so I went, but I was still on my high horse. And Dad was on a horse just as tall. We went through the motions for the other guests, but we weren't getting anywhere even after Thanksgiving prayer. In that mood we might never have got anywhere if a heavy snow hadn't started to fall. Within two hours the roads were impassable to sleighs. It was snug at Uncle Emanuel's, and there was plenty of room, but back home there were the milk cows and chickens that had to be cared for that night.

The final arrangements were that the women would stay, and the men would plow their ways back on foot to care for their livestock. Somehow that put me behind my father who was breaking trail on the long hike clear across town.

We plowed along in silence. We got along better that way. In fact we got along so well that pretty soon we were taking turns breaking trail and even laughing when one or another of us fell down. But when we reached our house I was still prepared to go on to Mrs. Spagmo's.

"Better come in, Bob," Dad said. "You can be sure Mrs. Spagmo has already taken care of her stock."

I was pretty cold, and that extra mile alone did look like a long way. I went in, and had some hot milk, and helped around the barn, and even enjoyed it. In the morning I helped with the chores again, and discovered my father could make a fair batch of pancakes when he had to. That led to my helping him cut wood to pay for my breakfast, and on that job I made another discovery. As long as I was an eager and willing worker, and not going out of my way to plague him, Dad could be a mighty fine fellow. By noon I saw my running away from home and rebellious stand in all its pettiness, and I was one repentant boy. I started to say so, but Dad stopped me.

"Don't say a word," he said. "I know what you've been going through. I've been going through it myself, so we're both wrong."

What a lesson that has been to me all my life. Discovering my father's love changed my whole attitude, and chores that I had hated and fought against resentfully, I now did cheerfully because I wanted to serve him. It's like that, only more so, when you discover the Lord. And you don't grow up and move away from your Father in Heaven. He is with you always and everywhere. If you aren't serving Him now, it's because you don't know Him, like I really didn't know my own father. But when you do know Him, you'll love Him, and when you love Him you'll serve Him, and find the greatest happiness in doing so that you'll ever know.

I was a changed character around the house after that, but it would be too much to say that my attitude toward school had improved. I still found it to be an enormous waste of time, and there was nothing around the house to really occupy my mind unless it was trying to repair a clock, or pipe the spring to bring it closer to the house, or endlessly question Harold about the horseless carriages that had motors in them powered by gasoline. If I had any recreation at all, as we know it today, it was in going to the docks in Duluth to watch the ore trains come in with their red loads and transfer them to ore boats. There were steam locomotives, and steam shovels, and steamboats moving thousands of tons of ore in the most massive display of power any kid could hope to see. The man who brought the ore trains out on the long trestle and dumped them into the hoppers that fed the ore to the boats below must be, I thought, the happiest man in the world.

That winter of 1901-1902 I was considered to be sufficiently grown to work with Harold and Bill on Dad's construction jobs. I think it was then, for the first time, I began to appreciate what Dad was up against in raising Harold, Bill, Mattie, Sarah, Louis, Marie, and Phillip—Phil was born in 1900—without getting a lot of back-talk out of me. I remember one bitter cold day we borrowed Uncle J.'s team of carriage horses to haul some lumber from a freight yard to a warehouse Dad was building. While we worked with painfully cold fingers to load the heavy timbers—if you banged a timber you felt your fingers must break off like glass—a man inside the freight office watched us through a frosted window. When we were loaded he stepped out and called Dad over for

18

a brief talk from which Dad returned mad enough to be walking on stilts.

"What's the matter?" I asked.

"You kids," he snorted. "I get mad enough trying to train all of you to do the Christian thing, so when I meet a grown man like that I don't have much Christian patience left."

Not knowing what to say to that, I said nothing, which showed I was learning.

"He wants to borrow the team," Dad continued. "Now don't forget this, Bob. If you ever want to borrow a team, don't be afraid to get out in the cold and help the owner put on his load. Don't step out after the sleigh is loaded and ask to borrow the team."

"Yes, sir," I said. "Did you lend it to him?"

"I had to," he said. "I had to set a Christian example for you kids. That's what makes me mad."

That was Dad. Going out of his way to set an example for his children, and there I had been, trying his patience to the point of exhaustion, and then jumping in with an argument, or some stubborn act of defiance. I had a lot to make up for.

In addition, that winter was a brute. Then a letter arrived from Mr. Walker, a member of the Plymouth Brethren, who had gone west to Portland, Oregon. Like Dad he was a building contractor, and his report stirred up Dad's restless desire to move. In Oregon you had outdoor construction work year-round if you didn't mind a little warm rain. No snow, the biggest roses you ever saw, a big boom going on, and a shortage of carpenters.

Uncle J. couldn't understand why anyone would ever want to leave Duluth. Uncle Emanuel and Uncle Bob Gilmour, with a thriving partnership in a blacksmith shop and warm forges to work over all winter, felt the same way. But Dad had had enough of pounding nails with frozen fingers.

We moved as soon as Dad finished the house he was working on, with Harold electing to remain behind to enter the University of Minnesota. Mother got a little tearful about that, the first of her children to leave the family roof. "But I don't have to worry about Harold," she said to assure herself. "He's the steady one." From the way she looked at me, I knew what she meant.

As for me, I was glad to be gone. If my attitude around the house had improved, I still resented the outside world, and going to church was a duty I performed only because it pleased the family. About all I knew of religion was that I didn't have it, and that if you didn't have it you were going to Hell. Maybe, I thought, in a new town where I wasn't known as "that stubborn LeTourneau kid," I could make a fresh start. I still had to learn that without God a change in geography isn't going to change a man's soul any more than travel with a circus will change the spots on a leopard. But we do have one advantage over the leopard. He can never change, but we, by finding God, Who is everywhere, can change our souls, and with them our whole lives.

3

Portland in 1902 was not any tougher than Duluth, but it worked at it harder. In Duluth when the harbor froze over and the iron mines shut down, there was always a lull during the long freeze. Even the lumberjacks were back in their camps, not to be seen until the spring drive. But Portland was a lumbering town with a Skid Road that boomed all the year round. The Willamette River was jammed with logs and steamboats. Its shore was lined with sawmills and lumber yards. The wooden sidewalks along the river front were crowded day and night with lumberjacks, rivermen, millhands, teamsters, Chinamen, Indians, and the bums from everywhere. So many bums that the road over which logs were skidded by horses and oxen lost its meaning as Skid Road and became Skid Row, a name now used everywhere to describe a run-down street where human derelicts collect.

Skid Road was no place for ladies, and certainly no place for a 14-year-old, overgrown hick from Minnesota, but there

I was, fascinated and bug-eyed. In Duluth my folks had managed to keep me in school, but Portland was a horse of many other colors. With my first glimpse of the excitement, I knew I was not going to squeeze my six-foot, 160-pound frame behind a desk made for little eighth-graders.

I made my stand at home that evening, knowing what I was up against. Like many uneducated men, Dad was determined that all his children would get what was denied him, and he was a very determined man. I am sure he regarded a high-school diploma as some magic passport to success, and a college degree as an awesome thing that made success inevitable. When on that subject, he could out-talk any educator I've ever heard, and I've made a point of hearing many. So I was braced. I knew I couldn't out-argue him, but I was resolved to outlast him.

Dad and I went round and round. I had only one line, but I worked it for all it was worth. "I'm a man growed," I recollect repeating at every opportunity. A couple of hours of that, and I could feel victory ahead. Then Dad said in his New England accent, "Wal, we don't have to do it all in one piece. We can sleep on it."

I had won. The trouble was that after lying sleepless in bed for an hour or so, I knew my troubled parents were praying for me. That hurt, because I knew if I could resist their prayers, I was pretty far gone. I kept assuring myself that the break had to be made sometime, but for a "man-growed," it was one worried boy who went to sleep that night. Had the argument been resumed the next morning, six-foot "Bobbie" LeTourneau might have answered roll-call in the eighth grade.

Instead, at a breakfast of buckwheat pancakes and corn syrup, standard fare because it was cheap and filling, my parents were quite serene. Not for two more years would I find out why. I was left to wander around uncomfortably, wondering, now that I had made my stand, what I was going to do about it.

On Sunday we all turned out to go to the Plymouth Brethren Assembly. Although Dad was a newcomer, his reputation as a building contractor in Duluth had preceded him. He had been welcomed by the elders as a man much needed in the community. And after church he was detained by several prosperously dressed and bearded men. The beards didn't deceive me because it was common knowledge among boys that the beards saved the cost of shaving, stiff collars, and neckties while being a great relief to the neck. What did impress me was that these important men glanced several times in my direction, sort of sizing me up. I suddenly realized that my brother Bill's coat, handed down to me, failed to reach my wrists by at least four inches.

Dad said nothing when he rejoined us. "No business on Sunday," was his rule, just as it is mine, but I have noticed that thoughts do come on Sunday that change the whole course of the working week, or even a working life. Some of those thoughts had been exchanged that day. I can't say they changed the course of my career, since I had none, but they directed it in no uncertain terms.

At 5:30 a.m. Monday, what had been "after church conversation" for Dad became harsh, cold business for me. I still think it was a plot, and Dad never downright denied it. "Get up," he shouted. "As long as you are a 'growed man,' you have to be to work at six-thirty. Don't want to be late on your first day."

It didn't come all at once, but by the time I had stowed away a dozen pancakes I gathered I was on my way to learn the iron business as an apprentice molder. It turned out that a Mr. Hill, one of the bearded men with whom Dad had been talking, was the owner of the East Portland Iron Works. Then Dad got in his dig. "Mr. Hill's had some trouble, what with his apprentices complaining about the hard work an' quitting before noon. I told him he wouldn't have that trouble with you, you being a 'man growed.' "

I didn't know what an iron molder was, but that remark was better than ambition to keep me going. All the long bicycle ride from the northside to East Portland I kept telling myself the horse hadn't been born that could pull me off the job. It was well that my stubbornness had been rasped the wrong way because, at my first glimpse of the foundry, I needed something for support. That was no playground in front of me.

Even today, with my own steel mill, I find something mighty impressive about everything concerned with molten metal. As a boy seeing my first foundry close up, and knowing it was there I would be made or busted, it was terrifying. Nor was it just my imagination. Compared to a modern, ventilated, well-lighted, safety-conscious foundry, the East Portland Iron Works—and all other foundries at the turn of the century—filled the bill for Dante's *Inferno* as close as I want to come.

Mr. Hill, when I came to know him, was a little, softvoiced Englishman, always neatly dressed even to a collar and necktie under his beard. The first meeting was something else. I remember I followed some railroad tracks into a huge building made of tin, soot-blackened and rusty. Smoke billowed past me, pushing the daylight back through the open doors. There were some electric light bulbs, I discovered later, so maybe they guided me past some ominous dark shapes to where I could make out four or five men standing near what even I knew was a furnace. I could feel its heat.

Mr. Hill saw me first and came toward me. At the same time one of the men tapped the furnace. What I saw against the white glow of the molten stream was the black silhouette of a giant, while the sparks flashing and popping behind him seemed to be leaping right out of his hair and beard. I was to be hired many times later, and do some hiring on my own, but after that first impression when anyone mentions the word "boss" to me, I think of Mr. Hill.

He welcomed me with one of the age-old cracks of the iron business, fortunately no longer true. "This is a job for a strong back and a weak mind. There's a gondola full of sand out in the yard. Just shovel it into a wheelbarrow and bring it in here. Joe will tell you where to dump it."

I hadn't wheeled ten barrows of the stuff that had soaked up about two weeks of Portland's rain before I was hunting for an easier way of moving dirt. Furthermore, I had achieved an enormous respect for a cubic yard of sand. The ten wheelbarrow loads had just dented it while making no impression at all on the carload.

Joe gave me some advice. "Pushin' is a rest from shovelin'. Shovelin' is a rest from pushin'. Then there's the trip back with an empty barrow where you don't do nothin' at all. Kid, you got yourself a job that's just one long rest."

I staggered home that night, my hands swollen to the size of hams, still trying to find the fallacy in his argument. I never did find it. A painful month later, during which I grew up, I discovered that shoveling did relax the muscles after pushing, and vice versa. I could even look around a little to see where I was.

I was in an iron foundry with one cupola furnace that could melt down about 25 tons of pig iron and scrap a day if all went well, as it did often enough to make Mr. Hill a very important person in town. For the most part we made gray iron castings for sawmill machinery. If I remember correctly, castings made up 73 per cent of the weight of sawmill machinery, so with new mills going up almost as fast as old mills could burn down, we were busy. Then we had a standing order from the booming railroads for all the freight car wheels we could turn out in our spare time. If that was not enough, we could always turn out castings for the steamboat trade, steamboats burning up about as often as sawmills.

My lessons continued. One day I was stirring up a mixture of sand, clay and water to the heavy consistency required if it was to hold its shape as a mold. I had about a ton of the stuff in the batch, shoveling it over and over again to mix it. As I heaved away, the shovel moving sluggishly, I became aware of Mr. Hill at my shoulder.

25

"I don't want you to work hard, son," he said.

I stammered something about the stuff being thick.

"Don't work hard, son," he continued. "Just fast."

Another day I was filing the burrs off a casting, bearing down hard with short, choppy strokes. Again Mr. Hill appeared.

"Y'know, son, when I bought that file, I paid for both ends," he said.

I stared at him blankly.

"That's right," he said very kindly. "I bought 'em so you could use both ends as well as the middle. Now—" and his voice crackled—"take a LONG stroke."

Two priceless lessons that have worked for me all my life. When I was hiring out for pay, I made it a point of stepping along a little faster and finding ways to do a job a little quicker. When I started building my own machinery, I became one of the first outside the aviation industry to use my own airplane to serve my customers.

The simple lesson of the file was equally valuable. It's the long, full stroke, not too fast, that keeps the file sharp and gets the work done quickly and easily. Yet it's amazing how many men still use only the middle of a file instead of working it for all it's worth. The same is true of machinery. The first, second-hand Holt tractor I bought had the power of 75 horses, but in dragging a three-yard scraper, it was only using half its power. I was using the ten middle horses instead of all seventy-five. So I put both ends to work, including the flywheel, and before I was through I had a machine that moved twelve yards of dirt while the tractor didn't even raise a sweat. Today the first question I put to any new machine is, "What more can you do better?" According to outside reports, the results have been astonishing, but we'll never stop asking that question.

My education continued. The day came when I could deliver sand faster than the molders could use it up. I can't say they wanted to educate me. They just didn't want to see me leaning on a shovel. We were casting freightcar wheels at the time, so they graciously let me help, Joe and Tim Gothe being the journeymen molders in immediate charge of my apprenticeship. Joe's last name I can't remember, but Tim had two beautiful daughters whose last name is unforgettable.

"Get a pattern," said Joe.

I went back through the familiar smoke to one of those gloomy piles that had so alarmed me on my first day. Here, stacked together in a manner that would horrify any modern stockroom man, were wooden patterns of everything from steam boiler beds to cast iron Christmas toys. I found a wooden duplicate of a car wheel, and because it was heavy, I started to roll it back to be moving fast. That display of energy was met with an explosion of profanity, ending with, "Don't you know that every dent you put in that pattern will show up in the casting?" I think my dislike of castings began then.

Because I don't like castings, I won't go into the details of making one. It's an art, and as a beginner, I made the mistake of making my first one almost right. At least it held its shape.

Joe and I picked up an empty ladle weighing about 100 pounds. The heat for the day was being poured from the cupola furnace, and other molders were standing in line with their ladles, about which I must say a word. No meaner instrument has ever been invented. Two iron bars extended from one side of the ladle like the arms of a wheelbarrow, and Joe held those. One iron bar of the same four-foot length extended from the other side, and I, serving as the wheel of the barrow, held that. When our turn came, we marched into the heat of the furnace and let 150 pounds of the fiery liquid pour into the 100-pound ladle.

I might also add that the handle I picked up was hot enough. We wore no gloves, any protection of that sort being regarded as sure traps for the droplets being sprayed out by the bursting bubbles in your cauldron. Such droplets striking your bare skin caused only the glancing burns we dismissed as "freckles," whereas a hot drop caught in your glove could fry you to the bone.

The handle was both hot and heavy. Between us we were carrying 250 pounds through a cloud of smoke after being half-blinded by the glare of the pour. Worse, in those days of careless housekeeping, the uneven dirt floor was a litter of tap rods, chunks of slag, piles of molding sand, and rejected castings. Staggering into that gloom, I had the uneasy feeling that one stumble would dump 150 pounds of iron into my ample shoes. We wore laceless shoes out of which we could jump in a flash, but that was small comfort.

We survived that trip as so many often did, and as so many often didn't. At my mold we lifted our 250 pounds shoulder-high for pouring. Then, for the first time, I realized what it took to pour a ladle. With me holding my single handle, Joe put all of his strength into his two handles to tilt that enormous, off-center weight into the pouring basin of the mold. They were tough, strong men, men like Joe.

The stream flowed down the sprue, into the runner and through the ingate. There was a rumbling and a popping inside that was not pleasant to listen to.

Tim backed off, shouting advice. "Pour faster! Get enough heat in there and maybe you can save her!"

Joe, with the ladle half empty, dumped the rest with one wrench that twisted off half my callouses. There was a gurgle I recognized once again when years later I heard Old Faithful go off. Whoompf! The whole pour exploded to the roof of the foundry before raining down on us. Chilled shot, they call it, but there was nothing chilled about the drops that went down my collar.

Joe and Tim both turned on me, apprentices being hired to get the blame as part of their duties. "Now see what you did. You put too much water in the sand. When the pour hit it, the water turned to steam and exploded."

They didn't say that at all. What they said can't be printed, but that is the gist of it, boiled down and expurgated.

Because I have spent much of the last 25 years testifying to the power of our Lord, many people have the impression that I have led a cloistered life. All I can say to that now is that my testimony wouldn't be much good if I hadn't been there. I've had my ears pinned back with words that leave me grateful I have any ears left. At the same time, to pass on an overheard remark, "That LeTourneau can cuss harder without swear words than any man I ever heard."

One of the most important factors in my apprenticeship was the timeliness of my arrival. In their processes, foundries had been much the same for hundreds of years, but with the arrival of the twentieth century, everything, as Joe said, "changed faster than time on your day off." The whole science of metallurgy came into being and was dumped on us without warning. One day we would be charging the furnace with coke, shattered pig iron (shattered by me with a sledge hammer), and whatever scrap we had in the yard. The next we would be measuring manganese, copper, and all sorts of metals out by the ounce to make the alloys our customers were demanding. I couldn't see much difference myself, and said so to Mr. Hill.

"Son, in this funny business you learn new tricks or you don't live to be an old dog," he said. "In my shop, what the customer wants, the customer gets. The time was I could tell him what he wanted. Now he doesn't ask me; he tells me. At my age I don't like to be told, but that's what happens when you get a jump behind instead of a jump ahead. Don't let it happen to you."

By that time we were better acquainted and could talk a little. He even as much as admitted that he had worked me a little hard the first few weeks, the idea being that I'd quit and go back to school where my father thought I belonged. When that strategy hadn't worked, he began to hope that he had found the apprentice he had been looking for.

"I still don't see any difference," I insisted. "What is this alloy stuff, anyway?"

"It's a way of combining metals to get more out of 'em than they have alone," he said carefully. "You won't see it much making castings, but you'll see it in the machine shop. That is, if you want to look."

That is as close to an invitation as Mr. Hill ever came. He wasn't telling me I could take some time off from my foundry work to learn the machinist's trade. He was saying that any time I wanted to spend in the machine shop, after my ten-hour day, would have his approval. Only someone familiar with the cost of machine tools and the jealousy with which they were guarded can realize what a great privilege was being offered me.

I had a machine shop in a trailer one time that was bigger than Hill's entire layout. I remember he had one small engine lathe, a drill press, a blacksmith's forge, some hammers, files, and a couple racks of stock. One old German, whose experience in a Frankfort steel mill made him think he was a Prussian general, ran it. Even Mr. Hill called him "Sir." He was such an autocratic old crab that no one would talk to him. What surprised everyone was that he and I got along fine, mainly, I think, because the old tyrant had been left to himself so long he was lonesome.

His work was never pressing. Hill kept the shop mainly as an accommodation for small customers who had no machine shops of their own, so beyond machining a few castings and drilling some holes, there was not much to task the old man's real ability. As soon as he discovered I was serious about learning his trade he used to save work so I could watch him set up a job or finish it while I crammed sandwiches into my mouth during the 30 minutes for lunch.

One day he said, "Bah, this is nothing. You watch the lathe go round and you learn what comes out. Shavings. To learn something, you must make something."

I was willing. "What?"

"A small steam engine," he said. "You work with brass, copper, nickel. You work with gray iron, white iron, and steel. You make something, and when it is finished, you know how to work metal, and you know how to work steam engines."

The project, fascinating though it was, offered problems. As a growing boy who needed every minute of his lunchtime to stuff in food, I couldn't tackle such a job at noon. It meant evening work, but that didn't matter to me. I started to build a small steam engine, riding my bicycle home at midnight.

Hardest hit during the two years before my 16th birthday was my spiritual life. I went to church with the family on Sunday, sleeping through the sermons, so I know some form of spiritual life was there, but to say the best I can for it, it was dormant. Nor was I worried about myself. If the iron molders of a half-century ago were a profane lot, with a great addiction to a few gallons of beer to quench the thirst and wash down "the dust and fluxes," they were the biggest-hearted rascals in the world, and I wanted to emulate them. It was Mr. Hill who saw to it that I didn't. A great Christian and churchman, Mr. Hill had let it be known through the foundry that anyone offering me the other side of his bucket of suds was asking for trouble if not dismissal. So in that respect you can say I led a sheltered life.

What brought me up sharp was not the loose congeniality of my seniors. Being my heroes, I didn't think they could do any wrong anyway, even when they'd hand me a wet rod to skim off slag, and howl with laughter when the steaming reaction splattered me with a burst of molten iron. What got me was the trouble apprentices in other shops were finding.

In spite of the fact that we worked hard and long hours, we apprentices were well informed on what our counterparts in rival shops were doing. With no radios, movies, or television to intrude on our time, the doings of others were of far more significance than they are today. If Jack of the Portland Steam Boat Works got drunk on green beer and fell into the river, it wasn't a matter of passing interest. We would mull over such items while shoveling sand, while tamping a mold,

31

while charging the furnace. It was an event, and we worked it, and weren't satisfied until we had figured out all the details down to how green was the beer and how cold was the water. And would Jack be fined, fired, or set back a year in his apprenticeship?

It was only days after my 16th birthday that the police came to me for information on the whereabouts of a friend of mine wanted for assault and battery. Then in rapid succession three other friends got in trouble with the law. One who had stolen some tools from a steamboat, I remember, was wanted for piracy.

This sudden accumulation of trouble brought me face to face with myself. I could tell myself all I was doing with my spare time was making a model steam engine, but I couldn't escape the fact that my closest associates were enrolled with the police. "A man is known by the company he keeps," said Dad. I said the only company I kept was maybe on a Sunday afternoon at the ballgame. That got me nowhere with Dad, but I didn't seem to be affected by that. What really got me was my mother's worry that she was turning out one of the pioneers of juvenile delinquency. My chance to do something constructive came during the Christmas season of 1904.

For many years, Portland had prided itself on being a town in which "anything goes." So dominant was the Skid Road element that the respectable element further uptown was satisfied to fight a rear-guard action to preserve itself. Down on the river-front only a couple of missions made a poorly-supported effort to work with the bums, jungle buzzards and mission stiffs who were in themselves sort of proud of their resistance to reform. Just who it was that decided Portland should become respectable all over I don't remember, but he must have been a great organizer. Somehow, for the first time in the city's history, he got all of the ministers of all denominations to work together in a common cause. The whole week before Christmas was set aside for a city-wide revival on a scale I was not to see again until Billy Graham gained his stature.

Every day and every evening there were parades and floats leading to one church or another, or to open-air services around the bandstand in the park. They had full bands and cornet soloists, choirs, quartets, and sopranos, and on Sunday they were all massed together. One evening I gave up working on my steam engine at the shop, and decided to see if the revival could do anything for me. Everywhere people were being saved, by street-corner sermons as well as in the big churches. As a matter of fact, while I don't know that any saloons went bankrupt, Portland was a different city after that week.

What terrified me was that after a week of concentrated singing, and listening to sermons, I didn't feel even a tremor of response. I was a blank, regretting the time I could have spent on my steam engine. I confessed as much to my mother before realizing I could have hurt her less by stabbing her with a blunt knife. The look on her face, not reproaching me but herself for having failed me, was what I had to take to bed with me that night just before Christmas.

I gave myself a working over that night. In my bitterness at my own calloused feelings I don't remember that I had to ask God for help. I could reproach myself thoroughly without asking for outside assistance.

No bolts of lightning hit me. No great flash of awareness. I just prayed to the Lord to save me, and then I was aware of another presence. No words were spoken. I received no messages. It was just that all of my bitterness was drained away, and I was filled with such a vast relief that I could not contain it all. I ran to my mother.

"I'm saved," I cried. "It happened. You don't have to worry about me any more. I have felt the love of our Lord Jesus Christ."

There was a long silence, followed by a deep sigh. A sigh of vast relief. Then, "Robert, we knew it had to happen. Two years ago, when we discovered we couldn't guide you, we knew God would. We have left it in His hands ever since,

33

praying every night that He would help you." She wouldn't have been the disciplinarian capable of raising a family like ours if she hadn't added, "But He sure kept us waiting a long time."

4

I entered the new year of 1905 full of high hopes and loaded with good resolutions. At church I joined the choir and the Young People's Missionary Society in which my sisters were leaders. In both I was an asset of doubtful value. My foundry-trained voice was deep enough if I could launch it on the right note. When that failed to happen with any regularity, the choir became markedly nervous, so in the end I made my biggest contribution to the choir by resigning. At missionary society I was so painfully inarticulate that when my sister Marie asked me to open a meeting with a prayer, I couldn't even stand up. For nearly 30 more years the torment of self-consciousness would be with me at meetings, an oddly silent beginning for one who has since addressed hundreds of audiences.

If I felt awkwardly out of place in church affairs, at the foundry I was becoming more and more at home. A lot of the old timers resented the changes being made after the turn of the century. They had been doing things the same way for so long that change made them feel insecure. The effect on me was quite the opposite. I was growing up during the most exciting part of the revolution in the iron and steel industry. Change did not upset my routine. I was one of the lucky ones trained to accept change *as* routine.

For an apprentice, my set-up was perfect. While in other foundries boys might have to work for months on mixing sand, I was big enough and apt enough to be moved around until in a matter of months I could substitute for any of the men sick or "laid up with a bad back," the usual term for a hangover. Especially did I like firing up the big furnace, or running the steam engine that powered the shop.

The more I learned about the steam engine in the foundry, the more room for improvement I saw in the model I was building in the shop. As a result I was constantly discarding finished parts in favor of new designs, some of which might have been good. My German friend was not so sure I was designing the engine that would wipe out the Stanley Steamer. At last, in some disgust, he said, "Parts you keep making, but no steam engine. What is? You don't want to finish for fear it won't run?"

He was probably so right that I denied it with more heat than necessary.

"Ach, so," he sighed. "But better a poor steam engine that runs than a good one never finished."

It was a good lesson that was to cause me plenty of trouble before I learned that one good lesson isn't always the full course. Sixteen years later I got the rest of it. I was leveling land for an irrigation project in central California when one blistering hot afternoon an idea for a new scraper hit me like a sunstroke. Mindful of the old German's warning that an unfinished machine never works, I started construction on the scraper that night, not even delaying to draw up plans. With my welding torch and plenty of scrap iron I could build a machine faster than I could draw one on paper anyway.

Both the old Holt tractor and my new scraper offered plenty of surfaces on which to weld my electric motors and controls, though not always were those surfaces in the most convenient places. Still, for me it was a good machine. I knew where everything was, and if I had to jump around a little to keep everything coordinated, what was a little activity compared to the fact that I could move three times as much dirt as any one man had ever moved before? I was so proud of the beast I named it the Gondola, not after the dainty Venetian boat but the ungraceful iron gondola used by railroads for moving coal, gravel, and the like.

Buoyed up with the thought that I could move three yards of dirt for the price of one, I put in a deliberately low bid on the job of building a half-mile horse racing track for the Stockton County Fair Board. The board expressed some doubt that I could do the job for that price and within the time limit, but when I did, I got my first taste of glory. The board chairman asked me to put the Gondola on display for the fair as the machine that had built the race track in record time. Right on Machinery Square he put me, along with such Stockton greats as the Holt Tractor Co., the Best Tractor Co., Harris Harvester Works, and others. All free, even to the placards the fair board draped on my machine.

Stockton and Fresno were nationally and internationally famous as builders of tractors, farm machinery, and earth moving equipment, and you can imagine it was one proud young man who strutted around the machine that was the star of the exhibit. I had delusions of selling the Gondola in gross lots.

Certainly the tractor companies were not going to find fault with my machine. If it did sell, it would need their tractors to pull it and power its electric motors. It was left to Mr. Harris of the Harris Harvester works to bring me back to earth.

He came up to me after one of my dry-run demonstrations.

"A nice machine, son," he said, "when you get the flaws ironed out. If you don't kill yourself first."

I'm afraid I got a little huffy at the suggestion Gondola might have some faults.

"Get off your high horse," he advised. "If I didn't like you, I wouldn't talk to you." That brought me up short because Mr. Harris was a *Big* man, with a harvesting machine that cut a swath 30 feet wide. "I notice you need about five acres to turn around in," he continued. "That's perfect for round race tracks, but what do you do on a job with tight corners?"

I hadn't thought of that.

"Another thing I noticed," he said, pouring on coals. "You're young, and you can run around on your machine like a monkey. But I can't turn out my harvesters for acrobats. If the farmers who buy my harvesters had to jump for the controls like you do, I'd have more farmers falling into the machines than grain."

Then he gave me the second semester of the course. "When you make a machine for yourself, that's your baby and you won't mind if it cries. It's your brain-child and you're proud of it. But the contractor that buys it won't stand for its crying."

It was a hard way to learn that my old instructor had been right as far as he went, but that he only went part way. Today I would add to his sentence thus: "Better a poor steam engine that works than a good one never finished, because until the good one is finished, its development can't begin." I was to lose a lot of money and hurt a lot of customers from time to time before the full truth of that statement finally sank home.

I had no such worry in the fall of 1905. Mr. Hill was getting in large shipments of coke and pig iron from the East in preparation for the uncertainties of winter shipping. The coke bunkers in back of the furnace were filled to the top, with more coke piled outside. The yard bulged with billets and scrap. When I wasn't piling one load here, I was piling another there according to the bidding of whatever foreman was in charge. By the first of November the whole East Portland Iron Works was as perfectly charged with coke and iron as ever its furnace had been.

No one knows how the fire started that Saturday night. Later a passerby reported having seen smoke and flames in the foundry around midnight but had thought nothing of it, smoke and flames being a foundry's stock in trade.

Not until 3:00 a.m. was an alarm turned in. By that time the tin roof had melted, and the unconfined flames were shooting high enough to light up the city. When I was awakened by a steam pumper clanging by, the glare was so bright I thought the next block was on fire.

In a lumbering town where all the houses were made of wood well-seasoned by a dry fall, one didn't have to be a fire buff to turn out for a blaze. I didn't catch up to the fire horses before they reached the scene, but I was gaining. We were all stopped hundreds of yards short by the heat. I remember saying, "There goes my model steam engine."

A Hook and Ladder company pounded up, scattering us. Those horses weren't going to the fire; they were going through it. The firemen who didn't jump off first fell off when the driver set the brake. The horses piled up in a heap. That was a night.

The slag pile that had once been the East Portland Iron Works was a week in cooling off, which was about as long as it took my excitement to die down. I suddenly realized I was unemployed. I think that that realization hit me harder than the loss of his foundry had hit Mr. Hill. All of my life and all of my ambition was in that slag heap. I was the apprentice who was going to work my way up to owning the place, and there it was—slag.

One advantage of an education is that it gives a young man a broad look at many vocations before he determines on his own. In the days of long apprenticeships a lot of us youngsters were committed to a career before we knew what it was all about. If we were on the wrong track, we were so long finding out about it that most often it was too late to start over. I don't think I would have made a good foundry owner. I don't like castings. The fire arrived just in time to broaden my education. Which reminds me of the comment of another graduate of the School of Hard Knocks. "Our school colors are black and blue," he said grimly, "and our school yell is 'Ouch!' "

I covered Portland from the east end to the west and back again, but there was no work for a half-finished apprentice. Most of Mr. Hill's other men got jobs, but there was a stern rule in the iron molders' union governing apprentices. One apprentice to every seven journeymen. If a foundry employed 11 journeymen, it could train only one apprentice, and not one and a half, of which I considered myself to be the half. When I argued the point with a foundry superintendent, seeing some justice in it, and heard myself called a "back-talk smart-alec," I began to suspect I was not going to get a job in Portland.

I couldn't have been righter. The year that had started out in high hopes ended with my appetite planted at the family table, mooching free meals. Big, dumb, broke, unemployed, and unemployable.

Late in January, Dad got a letter from Tim Gothe. "I am with the Moore and Scott Iron Works in San Francisco," he wrote. "They could use an apprentice like Bob."

Here was opportunity, but it meant leaving the family for the first time in my life, not counting my run-away. Even under the best of circumstances my folks would have found it difficult to turn their 17-year-old loose into the cold world. These were not the best of circumstances. At its wildest Portland could only brag that it was the San Francisco of Oregon. San Francisco was the real thing. In describing the delights of its Barbary Coast, it could describe itself as the New York of the Pacific. Beyond that, for temptation, imagination could not go.

I know Dad and Mother did not think of me as a wild one. They just knew San Francisco was bigger than I was and that I wasn't going to make it without calling for outside help. God's help. I assured them that ever since the Christmas week of 1904 I'd had God on my side, and would not hesitate to call on Him for help. They let me go, by day coach, with Mother packing enough cold beef, ham, corn bread and pickles into a wicker basket to last me through the trip and the whole week before payday. Twelve years later I was to learn how smug I had been in thinking God was on my side. Ever since then, with His help, I have tried hard to be on His side.

I can recall little of interest during those first months in the big city. I was too tired. Tim Gothe got me started at the foundry and for an old timer gave me some advice considered heresy in the trade. "All you'll learn in the shop," he said, "is how to do things in the same old way. Anything new you pick up by yourself, and most likely pick it up rear-end to. Get yourself some book-learning. I hear the vocational courses at the downtown Humboldt High School are real good, and don't give me any back-talk on school. I'll tell you that if I'da had a chance to go to school, I doubt it woulda hurt me a little bit."

When put that bluntly, I got the gist of it. I found a room on the second floor of a frame house near the corner of Fifth and Mission, close to both the school and the foundry. To my surprise, I found I liked vocational school. What I learned in class I could see in practice around me at the factory, and now that I was learning why a foundry operated the way it did, I had no trouble handling the complicated jobs usually delegated to older men.

On Sundays I went to the Plymouth Brethren Church and in the evening attended a nearby meeting of the Young People's Missionary Society. There I met an uncommon young man with the common name of Elmer Jones. He had been born in China and spoke fluent Cantonese, a feat that fascinated me because I had listened to my sisters Sarah and Marie, studying to be missionaries in China, trying to pronounce the words, and I had come to the conclusion that not even the Chinese could learn their language. In time I met his father who, after years in China as a Christian businessman, had returned to California thinking he would retire. Instead, he found himself on constant call to serve as court interpreter for the Chinese in San Francisco. Through the Joneses I got a glimpse of a world larger than an apprentice molder's sand pile, and from them, too, stemmed my desire to do something to improve the lot of underprivileged peoples.

I was thinking my first big thoughts of maybe going to China and opening my own foundry to make farm machinery when the quake struck, changing a lot of plans.

At the first tremor I thought I was in Duluth, being shaken awake to deliver the morning papers. At the second shock, and I was right in the midst of it, the noise of crashing buildings, and falling brick hit my ears with stunning violence. Then came the shock that dropped my room ten feet while my bed and the bureau swapped places.

I thought to myself, "This is the end of the world. Thank God I am saved and going to Heaven." Then I found the blankets on the floor and pulled them over my head.

In my talks around the country, I have always emphasized that in placing myself in God's hands, I have complete confidence in His rightness when His will is done. That is a very reassuring thing that averts yielding to senseless panic. At the same time I freely admit that in moments of extreme peril, while awaiting the commission of His will, I have found things getting a little tense. The quake provided one of those moments.

My next recollection is of a weird stillness. Not a silent stillness. The brickwork of nearby big buildings was still toppling with the rumble of landslides. It was the stillness of a motionless earth. I thanked God for sparing my life and got up, finding it hard to stand on the tilted floor of my room.

I went to my window. It was on the side of the house, separated from the next building by a narrow alley-way. Now both buildings were leaning together, my window pressed tightly against the adjacent wall. I remember dressing and packing my canvas bag, saying to myself aloud, "Well, you won't be using this room tonight. It's time to move."

Out in the corridor, I found all my fellow boarders milling around, some in a state of shock, but all alive. It took me some time to realize what had happened. In our house the basement was for storage, the ground floor consisted of parlor, dining room and kitchen, and the sleeping quarters were on the three floors above. On the big shock our ground floor, unoccupied, had slid into the basement, dropping us one story but leaving us unhurt.

Now I was worried about friends—Tim Gothe and his family, Elmer Jones, the girl in the young people's society. I ran to the front of the house, climbing out of the second story window that was now at street-level. Everywhere people were clawing at the debris of what had once been homes. Sometimes I stopped to help, but my main concern was to get to friends who might need me. I remember one awful moment when I saw an ice wagon headed south in the direction I was going, the driver lashing his horses to full gallop. I made a run and jumped on the foot board at the rear. The wagon bed was covered with the bodies of the injured and dying. I dropped off, feeling sick. They were hospital-bound, and there was no hospital.

I found my friends all safe, and reported to them the condition of the downtown district. Already efforts were being made to get rescue and salvage work on an organized basis, but as Tim said, voicing the dread of all of us, "If fire breaks out down there—"

Fire couldn't help but break out down there. Every stove, every shattered steam boiler, every toppled blacksmith's forge, every kerosene lantern—fire sources beyond count. All we

43

could do was gather on the surrounding hills and watch the city burn.

There should have been plenty of work after that rebuilding the city, and for a time there was. The city fathers talked big about plans for the *new* San Francisco, one of which I remember well because it concerned Chinatown. In the *new* plan the site of Chinatown would become the heart of the city, and the Chinese, without a word to say about the condemnation proceedings, would be moved to some valueless land on the outskirts of town. I don't know if Mr. Jones had anything to do with it or not, but the Chinese came up with a carefully worded counterproposal. If they were forced to vacate, they would, as law-abiding citizens, move out, all the way to Los Angeles, taking with them all their trade with the Orient and their enormous value as a tourist attraction. Very hastily plans for a new *new* city were drawn up, and Chinatown is still the heart of San Francisco.

My first job after the fire was with the Pacific Foundry in the unharmed part of San Francisco. But the big contracts expected to come out of reconstruction work failed to materialize. Money was tight, they said when they let me go.

I got another job with an Oakland elevator works that was booming on promises of all the elevators it was going to build for the new skyscrapers across the bay. San Francisco remained a shanty-town, and the desperate need for elevators faded away. Again I was fired, but not until I had completed the four years of apprenticeship that made me a journeyman molder. At last I was a full-fledged member of the iron workers union, and on the strength of that I got a job with the Judson Iron Works. I even had some money in the bank when the Panic of 1907 hit the West Coast so hard that the banks closed without bothering to ask if they'd been hurt.

I walked the streets for days. You couldn't buy a job even if you could have got your money out of a bank to buy it with. In this extremity I got a letter from my brother Bill. He was the business-minded brother who could, Dad used to say admiringly, "go out in the morning with a jack-knife and come back for supper on a bicycle." This time he had started out with a couple of city lots in Portland and ended up with a section of cut-over land near Rex, Oregon. As long as I wasn't doing anything anyway, would I come up and pull his stumps? Cash money, of course. Small, but cash.

If being broke wasn't enough of a spur, I was further goaded into taking the job by the unreasonable attitude of a girl in San Francisco. It was her candid opinion that anyone who had worked in three foundries and an elevator works and still couldn't hold a job was not worth waiting for. I felt the need of communing a few months with stumps to heal the wounds on my injured heart and wallet.

Bill had traded his way into more than a section of stumps. On hand when I got there was a small cook shack that provided fine living quarters for myself and a few chipmunks. Also left to me was a lone tree in the center of the clearing, formerly used by the lumbermen as a spar. Today I build a portable steel tower to do the same job, with an electric winch at the base, a pulley block at the top, and a steel cable that can be drawn into the forest to snake out logs that can't be reached by teams or tractors. The spar tree I had, with a pulley block 60 feet up its trunk, was a far cruder arrangement, but I figured that if the lumberjacks could use it to skid logs, I could use it to pull and skid stumps.

At a nearby stone quarry that was closing down, I was able to buy a few drums of cable and a steam-powered machine that was bragging when it called itself a donkey engine. A burro engine would be more like it. With the burro engine and cable drum installed at the base of the tree, and with an ample supply of pitch-filled bark for fuel, I started to work. In one week I encountered every form of obstinate root a stump can possess. I climbed the spar tree so often, replacing snapped cable and setting up new combinations of block and tackle, that I came to know the knots on its trunk by name. I had no mathematics to guide me in threading my block and tackle, but when you have to climb a 60-foot tree every time the cable snaps, you learn about such things much faster than in school. I also learned that what I couldn't accomplish by a direct pull from the spar tree, I could accomplish by threading the cable through sheaves attached to stumps in one direction or another from the stump being pulled. With plenty of cable to work with, I worked out a network running through sheaves from one stump to another so complicated that it resembled a spider's web. I'd stand at the burro engine at the base of the spar tree and take up slack on the cable drum. Cable would get humming-taut in all directions, and the engine would falter. I'd tie off the safety valve and throw in more bark. The cables would sound in the breeze like violin strings. More bark into the firebox and the spar tree would bend in the direction of strain. Something had to give, and often it was the stump I intended to pull. Once it was three other anchor stumps. Instead of being gratified that I was pulling three stumps for one, I wasted an entire day trying to figure out where my leverage problem had gone wrong.

I miscalculated often, learning by doing so, and only once was it serious. I had cleared all the stumps within 300 yards, and was really reaching out for the rest. I put the power to the cable drum, boosted the steam pressure on the boiler well past the safety limits, and was getting no results. The cable had that warning hum, and I glanced up at the spar tree to see how it was doing. Boing! I hear that "boing" sound on television as a gag, but that was the sound I heard, and it was no gag. Before I could twist my upturned face away, the snapped cable dropped across my mouth. Like that, half of my front teeth were gone. Yards of falling cable wrapped around me like wet string. By the time I untangled myself, and dusted myself off, and discovered I was still alive, I was beginning to get the idea that on hazardous jobs in the wilderness, a man ought to have a partner. Somebody to tell the others how you had been killed, and maybe save them from the same mistake.

My bill for the solid gold smile the dentist gave me just

about equaled what I had made pulling stumps. It was to cost a lot more back in San Francisco getting a dentist to replace the gold with less spectacular porcelain caps. Right there began my feud with doctors and dentists that I have carried on ever since. I number many doctors and dentists among my friends, as long as they are not working on me.

5

When I returned to San Francisco during the summer of 1908, business in general was showing improvement, but jobs for young iron molders were still scarce. Fires had swept two more foundries, releasing a score of molders senior to me. That put me at the bottom of the hiring list with no assurance that more foundries wouldn't burn before I got to the top. I began to wonder if I had been wise in choosing a profession so combustible.

My old boss at the Judson Iron Works kept me in eating money with occasional odd jobs, but a few hours of work now and then was no release for the energy pent up in this boy fresh down from the hills. In my free time I walked every hill in San Francisco and Oakland hunting work, continuing my pacing in my room after returning discouraged at dark. The family I was boarding with was being driven crazy by my restlessness, nor did I help matters by fixing everything in the house, whether it needed it or not. They were friends of my family, having been members of the Plymouth Brethren. Grunigen was their name, good people who deserved better than to be kept awake nights by my floor-pounding. Later, through their son Arnold, I was able to repay them a little for their consideration. With Arnold supplying the brainwork and me the energy, we were to get the Christian Business Men's Committee flourishing on a national and international basis, leading the senior Grunigen to claim with some pride that that great organization had gotten its start in his house.

Nevertheless, I am sure he was relieved when I finally got a job before I demolished his house with my repair work. The new job, like my meeting with Arnold, was to have lasting repercussions in my life.

I joined a line of men standing in front of a "Man Wanted" sign posted on a side door of the Yerba Buena Power System. I didn't know what the power system was for, nor why a man was needed, but I did know I wanted a job. "Know anything about melting lead?" I was asked. "I know it melts quicker'n iron," I answered. "Hire that guy," said someone. "He's the first one to know that much."

The electrical trades no longer have a bottom as low as where I started. I began as the scraper of the fouled lead plates taken from old storage batteries. And by no means were these ordinary plates and batteries. As I was to learn in time, the Yerba Buena Power System supplied direct current electricity to the trolley lines of Oakland. To produce an even and reliable flow, its erratic generators were used to charge scores of huge batteries, and it was from these banks of batteries that the current flowed to the streetcars.

My job was created by the fact that once every five years the batteries had to be reconditioned, one at a time, so as to cause no interruption of service. Each battery was eight feet by four feet by four—exactly the size of a cord of wood—and each lead plate was the hefty size of a table top. And after a year's service those plates were foul. Some were eaten by corrosion, and others were scaly with chemical accretions.

The job of the reconditioning crew was to clean the plates still usable, and save what we could of those eaten by corrosion. I was the cleaner.

It was a dirty job and dangerous. Working away with scraper and wire brush, I filled the air with the dust of lead, corrosion, and dried chemicals, a dust that ate the clothes right off our backs. I wore no mask, health regulations were unheard of, and if I got lead poisoning it was my own hard luck.

Yet that was the job that introduced me to the welding torch and led to my being known at one time as "Tobin-bronze Bob, The One-Tool Mechanic." Beyond that, it led to my taking welding out of the "repair work" class, and making it a universally accepted manufacturing process. I wasn't alone in that, of course, but I will say that our company is unique in that we never use a bolt where a weld will do.

The way it worked out at the power plant, as fast as I cleaned a plate, I passed it on to the man next to me. He was not called a welder, but a lead burner. In his hand he held a fascinating instrument called an oxyhydrogen torch and with that he heated the lead plate to exactly the right temperature for "burning" it back into place in the battery cell. From the moment I saw him burn in the first plate, I wanted his job, and not entirely because I wanted to get out of my own.

Thanks to my iron-molding background, I was able to give my lead burner better service than an ordinary helper, and he, in turn, was very gracious in letting me try my hand with his torch. I soon discovered why lead burners were in a class by themselves. Lead is one of those deceptive metals that doesn't change appearance when it nears the melting point. It looks cold right up to the moment it becomes liquid and runs away like quicksilver, yet it is precisely at the moment the lead is about to become liquid that the plate can be fused to the bus bar of the battery. To determine that split-second in those days, the burner had only his instinct to guide him. I remember my astonishment when my first efforts melted away before my eyes, leaving gaping holes in the plates I had so painfully cleaned.

Then one day when my lead burner was gone from the battery room, I said to myself, "It's time to quit fooling around, and really do a job." I lighted up the torch, fitted a clean plate into the battery, and started burning it to the bus bar. I put my mind to my work with such determination and concentration, that I didn't know what was going on around me. I got a good scald on the job, and stepped back to admire it. There was the big boss, right behind me. I thought it was the end for me. Lowly scrapers just weren't allowed to put a torch to the bus bar where the damage could be considerable. But what he said was, "I'll get you a torch."

I felt as though I had been knighted. A week later, so naturally did a torch fit into my hand, I was promoted to the full rank of lead burner after the shortest apprenticeship on record.

We worked our way through the batteries of the Y.B.P.S. in about three months, during which time I had learned a lot about oxyhydrogen welding and the rudiments of electricity. Then the reconditioning crew was off to its next job in Los Angeles. I was offered a chance to go along, but everyone in San Francisco knew Los Angeles was a sorry town with no future. I decided to take my chances on construction work, now beginning to boom again.

Brick layers, I next discovered, were as aristocratic within their own trades as iron molders and lead burners. Again I started at sub-bottom, aided only by the fact that my experience mixing molding sand entitled me to mix mortar for the bricklayers and carry it to them in a hod up several flights of ladders. By the time the brickwork of that building was finished, I had learned how to mix a mighty fine batch of concrete.

My letters home contained none of this depressing information. To eliminate any possibility that Mother might worry about her wandering boy, I loaded my letters so full of golden opportunities that Dad began to wonder what he was doing in Portland. He wrote as much to Uncle J. in Duluth, and the next thing I knew both were in San Francisco, wanting to know where to start.

Joshua Jehosophat LeTourneau—there was a name, and there was the man to go with it. He was J.J. for "Jumpin' Jehosophat" in the fullest meaning of the term. Within a week of his arrival at the Golden Gate, he had been steered to so many gold mines he didn't know which one to buy.

And my father, Caleb Thucydides LeTourneau was also the man to live up to his name. For brothers they were as unlike as any two men I ever met. Uncle J. was the man of finance. Dad was the executor of the work that carried out his dreams. Both worked for the exhausting excitement of working, with Uncle J. wanting his dividend in cash, and Dad wanting it in whatever the Lord would provide. My father hadn't been in town a week than he was all for vineyards, prunes, and almonds, with his dreams based on a magic promise called irrigation.

Uncle J. ended up by buying the worked-out but still producing No. 5 Exchequer Gold Mine in the Merced Valley. Dad had no objection to mining for gold, as long as his share would be applied to buying the lands he wanted to bring into bloom. There remained the problem of who would do all the work. At this point both father and uncle looked at a young back made powerful by iron molding, lead carrying, hod toting and stump wrestling, and I was elected.

Two things about gold mining have equal impact in my memory. The No. 5 mine had been worked originally from a vertical shaft sunk from the top of a steep ridge. At the 300-foot level its operators had found it more expedient to run in a horizontal shaft at the foot of the ridge. Thus between the two shafts enough rock formations were exposed to provide for me a highly practical if unacademic course in geology, a fact that later was to save my skin when I took a big road-building contract at Boulder Dam. At the same time I became an expert in the use of dynamite, an art that was to serve me well on scores of contracts.

While we never did find the big gold vein that was supposed to be there, I managed to get out enough low grade ore to more than meet expenses. Dad was able to put a down payment on his dream ranch on the banks of the Stanislaus River just outside Escalon. Again there was that matter of having a strong back to set out the grape vines, and break soil for the wheat crops, and milk a couple of cows, and clear about ten acres of scrub oak that he saw as desirable almond land. Figs, too, he had in mind, if I had the strength to clear another ten acres of oak closer to the river. Wages? "Tell you what I'll do, son. You clear the land for Uncle J. and me, and you can keep what you make sellin' it off as cord wood." He was a dreamer, but he was a New England, Yankee-type dreamer, so that was the best I could do.

I was more than a year on the gold mine-farming venture, an important year in many ways. In hand-shoveling an irrigation ditch from the river to Dad's fig sprouts, I learned how to calculate the lay of the land practically to the ounce of earth moved. Equally valuable was my experience cutting oak with an axe. Maybe you don't have to move earth with a hand-shovel to learn how to make earth-moving machines, and maybe you don't have to cut oak with an axe to learn how to make jungle crushers, but I've never stopped being grateful for the experience.

One day in the grove I hauled off for a full swing at a tough old oak and hit a knot. The bit of the axe rang, my hands were left numb by the whip of the handle, and I knew I had done something very bad. I took time and courage to glance down. Instead of having cut off my leg, as I thought I had, I had pared the calf of my leg from the bone with a vertical slash, not an amputating horizontal one.

While the wound was healing, I had time to ask myself what I was doing. I was just past 21, and by the time I was able to hobble around, I was able to realize that my career was hobbling, too. I was in many ways an iron molder, lead burner, brick layer, carpenter, gold miner, stump puller, irrigation ditch digger, farmer and oak chopper. Everything the hard way, by hand, or, with the exception of the oxyhydrogen torch, by tools that hadn't been improved in centuries. The more I thought over my past jobs, the less I wanted them in my future. What was I? As far as I could see from the record, I was a washed-up bum.

A correspondence school ad in the back of a magazine caught my attention. Most of it was devoted to the glowing future of the automobile and the riches that would be literally thrust upon the mechanic who understood its innards. Well, I was willing to be forced to get rich through mechanics. I sent for the course.

When the first lessons arrived, I tried studying them by lantern light at night in the tent I had set up on the job. I don't know how Abe Lincoln managed to study by firelight, but after a day of oak chopping, I fell asleep. I reversed the process by getting up at 4:00 a.m. to study by lantern light until dawn. The trouble with that program was that I'd get so interested in a lesson I'd forget about breakfast. Noon would arrive, and still no wood cut. I finally worked out a schedule of early morning chopping followed by four hours of study between ten and two, and then back to the axe to work off my remaining energy. In that way I worked my way through four correspondence courses that winter and cut enough wood to buy a one-cylinder motorcycle and had 100 cords left over. When I could take the motorcycle apart and put it together again in one day, I held a one-man graduation ceremony for myself and gave myself a B.M. degree for Bachelor of Motorcycles. That ended my education.

I was amazed to discover that none of the garage owners in San Francisco were overwhelmed by my self-conferred degree in mechanics. The best I could get was a job tending the stationary gasoline engines for a crew building a bridge across the Stanislaus River. I soon had the engines on the pump, hoist, and concrete mixer running as smooth as silk, and then I began to look around. I didn't see anything I liked.

Construction work in 1909 was man-killing in the full meaning of the term. Steel beams still had to be man-handled when mule-drawn loads bogged down in the mud. Accidents on the ground were frequent even before the clumsy steam cranes began lifting the beams to the riggers waiting on the structure. The best of crane operators, jerking at a confusing array of long handles, and tromping on foot pedals, was lucky to line up a beam within inches of where it was to be placed, after which the riggers, working with no safety devices or nets, had to use their own weight to get it into position. The steel hanger with three years' experience was greatly admired in those days. Not for his skill. For his survival.

The other side of bridge building—the construction of the approaches—was just as appalling. On our little job of bridging the Stanislaus, we had a high bluff to cut through on one side, and a wide stretch of bottom land to fill on the other. Today we would just rig a conveyor belt across the river, and use the dirt from the bluff to fill the bottom land. In 1909 the contractor cutting through the hill hauled his dirt away from the river, and the contractor on the other side, filling the bottom land, hauled his dirt to the river. It all seemed right and proper then.

As the young man who was to become a manufacturer of earth-moving equipment, I marvel that what I saw on the Stanislaus didn't turn me away from the field forever. As it had been ever since the invention of the wheel, the first earthmovers were the men with the wheelbarrows and shovels. They prepared the way for the teamsters to get in with their dump carts and larger crews of shovelers. But we were also keeping up with the march of progress. With us also was a newfangled thing called a Fresno. A whole score of Fresnoes, in fact.

In earth-moving history, the Fresno must occupy a place second only to the wheelbarrow. It was invented around 1880 by Abijah McCall, a blacksmith and part-time digger of irrigation ditches. His machine, named after the town where it was manufactured, made possible the swift expansion of the railroads and highways from the turn of the century right into the twenties. As the saying went, the Fresno moved more dirt than Gossip.

It was, in brief, a mule-powered scoop shovel. It came in widths of from three feet, for two-mule power, up to five feet for a four-mule team. The handle of the shovel was an iron bar up to eight feet long that was operated by the mule skinner. In action, the mules dragged the empty Fresno along the ground on its bottom until the operator reached the point where he wanted to scoop up some earth. There he lifted up on the handle of his shovel, tilting the blade into the ground. The mules groaned, sometimes kicked resentfully, but usually pulled if the operator was a real mule skinner, meaning one who could crack his whip and lift a patch of mule skin from where it would do the most good. Four mules on a five-foot Fresno could scoop up half a cubic yard of dirt, at which point the skinner threw his weight down on the handle and tilted the blade out of the ground.

It sounds so simple, and it was in beach sand. But put a few rocks in the way. Then the operator, shoulder under the handle trying to dip the blade into the ground, could get his head slapped off by the unexpected resistance of a rock at the far corner of the scoop. Or, should he be resting his full weight on the handle in an effort to tilt a full load out of the ground, a jarring encounter with a rock could kick him in the midriff hard enough to knock him windless, or rear-end over tea kettle, or both. Mule skinners had many colorful descriptions for such incidents.

On our job, the Fresnoes were used to cut down the hill approach. At first they had but a short haul, cutting into the back side of the hill, and dumping into a convenient valley. As the cut grew longer the hauls increased from ten minutes for a round trip to 20, and finally to a half hour. Four mules and one man to move one cubic yard of dirt an hour, if there were no balky mules to block traffic, as there usually were. I might also add that because the Fresnoes were skidded along on their bottoms, both empty and loaded, they wore out fast, presenting a substantial replacement cost at $40 apiece. I can hear some of my customers snickering when I say $40 represented a substantial replacement cost. I sell machines now for which the replacement of just one tire costs $3600, and that's one of my medium-sized tires.

The bridge was completed in September. With $100 in cash, a motorcycle, and 100 cords of wood in reserve, I was richer than I had ever been before, and felt reasonably secure if I didn't get another job all winter. In that confident frame of mind I rode across our completed bridge, through our completed hill approach so recently jammed with mules, and by nightfall was in Stockton. To me it was just another town. I ate in a hash house there while I debated with myself whether I should try the dirt road to Oakland at night or wait for morning. With four or five pork chops under my belt, I decided I was in no hurry. I put my motorcycle in a garage, and got a room in a place that called itself a hotel across the street. As casually as that did I turn one of the most important corners in my life.

6

As the crow flies, Stockton is only some 60 miles due east of Oakland, but because of the Dublin Mountains in between, few crows are willing to make the trip. I had a contract some years later to build a road through Crow Canyon to provide a more direct route between the two cities, so I know how the crows feel. On that rock-strewn, gully-sliced, rattlesnake-infested job I had to invent the first mechanical bulldozer to break even. Strangers going east over that highway are always surprised to find that Stockton isn't in the middle of a desert like the Mojave. Instead, it is in a rich valley, not far from where the San Joaquin River empties into San Francisco Bay. Because of that, Stockton has long been the headquarters for the makers of farm machinery and dirt-moving equipment.

My own company had no such logical reason for starting there. I started there because I parked my motorcycle in a Stockton garage overnight. When I went to reclaim it in the morning, the first man I met was an iron-molder named

Jensen, last seen when I worked with him at Judson's. It turned out he was a half-owner of the garage in partnership with a man named Cap. Under the circumstances, I was not long in informing him that I had read through four correspondence courses in automobile mechanics and had graduated myself at the head of my class.

His partner Cap was dubious. "Is that all you know? I mean no other experience?"

"I can take a motorcycle apart and put it together in a day."

"We don't handle motorcycles," said Cap.

But Jensen, knowing I was a good worker, was more charitable. "We can put him on as night man, answering the phone and maybe towing in a stranded car. He won't have to be doing any repair work."

A mechanic at last, even if I was not supposed to do any repair work. As night man my main job was to go to the rescue of customers whose cars had broken down. There were a lot of them, and what they had to say about me, Jensen, Cap and the automobile world in general would have fired up a dozen cars if we could have put it in the carburetor. Actually, in most cases, the cars were not to blame. In 1910 the gasoline we were getting in California was not the best, nor were our delivery and storage tanks much better. Moisture had a habit of condensing in them by the bucket, creating a lot of rust that invariably found its way into one carburetor or another, usually, I was to discover, at night.

The big advantage of my job as night mechanic was that I could sleep in the back seat of a car between phone calls. That left me pretty well rested up during the day so I could wear off some of my surplus energy giving the boys a hand in the shop. That was all right with Cap. As long as he paid me only for night work, I could put in 24 hours a day without bothering him.

No one asked me to help on simple jobs. But if a clutch had to be removed, or a motor lifted, or a new transmission installed, the call went out for me. With a little observation, I was not long in mastering the inner workings of Saxons, Everetts, Regals, Fords, Buick White Streaks, E.M.F.'s and a vicious monster we called the left-handed Cadillac.

I doubt there are many who recall the left-handed Cadillac with affection. It cranked backwards and kicked frontwards. No matter how you gripped the crank, and no matter which arm you used, a right-handed man was always off balance turning a heavy motor counterclockwise. And when you were off-balance to start with and the brute backfired, you were hospital bound with a broken arm, jaw, or both. I remember broken arms were so common the doctors had splints and casts prepared in advance for "crank-handle break," or "car starter's wrist." With my naturally husky build and iron molder's arms, I was luckier than most. I could hang onto a crank. What got me were the forward projecting fenders. A really solid backfire against my braced arm would snatch me off my feet and slam my ribs into a fender with a cruncher I can feel yet.

It was a call to tow in a left-handed Cadillac that gave the course of my life an unexpected turn. I found the stalled car about a mile out of town on a dark and lonely road, and as usual the owner was a very irate man indeed. He became more so when I informed him that I was just the night man, and was not supposed to work on expensive cars.

He was so mad he had forgotten all thoughts of a tow. He wanted that car to carry him in under its own power if he had to stay there all week. "If you can't fix it," he growled at me, "at least you can turn your lights on my motor so I can."

I maneuvered around and got a glow from my acetylene gas headlamps to shine on his motor. I offered to assist, but he was pretty short with me. "I paid a lot of money for this car," he said, "and I don't want any second-rate mechanic wrecking it for me."

He began work, taking out the spark plugs. The wrench slipped a couple of times, and he barked his knuckles pretty badly while barking his temper even more. Finally he was so beside himself he would have thrown the car away if he could have picked it up.

"Go ahead," he yelled at me. "Fix it yourself. I don't care if you make junk out of it. It will serve it right."

If I couldn't do anything else, I could clean carburetors. I was only a few minutes taking it apart. If any rust from the gasoline was plugging the needle valve, it was too small to be seen, but I polished the needle, blew through the jet, and put the carburetor back together. I cranked a couple of times to give the gasoline a chance to fill the float chamber, pulled the choke wire, and gave her a full left-handed twist. That was it.

I like to point out in my talks that little things, too small to be seen, can stop a motor just as effectively as a rod through the crankcase. And it's the little things that get into our lives—a small lie, a snubbing of our neighbor, a thoughtless taking of the Lord's name in vain—that can stop your Christian way of life as surely as the big sins. Yet the Lord is willing to cleanse you of all sins, large and small, if you will only ask Him. And when that happens, you will find everything running smoothly again.

As it turned out, the Cadillac owner was an influential man in Stockton, and he was so taken by the speed with which I had fixed his car that he bragged me up as the best mechanic in town. Jensen and Cap must have been impressed, because a few days later I was promoted to full fledged mechanic on the day shift. All told, I worked in the garage six months, rarely leaving it except to go to church on Sunday. The Plymouth Brethren were too few in number to have a church in Stockton, so we met in one home or another each Sunday, these calls providing my only social life. Under conditions like that, a young man can learn a lot about cars if he applies himself.

Thanks to my Cadillac friend, I had several customers who specified that I was to service their cars personally. One day, toward the end of my sixth month at the garage, one of them came to me with a proposition. "You know my son Parks, don't you?" he asked. (For once I am using a fictitious name for reasons that will become clear later.)

I knew Parks. At the time he was as fine a fellow as I have ever met—handsome, well-educated, loaded with personality, and with a business mind that was a shame to waste. He worked as a salesman for a rival garage, and though he was just my age, he had the reputation of being the best auto salesman in town.

"He's thinking of going into the garage business, and I'm ready to back him," the customer continued, "if he can find the right partner to manage the repair end. It occurs to me, you might be the man."

At lunch time I went over to see Parks, and we hit it off at once. Within five minutes we were deep into plans. A fifty-fifty partnership, with Parks running the sales and the business side, and me servicing the cars and handling the repairs. No livery stable converted into a garage for us. We had to have a new building. I'm not sure, but I think we had the first building designed exclusively for the sales and servicing of automobiles in that section of California.

We both had to put up $1,000, after which Parks' father would back our notes for the rest. Fortunately I had the 100 cords of wood I had cut the previous winter. Now well-seasoned, it brought $10 a cord, and I was in business.

We opened up our garage, not-so-modestly called the Superior Garage, in the heart of town, just down from the corner we called Information, Education, Salvation, and Damnation. To earn its name it had on its four corners the telephone exchange, a business college, the Y.M.C.A., and the town jail. Not much of a gag today, but in 1911 we could sure wow strangers when we told them what corner they were standing on.

The Superior Garage was a success from the start. With a modern show place on the main street, Parks had no difficulty in getting the distributorship for the underslung Regal, a real road scorcher that was approached only by the Buick White Streak and the "chummy" Saxon roadster, so called because a couple sitting in the narrow back seat got very chummy indeed on a rough road. Back in the shop I was doing such a good job of reconditioning the cars Parks was taking in on trade-ins that we were making almost as much money on second-hand cars as on the Regals.

The Stockton County Fair of 1911 was coming up, and naturally we wanted to be represented on Machinery Square where the prospering ranchers gathered to look over the latest in harvesters, tractors, and threshing machines. Autos were a big attraction, with a lot of farmers still arguing in favor of the horse, so I knew Parks would have plenty of chances to get in his sales talk. What bothered me was that my former employers, Cap and Jensen, would be out there selling their line of E.M.F.'s, which Parks claimed stood for Every Morning Fix. So would be the dealers in Buicks, Fords and Saxons. What we ought to have, I argued, was a sure-fire demonstration that would set up our Regal in a class by itself. Something that would catch the eye of the whole public instead of just the men visiting Machinery Square. A grandstand stunt.

Once I got on the track of that idea, I had to find the stunt, and while thinking about that, I happened to be driving past a flight of wide stone steps. Seeing was doing, and up the steps I drove the Regal, its underslung springs taking the bumps as nice as you please. That was it then. I went to the county fair board and offered as a grandstand act to drive a Regal up and down a flight of stairs 30 feet high. "Three times a day for free," I urged. "And just to make it interesting, I'll build the staircase to the exact width of my wheels, and no rails on either side."

So three times a day during the week of the fair, I poured everything I had into the Regal, racing up one side so fast my tires barely touched the stair treads on the down side. Parks, in the meantime, would be megaphoning his sales talk and challenging any other car dealer to duplicate the stunt. We were safe. I knew the Buick and the Saxon could climb the stairs as fast as our Regal, but there wasn't a driver to be found who would try it. Let the steering be as little as one inch out of line, and somebody would be in for a bad spill.

Say, did we sell Regals after that.

Our demonstration wouldn't work in 1912. Buick had imported a driver from the East who could not only climb my stairs but was ready to climb a guy wire if necessary. Still on our side was a higher gear ratio. Given the right driver, I suggested (and I didn't mean me) we could enter our Regal stock car against the professionals in the county fair races. I didn't know how we would make out against racing cars. My idea was that we challenge Buick to enter, too.

"Even if we lost to the professionals, we'll still beat Buick," I urged. "If he won't compete, you can claim we've got the only stock car fast enough to race with the pros."

I don't claim to have invented stock car racing—every man who ever owned a horseless carriage raced it at one time or another—but the entry of a stock car in a professional race certainly got us a lot of publicity around Stockton. The driver we hired was a young man named Percy Arthur. The Percy worried me. In our part of the west Percy was a name second only to Little Lord Fauntleroy for sissies. When I met him, I was not reassured. A pink-cheeked youngster with a downy mustache. Eyes so mild it was hard to believe they could look so cold behind a pair of goggles.

I started to become bald at an early age, and I know when it happened. It was with my first turn around the track with Percy Arthur.

I was the mechanic. We didn't know too much about souping up motors then, but I will say that if any specks of rust were to block our carburetor, they would have had to have been the size of walnuts. When our Regal needed gas, we got it. We rounded the circular one-mile track with our outside tires worn out. The tires on the inner rail side had barely touched the ground.

"This heap might do," said Percy approvingly. "We might even keep up with the pack if we can get more fire in the engine."

I changed to some "lightning bolt" spark plugs, opened the apertures in the carburetor still wider, added an air scoop for a sort of super-charger, and changed the worn out tires. Off we went on another test run.

The auto track—it was inside this track that later I was to build the half-mile horse track—had a plain rail fence on the inside. On the outside, for the protection of spectators, it had the same rail fence bucked up with steel cable rigged to posts as thick as telephone poles. We screamed around the far turn, and came into the stretch past the grandstand. We didn't skid. It was just that our high-bodied stock car couldn't corner like the racers Percy was accustomed to. We took out sixteen posts and all the rail and cable in between.

They told me later Percy was still steering for the next lap when they pulled him out of the wreckage. They didn't worry about me. They thought I was dead.

From what I can gather, they got around to me when they discovered I was still warm long after the crash. I came to in the Stockton hospital. I didn't say, "Where am I?" I asked, "Where did I get those curtains?" For the two years I had slept in the storage room of the garage I hadn't seen a curtain, and their presence alarmed me. Then I saw the nurse, and, completely bewildered, asked, "And where did I get you?"

I was pretty generally shattered, the most serious of my injuries being a badly broken neck. They didn't know much about traction in those days, nor did they have any of those padded leather collars for neck injuries. They tried to straighten me up with a rope arrangement that was first cousin to a hangman's noose. It didn't work. No matter how they tied my neck in place and lashed my aching body to the bed, they'd find me in the morning with my head lying limp on my shoulder. "He looks," said a doctor one day, "like a chicken trying to put its head under its wing—if he had enough neck."

The doctors were doing their best. I know they were doing their best. Every day they would take that broken neck of mine and try to work it back into place. Still, a 180-pound doctor bearing down with his full weight on a broken neck trying to get it into place is not building up love in his patient. Not in this patient. Especially when, after weeks of being reduced daily to a lump of agony and cold sweat, I was released from the hospital carrying my head on my right shoulder like a tote sack.

I tried everything with no result. My head rested so heavily on my shoulder my ear was being rubbed raw. In desperation I again went to a doctor, this one a bone specialist of high repute in San Francisco. I don't know what he did, but from the shock of pain that hit me while I was strapped face down on his table, I think he jumped on me with both feet from a step ladder. Right there I vowed they would never get me to a doctor again unless they carried me, as they were to do from time to time.

As a joke Percy, who had emerged reasonably sound, suggested we hit the fence from the opposite direction, and break my neck back into place. A joke, and we could laugh at it, but it was the most sensible suggestion I'd heard. A few months later, during which I had been massaging my neck regularly and had restored some strength to my neck muscles, I took a nasty spill on a motorcycle to avoid hitting a dog. I felt the sharp pain in my neck, and said, "Oh, oh. Back to the hospital again." But that was not the case. I had actually wrenched my neck a couple of notches in the right direction so that my head no longer rested on my shoulder.

More months of massage and muscle training were to pass before I could really hold my head up, and you can be sure that when I did succeed it was through the help of God. The only trace left now is after a long day. Then my head tends to list to starboard a little. My wife tells me I look as though I have my head cocked over attentively, which is a nice way of putting it.

And having mentioned my wife, I will continue by saying that it was at this point in my life that I met her, though scarcely noticing the event. After my release from the hospital I was in no shape to go back to my bed in the garage, so at the invitation of Uncle Bob Gilmour and his wife, I moved into their back room. Uncle Bob, at the urging of my father, had finally forsaken the winters in Duluth, and was now using his blacksmith talents to help us out at the garage while also doing some work for a big draying company owned by another ex-Minnesotan named Oscar Peterson.

Mr. Peterson was a second-generation Swede, born in Minneapolis to parents who were among the first Swedes to arrive in that city. In time his father had moved the family to Stockton where he went into the moving van and general draying business. He and Oscar kept their horses in a barn behind their house, and while they were big, beautiful animals, Oscar was trying to replace them with modern motor vans. It was a necessary step, and one we favored at the garage because it meant business for us.

On the other hand, the Teamster's Union was opposed to trucks, seeing them as something that would put teamsters and horses out of business. One night a few hot-heads ganged up on Oscar, and if I hadn't arrived with my bulk, things might have gotten a little rough. I accompanied him to his home that night, and then when there was no relaxing in the tension, for several nights thereafter.

Finally one night he said, "Bob, maybe I'm a stubborn Swede, but I'm going ahead with this. As long as you're coming out here every night, why don't you just move in with us? We've got an extra room that isn't doing anything."

I moved in, and then began to wonder why. His oldest daughter Evelyn was a twelve-year-old in high button shoes, gingham dress, and two huge hair ribbons tied to long, blonde braids. She was full of questions like, "If you broke your neck, why aren't you dead?" Or, "When your head tilts over like that, do you see things sideways or like I do?" What questions she didn't ask the younger ones—Ray, Howard, and Edna—did. A fifth child, Buster, arrived some years later, weighing in at 13 pounds. He was christened Robert, but Buster he was called, and Buster he is to this day.

The one calming influence in that house was Mrs. Peterson. She was as different from her husband as the positive and negative poles of a generator. America Butler was her maiden name, of the Butlers who came over on the *Mayflower*, and also of the Butlers who arrived in California among the survivors of the ill-fated Donner Party. You may remember that was the party that was snowed in for the winter at what is now called Donner Pass. As the history books have it, some members of the wagon train survived by living as cannibals on the bodies of those who had starved or frozen to death during the long ordeal. The history books also show that the Butlers were not among the cannibals, though they reached Sutter's Fort—now Sacramento—that spring more dead than alive.

Being not only a native daughter of California, but the daughter of a native son, Mrs. Peterson had one of those broad, liberal minds that could cope with anything, including me. I remember one time her oldest son Raymond came home with a dead cat and began digging up some tomato plants in the garden I had flourishing in the back yard. From the kitchen window she watched as he buried the cat and then carefully replaced the tomato plants on top of the grave. Then she strolled out to demand an explanation.

"Why," said Ray, "I'm going to help Bob raise catsoup."

Being the hero she was, she never batted an eye.

Life with the Petersons was never dull, on top of which it was my first family life since I had left home nearly six years earlier. I learned how to eat with a fork again, and how to drink coffee out of a cup instead of a saucer. As my neck healed and my head began to stand straighter on my shoulders, I was able to look around with new interest.

The year of 1912 was an exciting one in the automobile industry, with many radical improvements in ignition, carburetion, lighting and suspension. Each improvement was more complicated than the last, and we garage mechanics were united in the conviction that the whole thing was a conspiracy to make our jobs impossible. Just to open a gear shift housing was to drop a pile of springs and gears on the floor that would defy a Chinese puzzle-maker to put together.

The early self-starters were the most fiendish of the new improvements. I recall a spring starter that you cranked up like winding Big Ben. When you released the spring, it engaged the motor and spun it over. The only nice feature I can remember of that device was that if the motor kicked, it broke the spring instead of your arm. But try to fix that spring. I opened the housing of one one time and the spring shot the length of the garage, knocking out a window instead of me.

Then there was the Presto-Lite starter, made by the manufacturers of the acetylene headlights that were the feature of the day. This contrivance charged the motor cylinders with high-explosive acetylene gas instead of gasoline. Turn on the spark and you got instant combustion. If you didn't blow the head off the engine block. It added a certain excitement to starting a car, but I couldn't recommend it for ladies, or men with weak hearts.

With my changed attitude, I was able to accept these improvements as challenges, just as I had been able to accept the introduction of new methods in the foundry. Aiding me in this was a young, bespectacled friend named Henry Rogers. Hank was a real inventor, a living example of our famous fiction hero, Tom Swift.

Hank was building an electric self-starter for an old Ford he had. It was his idea that he would use the electricity from a battery to turn a starter that would turn the engine until it fired. Then he would use engine power to turn the starter until it replaced in the battery the electricity it had used. In short, he had a motor that could serve as starter or generator.

It had some bugs. It was bigger than the Ford engine it was supposed to start, a tail-wagging-the-dog sort of thing. My own hunch, now that I have my electric wheel, is that he might have done better if he had used a Ford engine to generate electricity for his starter, and used the starter to power the car. It also had a bad habit of buckling the plates in the battery with an overload. To my surprise, I, the dumb mechanic, was able to help Hank, the intellectual, by calling upon some of my half-forgotten experiences repairing batteries in Oakland. Between us we invented a cut-out that prevented overloading once the battery was fully charged.

"You have a knack for electricity, Bob," he said to me one day. "Why don't you study electrical engineering?"

"When and how?"

"You can read, can't you? That's all it takes. Anybody who can read has all it takes to study." He was a very earnest young man.

There's more to studying than reading. There is an awful lot of doing, too. That's why Henry Rogers remains in my mind as one of my most invaluable friends. The more I read about electricity, the more he had for me to do. Every time I'd get baffled by a wiring diagram, he'd have the real wires there for me to solder together.

I read, and I worked with Hank, and I worked in the garage, no longer annoyed by improvements but wondering why they didn't come faster. While I was deep in electric motors and generators, another big problem came up. A lot of our repair work at the garage consisted of cracked cylinder blocks or heads that had to be sent to San Francisco for welding. Sometimes we got the welded jobs back in a week, but a month was the usual rule. We knew we would be better off with a welder in our own shop, but the best welding school in San Francisco couldn't promise to turn out an acetylene torch welder in less than six months. Acetylene torch welding was brand new. It used a high temperature flame and was as tricky as all get-out. Unless the operator was highly trained, he could burn a hole through a cylinder wall quicker than he could repair a crack.

I read all I could find on the subject, and sent away to the manufacturers for more. When I had absorbed that, I decided it couldn't be a bit trickier than burning lead. It was time to quit reading and start doing. I went to San Francisco and bought a used torch from a welding shop with the understanding that I was to practice welding all kinds of metal under their six months' course of instruction. At the end of three days I had had it. I took my torch and drove back to Stockton, and there I hung out my shingle as a welder of all metals. I didn't know what a significant step I had taken.

7

My first successful invention was one designed for the hot-rod set of Stockton. Modern hot-rodders may consider themselves something new in this world, but they should have seen their grandfathers around 1915 when the roads were full of chuckholes and tires were inflated to a pressure of 75 pounds. The big difference then was that the elder crowd set the pace. There was something heady about moving up from horse and buggy to automobile that made even the old graybeards want to take off after three driving lessons and hit 60 miles per hour.

My invention was just the thing to catch on with these aging and not-so-aging hot-rodders. It was a cut-out in the exhaust pipe that could make a 30-mile-per-hour car sound like an express train on a down-hill grade. As usual, I made it with my welding torch, cutting a hole at the bend of the exhaust pipe just ahead of the muffler. When this hole was closed with a butterfly valve, also made with my welding torch, the exhaust gases were passed through the muffler and the car proceeded with reasonable quietness. But when the driver pulled a wire that opened the valve, the exhaust gases were funneled straight back with a trumpeting effect that was ear-shattering. Sleeping citizens, aroused at midnight when one of those things was turned on, told me what they thought about my invention, but I must have installed hundreds of them for hot-rodders, some coming from as far away as San Francisco. It was our biggest sideline.

Aside from being my first invention, the cut-out is important because it put me into another of those situations from which I could be saved only by Divine intervention. One day an elderly customer brought in his old Buick that he wanted brought up to date with a cut-out. He didn't want speed. He just wanted the sound of it.

I put the car over the grease pit, and climbed underneath with my torch to cut into the exhaust pipe. The whole under-carriage was a coagulated mass of oil and grease, that led me to believe that my torch might start a fire. I called to Uncle Bob Gilmour to stand by with a pail of water. Then I started to work. Sure enough, the oil-soaked floor boards caught fire.

"Douse her a little," I shouted. "It's getting warm down here."

He got excited and dumped in the whole bucket. Unfortunately, he had grabbed up a bucket of clear gasoline intended for use in cleaning automobile parts. Boom! The whole pit was filled with a sheet of flame.

Folks ask me what difference a man's religion makes as long as he is sincere, and I say it makes a big difference. The Bible says there is no other name under heaven whereby we can be saved but the name of Jesus. Uncle Bob was just as sincere as he could be, and he wouldn't have hurt me, his namesake, for the world, but his sincerity couldn't stop that gas from exploding, nor save me from being in the midst of the explosion.

How I got out from under the car I have never been able to

figure out. I know Uncle Bob ran for a fire extinguisher about 50 feet away. When he returned with it, I was already there with another extinguisher that I had snatched from the rear wall, several yards beyond his. Together we put out the fire with very little damage. Of course we got a lot of explanations for my miraculous escape. One was that the Buick had a canvas top, which offered no resistance, and so the force of the blast escaped upward instead of blowing the floor boards down through me. Other factors, too, were advanced to account for my unharmed state, but when I was on my knees that night I was not thanking a freak combination of physical laws for my deliverance. I knew I had been saved by the Lord Jesus, and all my thanks were directed to Him.

It was about this time that we dropped our dealership for the Regal car in favor of the up-and-coming Saxon. Now there was an automobile! Of all the cars I have tuned up and driven since 1910, that was the road-scorcher that is closest to my heart. It had everything. When we took over the Saxon agency, the company was one of the most promotion-minded in the country. Their stunt that year I still regard as a classic. It was a cross-country race against time, New York to San Francisco, with two company-trained expert mechanics riding along with all their spare parts as ballast. The big attention-getter was that the actual driving was done by local dealers along the way, as in a relay race. In the first place, the local dealer got a lot of publicity in his own home town for his participation in a national race. And in the second place, because the local dealer knew his roads as no outside professional driver could know them, he was able to set a blistering pace for his stretch that must have aged the two company mechanics considerably. I know in my case I set a record between Sacramento and Tracy that lasted until the road was paved eight years later, and all told, we knocked 16 hours off the existing transcontinental record.

What with one stunt and another like that, Parks and I were considered to be some pumpkins in Stockton by 1917. Our garage was rated as one of the best in town, my welding business had grown to include the repair of everything from pump handles to windmills and giant harvesting machines, and I even had some money in the bank. I was doing fine everywhere but in the direction it counted most. Oscar Peterson and I were not getting along at all well.

To go back some months earlier, Dad and Mother had arrived in Stockton and, finding a house to their liking, had moved in with the intention of making a home for me while Dad looked over the territory for something to do. It was nice to be at home with them, but at the same time I seemed to be spending a lot of evenings at the Petersons'. The Evelyn I had met when she was in high-buttoned shoes was wearing pumps now, and in a silk dress she was something to behold. What was more, she liked to go along for the evening drive when I road-tested the cars I had repaired during the day. It was Dad who suggested I was doing a lot more road-testing than most mechanics found necessary, and I remember telling him, "Don't go getting any wrong impressions. She's just my little pal."

Once he had planted the idea in my mind, however, I discovered how right he was, and after that Evelyn and I were not long in reaching an understanding. Mrs. Peterson, too, proved receptive to the idea, and even Oscar said yes, "if you want to wait for her."

The trouble began when his idea of waiting and ours failed to jibe by several years. After an appropriate wait of about six months, I again brought up the subject, and was met by one of those Scandinavian frosts that are said to freeze mountains. As far as Oscar was concerned, his oldest daughter was still his baby, and what Evelyn and I might think was of no consequence to him. "I said wait," he told me. "Talk to me in five years when she comes of age."

To Evelyn and me five years looked like a 100, so we made our own plans. On August 28, 1917 we were all set but for one slight miscalculation. Evelyn's folks picked that day for their annual shopping trip to Oakland, and she had to baby-sit for Buster, who was teething. I was parked in my Saxon in back of the Peterson livery barn, and I could hear Buster clear back there. From the sound of him, you'd have thought he was sprouting full-sized molars.

It was after dark when I heard the Peterson car drive up. In those days a good mechanic could recognize any car in town by the sound of its motor. I started up the Saxon for a fast get-away, and then waited. Fully an hour went by before Evelyn appeared, rather breathless.

"I couldn't bring it," she gasped. "I don't know—I think Dad suspects something—if he had seen me leave with a coat—" She didn't finish the sentence, and she didn't have to. I put the car in gear and away we went. Instead of going straight down the valley, I headed for the coast, hunting out the back roads.

Evelyn was still lacking several months of her 17th birth-day, a fact that California marriage laws considered important, but there was still Mexico.

Within an hour in the chill night air of California, Evelyn was paralyzed with cold. I stopped at an all-night garage and picked up a bargain in some old lap robes, but even wrapped in those she continued to freeze. I do have to admit one weak-ness in the Saxon roadster. Side curtains notwithstanding, it was just one big air scoop.

The dirt roads I was following did not help matters. The well-sprung Saxon took the chuckholes like a loping grey-hound, and by midnight Evelyn was car-sick. Excitement may have contributed to it, along with the clouds of dust that were coating her in layers.

According to my suspicions, later to be proved well-founded, Mr. Peterson would be telephoning every police chief and sheriff between Stockton and the Mexican border, warning them to be on the lookout for an eloping couple in a Saxon roadster. His actual warning was that they be on the lookout for the kidnapper of his little girl. From what I was told later this passed us through one town where an alert sheriff sized us up, but didn't think Evelyn answered the description of a "little girl." For my part, I was not taking any chances. As soon after daylight as the first hitch-hikers appeared on the road, I began picking them up, loading them in as though I were running a bus. At one time the chummy seat held a sheepherder and his dog while my bride-to-be sat on bony knees of two migrant fruit pickers. If the law was looking for an eloping couple, it would never see any romance in us.

In that fashion, still car-sick and dust covered, my bride arrived in Tia Juana. We were married within the hour in a civil ceremony. My plan was that we would drive on down into Lower California on a romantic Mexican honeymoon, but that was not to be. Even as I was carefully pocketing the Mexican papers that made us man and wife, one of the police in the town hall told us of the kidnapping charge. That made me so mad that we drove all the way back to Stockton. That was our honeymoon.

The truth is, we were in serious trouble. The District Attorney had Mr. Peterson's charge of kidnapping against me, and there was nothing in his California law books to make him look kindly at my marrying a California girl under 18 in Mexico. Evelyn was in tears before she convinced him that she had not been kidnapped. Some quiet talks with Mrs. Peterson, Ray, and Edna also served to allay his suspicion that I had crashed Oscar Peterson's house and stolen his daughter.

Finally he said, "All right, Bob, we're dropping the charges, but so help me, don't do it again." There was something so ridiculous in his last warning that we looked at each other for seconds before bursting into laughter. Besides, I was the only mechanic in town who could keep his Buick running, which may have helped more than anything.

Oscar Peterson did not speak to me for another seven years. One day in 1924 he came up to me in my Moss Avenue shop in Stockton, holding out his hand. "All right, Bob," he said. "You're all right, and my daughter is all right, and my grandchildren are all right. I'm the one that's wrong in holding a grudge. You want to shake hands with me?"

Did I? I nearly broke his arm, grabbing the way I did.

The feud was over, but Mr. Peterson was not the stubborn Swede he was without getting in the last word. "It isn't Christian, and I was wrong in being sore for seven years. But I was right the first three months. Kidnapping my little girl like that."

My bride and I didn't have much time to set up housekeeping. We got a room with a gas plate in it—bathroom down the hall—and everything would have been fine but for World War I. I am not a pacifist. I like to believe I'm like David, ready to fight for Right if only with a sling-shot. And it was pretty clear to me by September of 1917 that my country was putting up a righteous fight I had to be in on. Evelyn was in firm agreement with me.

My once-broken neck eliminated me from military service, but I was still a good mechanic and welder. I arranged with Parks and my chief mechanic to run the garage without me, and drove over to the Mare Island Navy Yard to offer my services for the duration. Just to be sure I got in on war work, I filled out separate applications for work as iron molder, electrician, mechanic, and machinist. Welding was still too much of a freak job to be considered a trade at the yard. To my dismay, all the jobs were reported filled.

"I came here to work for the Navy, and I intend to work," I told the man in charge. "What other jobs have you got open?"

He looked over my bale of rejected applications and seemed impressed. "You ought to be good for something," he agreed. "I'll put you to work in the shop, and when something in your line turns up I'll send for you."

That was nearly the end of me. It was my first experience with something as big and complex as the Navy Yard, so I worked my head off to make good. I wanted to be promoted as fast as possible and get to work on the actual construction of warships. But the harder I worked, the more valuable I became to my foreman, and the more care he took to see that I didn't get transferred. That might have gone on for the duration if I hadn't made a friend of a chief electrician. He put in a request for my transfer to his department, and then followed the request through in person to see that it didn't get lost on the way.

After that I was an electrical machinist, doing everything from winding coils and machining rotors to installing steam-powered generators in battleships. I loved it. I've been told there is a difference between like and love; that you can love people because they can return your love, but you can only like machinery because it is impersonal and cannot return your liking. Maybe so, but to me machines possess a responsiveness that is not impersonal at all.

I'll admit that at one time I feared my love of machines was becoming an obsession that was taking me away from my love of God. I went to Him for help, and was reassured. I was just a mechanic striving to translate His laws in terms of machinery, and as long as I understood I was just His follower, and didn't get to thinking I was operating under my own head of steam, I was on the right track.

At Mare Island, I probably had some of the best supervisors a man could get, the Navy being in the habit of getting its share of the best. At the same time the electrical system of a battleship is so complex that I know a lot of men who were too overwhelmed to try to grasp it. Ask one what he was doing, and he'd say, "I'm winding a coil," or, "I'm hooking up a generator."

Well, maybe I'd be winding a coil, or hooking up a generator, but my own idea was that I was building a battleship. You may consider that a small conceit, but I have come to consider it highly important. The coil winder who thinks he is building a battleship has added a lot more to his job than a few strands of copper wire. He is not winding wire but creating magnetic fields, and magnetic fields made the motor go

79

round, and the motors give life to the ship. By asking questions and reading textbooks on electrical engineering, Mare Island became for me both a job and one big electrical laboratory.

While I worked, Evelyn had solved the housing problem for us by installing us in an old farmhouse about 15 miles back in the hills. She had to pump her own water, and clean her own kerosene lamp chimney, and fight her own packrats, but I was home often enough to split the kindling and keep enough oak in the woodbox to fire up the kitchen range. That summer of 1918 she also raised her own vegetables and "eating ear" corn, and I brought home the store-bought groceries. By late summer, however, it was clear she would have to move closer to a doctor. We were about to make our parents grandparents.

Relations with Oscar Peterson being cool, to say the least, and with my folks having moved to Uplands to start an orange grove, we accepted an invitation from the Robert Gilmours, and Evelyn moved in with them in Stockton. I batched it at the farm, and made up for my lack of companionship and good food by working overtime to all hours of the night.

There was a refrain at the time that I didn't think applied to a big husky man like me. It went, "I opened the window and in flew Enza." The great Spanish influenza epidemic that swept across the country, killing people by the thousands, hit the Navy Yard so hard that by October we were down to less than a third of our working force. Still I didn't think it applied to me until I woke up one morning feeling as though I had been dragged through a knothole. I was so sore, and tired, and weak that I just lay there for three days alone in that farmhouse, drinking some water now and then, but wanting nothing to eat.

Finally I told myself, "This is silly. You've got to shake this thing off. Get up and go to work. As soon as you get up a little circulation, you'll be all straightened out."

I drove down to the landing, trying to follow a road that kept twisting away from me, and took the ferry over to Mare

Island. I told my boss I'd been sick, but that I would be fit in the morning.

"Been sick nothing," he told me. "You *are* sick. Get over to the hospital right now, and no fooling about it."

By that time I was willing to agree with him. I made it to the hospital all right, and up to a long room lined with men on canvas cots. There must have been a hundred of them, and I was told to take an empty cot at the end. I still remember how long that room was, and how I never thought I would get past all those men to the cot at the end.

By the time I reached it I was burning up with fever. My face had never felt such heat even in a foundry. I collapsed on the cot, and the next I remember was a doctor standing over me and calling to his assistant, "Come quick, this fellow is about gone." For once I didn't argue. I was as well aware of it as he was.

I don't know what they shot into my system, but within a minute the sweat was pouring out of me. Within a week I was back on my feet, and in two weeks I was back at work, but the stuff they shot into me didn't leave that fast. For more than a year all I had to do was lie down on a bed, and the sweat would pour out of me just as it did the day the fever broke. I didn't mind. Even though I've never had too much use for doctors, I have to admit they saved my life that time.

News of the Armistice reached California during our lunch hour. We had no radio, but the word flashed through the yard just as fast, and as though it were one motion all of us threw our lunch boxes up into the air. I well remember that most of the fellows had finished their lunches, but I was late in arriving and my box was full. Somebody there had no occasion to love me when the slab of pie came down.

8

Our first son, Caleb, had been born on October 30th, and I returned to Stockton and my absolutely beaming wife when he was three weeks old. For a week we did little more than hang over his crib, and marvel, and thank God that the war was over, and that we all could be together again. We are still grateful for that week.

You've all been at meetings where the speaker of the occasion is being introduced, and you know how the chairman making the introduction can get pretty flowery sometimes. Speaking as I do as often as eight times a week, I've heard myself introduced so glowingly that I wonder who is being described. And what do I think about when I hear myself presented as a "Horatio Alger character born to succeed," or a "gifted genius who does not know the meaning of failure"?

I think of the closing months of 1918.

I ran into the first trouble the day I returned to the garage and found we were bankrupt. I simply couldn't believe it.

The most prosperous garage in town had gone broke? Somewhat thickly Parks informed me that the shortage of new cars to sell during my year's absence had wrecked us. But when I looked around I saw that Jensen and Cap weren't wrecked. None of our other competitors were wrecked. If they had had few new cars to sell, they had worked overtime keeping the old serviceable. They were in excellent shape to face the 1919-1920 boom when new car sales broke all previous records.

"But what happened, Parks?" I pleaded. "How can we be so busted? Surely there must be something on the books—"

"Didn't keep any books," he informed me. "Books are for when you're making money. When you're losing, what you don't know, no one else knows either. Tell 'em you're rich, and they can't prove otherwise."

Talk about ostriches putting their heads under the sand. Yet that was what Parks had done, and the reasons were not long in coming out. I had known that Parks was not above taking a prospective customer down to the local saloon to warm him into a receptive frame of mind. I had closed my eyes to that, assuring myself that entertainment, as he called it, was his side of the business and not mine. I was wrong. As a partner condoning his practices, I was as guilty as he was. Oh, I know, because my competitors reported it with glee, that a few years ago some of my eager salesmen felt compelled to match rival "hospitality" with a little hospitality of their own. I can assure you some pertinent words were exchanged between the "old man" and his salesmen. If I was a little heated, much of it can be attributed to this experience with Parks.

What had happened was that Parks, seeing the Volstead Act coming, had not only filled his basement but himself. He had not made his drinking conspicuous around Stockton, where mutual friends might report it to me, but on "buying trips" to San Francisco and Los Angeles he had cut quite a swath. It hadn't taken long for a small town boy trying to act like a Hollywood big shot to go through a $40,000 garage business.

I thought we might get some of our money back from the

used cars Parks had taken in as trade. He had a long row of them filling one side of the garage that only needed a little work to put back in shape, but he was ahead of me there, too. Every one had been hocked to the bank, and the loan on most of them was far more than they could possibly be sold for. So I said to Parks, "Maybe you can do business this way, but I can't. I've got to know where I stand, and then the only honest thing to do is let our creditors know where we stand. I want to hire a bookkeeper and have it understood he's working for me."

Parks shook his head. "We can't even afford a bookkeeper. But why don't you and I keep books together in the evening until we get caught up?"

"It's a deal," I said, there being no alternative. "I don't know anything about it, but you do, and I can learn."

It took me weeks of working all day in the shop and half the night in the office to gather up the fragments, get the accounts in shape, and send out regular monthly statements. It was one of the most valuable experiences of my life, learning accounting the hard way, with each week revealing more losses as I uncovered more unpaid bills.

By January first our creditors were finally aware of our desperate situation, and began putting the pressure on us. In the shop I had things reorganized and back on a paying basis, but the revenue from my repair work was but a drop in the bucket. Especially was it discouraging to fix a used car, and sell it in tip-top shape for $300 and then discover Parks had borrowed $500 on it in a deal he had "forgotten to put down."

Every day brought more such discouragement, and by the end of January, after the longest hours and hardest work I had ever put in in my life, I thought I was about as low as a man can get. Then I returned home after midnight one night to find Evelyn pacing the floor nervously and Caleb whimpering in his crib.

"I've sent the neighbors for the doctor," she said. She was white with fright, and she didn't have to tell me why. Though late in arriving, the influenza epidemic was now raging through Stockton, taking an especially heavy toll amongst infants.

We had no time to prepare ourselves for the blow. On February 9th the doctor turned to us as he had turned to so many other parents, and said, "He's gone."

I held Evelyn, but when I could find words, it was to God that I addressed them. "What's wrong?" I pleaded. "What have we done that we should be so punished? We've worked hard. We've tried our best to be Christians. Oh, where have we gone wrong?"

That night, while we were still numb with sorrow, the answer came to me. "My child," the Voice said, "you have been working hard, but for the wrong things. You have been working for material things when you should have been working for spiritual things."

The words were few, but the meaning ran deep. All that long night I reviewed my past, and saw where I had been paying only token tribute to God, going through the motions of acting like a Christian, but really serving myself and my conscience instead of serving Him. Instead of being a humble servant, I was taking pride in the way I was working to pay my material debts at the garage, while doing scarcely a thing to pay my spiritual debt to God.

From my lesson that night I can now say that when a man realizes that spiritual things are worth more—and certainly they will last when material things are gone—he will work harder for spiritual things. I discovered then that God loves us so much that He wants us to love Him in return. He wants us to cooperate with His program. *Matthew 6:33* says, "But seek ye first the kingdom of God, and His righteousness; and all these things shall be added unto you." That I had not been doing. I had been seeking first my own way of life, and I firmly believe God had to send those difficulties into our lives to get us to look up into His face and call upon Him for His help and guidance.

I know that when I returned to the garage it was with a

new attitude. I had been furious at Parks for the weakness of his that had caused all the trouble, and had wanted nothing to do with him. Now, having been shown the light, I was able to use my influence, with the help of God, in getting him straightened out. He became his old personable self, and sales began to pick up.

Evelyn and I were still not happy with our spiritual life. The Plymouth Brethren had never been numerous enough in Stockton to support a church, and now, with several families having moved away, our weekly meetings at one home or another found our number down to about a dozen, with all of us feeling the lack of strong leadership. I was talking about this to Evelyn one evening when she said, "Oh yes, that reminds me. Do you remember Carolyn Jones?"

She still switches the subject on me like that. I remembered Carolyn Jones. She was a friend of Evelyn's, a tall serious girl who had been so impressed by the stories my sisters had told her of their missionary work in China that she, too, had gone to China as a missionary.

"Carolyn's coming to supper tonight with her husband," continued Evelyn. "She married a missionary, and they are just back on their first leave. Isn't it nice that they come from China? Rice is about the only thing we have for supper."

I have an expression for the kind of surprise that awaited me that evening. "You could have knocked me off the Christmas tree." I don't know where I picked it up, but this night, faced with a coincidence to beat all coincidences within my experience, it was literally true. It was also to again change our way of life. Evelyn's Carolyn Jones of Stockton turned out to be married to my Chinese-speaking friend, Elmer Jones, of San Francisco. That Carolyn's maiden name should also be her married name had never occurred to us, so even after a full banquet of rice we were still shaking our heads and saying, "Well, now who would have guessed it?"

I hadn't seen Elmer for ten years. During the interim he had gone to China as the representative of a big oil company, and with his ability to speak Chinese he had been fast headed for the top. Instead of being happy about his success, however, he had felt more and more the urge to do something to improve the living standards of the Chinese, and being a devout Christian, he had felt strongly that the biggest gift he could give them was the word of God.

"I couldn't lift them up all by myself," he told us, "but I knew that if they knew God, He would give them the strength to lift themselves. I joined a mission supported by the Christian Missionary Alliance Church. And who was there? Carolyn. Right then I got back more from the mission than I could ever put in. But that's enough about us. Tell us about yourselves."

We told them about Caleb, and the garage failure, and our dissatisfaction with the meagerness of our spiritual life, sparing neither the details nor ourselves. "We're trying to live like Christians," I said, "but we know that is not the same as being Christians. The thing is, we don't know what to do about it."

"Why don't you join the Christian Missionary Alliance, Bob?" asked Elmer. "We can use a man like you."

"And a woman like you, Evelyn," added Carolyn.

As members of the Plymouth Brethren all our lives, we found a step like that hard to take. To switch church allegiance was a serious matter with us. I remember asking Elmer, trying to make light of it, "You were a Plymouth Brethren, Elmer. How do you find these Christian Missionary Alliance folks?"

"We're all servants of God, Bob," he said. "What should interest you is that we have an active church here in Stockton, and we have a big program supporting the Peniel Mission houses here in California as well as in foreign countries. By working for the church and the missions, you work for God. You know, it is only through supporting His program that you get to know Him."

He then gave me my first lesson in the value of personal testimony. Quietly but convincingly he told us about the

87

Christian Missionary Alliance, a small, sincere group dedicated to bringing Christ to all of God's children regardless of color. "Ours is a working religion," he said. "We work for Christ, and Christ helps us. Bob and Evelyn, Christ can use your help, and you've already told us you can use His. I don't ask you to take this in all in one night, but I'll tell you one thing: We've found that our work sure works for us."

We had a sort of prayer meeting after that. Not much of a one. Just four young people down on their knees before God, asking Him to help us, and to help us help Him. Then the Joneses went back to the parsonage where they were staying, and probably raided the icebox for something more substantial than the rice we had fed them.

The following Sunday we attended the Christian Missionary Alliance Church, and as Elmer had said, they had work for us. Work that has shaped and guided our lives ever since. Evelyn was whisked at once off to the Sunday School where she began the teaching of children that was eventually to make her a leading figure in the development of summer Bible camps.

As for me, they sized me up for bulk, and gave me a different kind of job. Talk about politics making strange bedfellows. Religion has brought me into contact with fellows the politicians never meet, and provided me with an insight into human nature that has proved invaluable. I was assigned to work once a month with the Peniel Mission House, a job that needs a word of explanation. As in most towns in California, Stockton has that ideal year-round climate where the living is easy for bums, and we had our substantial share. Taking care of them for the most part were two dedicated spinsters who ran the Peniel Mission House. Today much of the work of the Peniel's has been absorbed by the Salvation Army and the Red Cross, but in 1919 it was the only hope of the down-and-outers. The two spinsters worked day and night at their task, and would have kept right on working without rest if it wasn't the program of our church to send down a relief team from time to time to give them some time off. I was put on the relief team, an honor I accepted willingly before I knew what it was all about.

I don't know what I expected the first Saturday night I reported for work at the mission, but certainly I did not expect to be handed a big bass drum and put through an hour's rehearsal with the trombone, trumpet, and tambourine players Then a very self-conscious LeTourneau was shoved out on a street corner with our band and gospel singers, and our crusade was on. It didn't help me any that in the singing I had the loudest parts to carry over the pounding of my drum.

The hope of the group was that I would also become their loudest orator, but there I was a disappointment. I tried. I tried hard, but my old fear of speaking in public was still with me, and I couldn't open my mouth. What I could do, however, I did well. When singing, preaching, and prayer couldn't penetrate the wine-fogged minds of the derelicts we called winos, I could just pick them up, one under each arm, and drag them off to the clean beds in the mission house.

For years, like most people, I had avoided these characters, regarding them as beyond redemption and never considering that they, too, were made in the image of God. Now I not only hauled them off to the mission, but when one or another of them woke up screaming with the delirium tremens, I was right there with them, helping them bat down the snakes and elephants that were threatening to attack. If I couldn't talk to a crowd on a street corner, I could talk to these suffering individuals. I must have been fairly convincing. Even today it is not unusual to have some fine man come up after one of my speaking engagements to tell me he had been put on the right track through one of my personal talks in Stockton.

Of course it wasn't my talk that had brought about the reformation. I had merely brought to the attention of these men the power and capacity of our Lord. Today Alcoholics Anonymous works its wonders. We can be His instruments, but only God can work the wonders.

Following up the same thought, I will add that it is for the above reason that I contribute not only my voice but 90 per cent of my personal and company income to the cause of Christ. My slogan, with the exception of one disastrous lapse I will bring up later, has long been, "Not how much of my money I give to God, but how much of His money I keep for myself." Or as I sometimes put it more bluntly, "It's all right to give God credit, but He can use cash, too." You know, they say you can't take it with you, but I say you can send it on ahead, and have it waiting to your credit when you get there.

9

By the spring of 1919 I had uncovered the last of the unpaid bills at the garage, the books were in order, and at last we knew where we stood. The picture was both good and bad. On the bad side was the fact that we were still $20,000 in the red. On the good side was the fact that I had reconditioned and sold the glut of used cars Parks had accumulated, recovering about 60 cents on the dollar. Furthermore my repair business was flourishing, and Parks was staying sober and selling cars. As far as I could see, in another couple of years we would be out of debt and ready to really get going.

I found no comfort in the prospect. Whatever attractions the garage business had held for me before Parks got us into the mess were gone now, wiped out by the overwork and experiences of the last six months. I had a fierce desire to get out on my own and make a fresh start.

I didn't know how to go about it, so I did the most obvious thing. I just called a meeting of our creditors, and told them

I wanted out. I remember Parks was there, and his father, and the real estate man who had built our garage, and our banker, and maybe a dozen others.

"I'm not trying to get out of my half of the debts," I assured them. "At the same time, we've got the garage going again, and I've got a half-interest in it that ought to be worth something. Now my idea is to sell out that half-interest, apply that on my debts, and then pay the balance if it takes me the rest of my life."

"What security have you got for the balance?" asked the banker.

That hadn't occurred to me. I simply held up my two big hands.

To my surprise, the banker nodded as though satisfied. For the next half-hour he and the rest went over the books I had worked on so long, while I helpfully pointed out the upward trend of recent months. Then came the decision. "If you will sign over your half-interest in the business to Parks, and promise to pay $5,000 to us over the next three years, we'll consider it a deal."

I accepted at once. I signed a note with the banker, transferred my half of the business to Parks and his backers, and walked out. I was 30 years old, unemployed, and $5,000 in debt.

The next day I met my old friend Ira Guy on the street. "I hear you're out of the garage," he said.

"Yes, I am," I answered.

"What are you going to do now?"

I had the answer for that, too. "I'm going to take the first job I can find that's good enough to pay my debts."

"Good enough," he said. "I know where there's a job to start out on."

And that's how, on that casual meeting, I got my start in the earth-moving business.

Ira Guy and his brother Bill, two chaps only slightly older than I, were big dealers in farm machinery, working both ends against the middle and then some. They had started out about the time I started in the garage business with one old steam tractor and a threshing machine, touring the county to thresh grain from farm to farm at so much a bushel. Now they had a fleet of Harris Harvester Company combines and Holt tractors, and contracts to thresh thousands of acres of grain a season, and never let it be said that if a rancher wanted to buy their machines for his own use, they wouldn't sell. They turned their threshing contracts into sales demonstrations, and they were going to town. If one of their machines broke down, I was the one they had called in as doctor, so you could say we were pretty well acquainted.

"What's the job?" I asked.

"Old man Grunaur is so mad he's walking on stilts," said Ira. "Four feet above ground. He claims the tractor we sold him is no good."

I had to admit that was serious. Grunaur, the senior partner of a big land company called Grunaur & Fabian, was one of the biggest customers the Guy brothers had, and if he was really mad, it could cost the brothers plenty. "What seems to be the trouble?" I asked.

"We can't figure it out. Bill has been out there four times, but no matter what he does, the thing breaks down a day or two later. I'd sure like you to run out there to see what you can do. I know you'll be able to find the trouble."

"Okay, I'll try it," I said, and walked on, feeling pretty set up at getting a job, even if it was a small one. I hadn't walked a block when I remembered something. When I left the garage, I had taken with me my welding torch and a few tools of my trade. The company car and service truck that I had always used before had been left behind as part of the deal, so I had no way of running down to Grunaur's Whitehall Ranch, some 20 miles away over old dirt roads. I was about to turn around to tell Ira I couldn't take his job after all when an old garage customer hailed me.

93

"Bob, I've got a deal for you," he said. "You know that Saxon I bought?"

I certainly did. It was a beauty. Bright yellow, with a sporty chummy seat, and I knew it was in perfect condition because I had serviced it once a month myself.

"Well, I tried to turn it in to that partner of yours, and he'd only give me $400 for it," he said. "And you know yourself we still owe $400 on it. He'd be getting it for nothing. I don't want that to happen, so why don't you take it over for the payments that are left?"

It was a tempting offer. I knew I couldn't lose, but at the same time my $5,000 debt was so huge I could only look at it around the edges. And what would my banker say if he saw his pauper riding around in a Saxon? It hurt me, but I turned him down.

My sister Sarah was visiting us in Stockton, and when I related the day's events that evening, she remembered that she just happened to have $400 saved for her return passage to Wei Hai Wei Mission in China.

"That's just too good a bargain to miss," she said firmly. "I'll buy it myself. The only thing is, be sure you buy it back from me before I have to buy my ticket."

Evelyn and I looked at her, knowing she was staking us to the car. Nevertheless, I had to protest. "What if we don't have any money?" I said.

"The Lord will provide," she said calmly.

I must mention here that there is a big difference between faith in the Lord and presumption. Had I made a statement like that at that time, I would have been presumptuous. Sarah, with her wonderful, serene faith, could say, "The Lord will provide," with absolute conviction. I must also add that her confidence in sailing on schedule was all in the Lord, and not in me.

I was filled with doubt when I took possession of the Saxon. A lot of people, knowing how broke I was, would think I was riding pretty high. That the car might create a beneficial impression never occurred to me until after I arrived at the Whitehall Ranch. Grunaur, seeing me drive up in my yellow beauty to repair his Holt tractor, thought it was Mr. Holt himself. I think it was the first time in his life that he ever addressed a mechanic as "Mister."

The ailing tractor was a huge, 30,000-pound, 75 horsepower job that was plain sick all over. The timer had been monkeyed with so often that even after it was adjusted it would hold only for a few minutes and then start drifting off. I solved that problem by simply welding the adjustment bolt in place so it could never drift again. Next I discovered that Grunaur's gasoline storage tank was so lined with rust that every time he gassed the tractor he poured more iron than gasoline into the carburetor. It took me a week to go over the whole machine, but when I was through it was as good as new.

"Now let's see if it will keep on running like that," Grunaur said. "I've got 40 acres I want leveled for irrigation, so you just go on down there and shave off the hummocks. If the machine is still running a week from now, I'll pay your repair bill and give you a dollar an hour for your work to boot."

The tract he wanted leveled was located in that section of the valley known as The Islands. Today the name is meaningless, but in 1919, before the vast drainage system was completed, the islands were real enough. Each spring the San Joaquin River would flood over hundreds of square miles of land, inundating all but those strange mounds. For the most part they were composed of sediment and peat, but some of the islands contained the relics of ancient Indian villages. When we land-levelers hit one of them, we called in the archaeologists of the University of California and let them do some of our leveling for us.

Before I could start leveling land, I had to repair the scraper. As I look back on it now, if that scraper had been in perfect working condition, I might never have gone into the manufacture of earth-moving equipment. As it was, there were so many things wrong with that machine that I practically had to rebuild it, and by the time I had it running I thought it was the most fascinating piece of machinery I had ever encountered. I don't know why. Some men go for airplanes, or electronics, or automobiles, or atoms. I went for the ugliest chunk of brute machinery you'd ever want to see.

Several writers have credited me with being the first to build powered scrapers, so right now I want to give that credit to the right man, Mr. T. G. Schmeiser of Fresno. In 1915 he patented a scraper with a blade that could be raised or lowered by compressed air. It was a cumbersome affair, but with one man pulling it with a tractor, and another man on the scraper operating the compressed air valves, it could move three cubic yards of dirt at the rate of about three miles an hour. By comparison, that was about what six mule-skinners driving 24 mules on six big Fresnoes could do.

Other manufacturers like Holt then came out with tractor-drawn scrapers, using a variety of belts, pulleys and gears to manipulate the blade. All shared the same weakness. When the blade hit a rock or a tough root, belts would slip, gear teeth would be stripped, or the compressed air system would either bounce the blade or blow out an air hose. As a result the land being leveled was left about as uneven as a field of drifted snow, and a lot of plowing, harrowing, and hand-shoveling had to be done to get the table-top smoothness required for irrigation. Of course, if they hadn't had this weakness, along with many others, there would have been no room for me to introduce my own scraper when the time came.

The tractor and scraper I used on my first earth-moving job for Grunaur were both made by Holt. I drove the tractor, and Grunaur's foreman operated the scraper. If he's alive, he's still hating me. I claim there is no surer way to turn two friends into enemies than to put one on a tractor and the other on the scraper behind. Everytime we hit a root that flipped him off the scraper, he swore I hunted it up on purpose. Everytime he socked the blade unexpectedly deep into the ground, stopping the tractor cold and cracking my neck like a whip, I was just as convinced he had done it deliberately.

Maybe I did hit some bumps too hard. By the end of my second day I knew I had found a job that satisfied me like none in my life. When I was in dry going, the track-type treads of the Holt threw sand and dust into my face. When I was down in the bottoms, they threw mud, and I loved it. When I saw a hummock ahead to be cut down, I charged it as though I were a knight in a tournament, and if my scraper operator bounced out without slicing off a good cut, I was furious. I wanted to move dirt. Lots of dirt.

Grunaur was so pleased with the job we did leveling his land that he invited me to overhaul all the rest of the land company's equipment. That included a steam tractor, threshing machine, hay mowers, gang plows, irrigation pumps, and several wagons and dump carts. For me it was a holiday. Many of the machines were so old that no spare parts could be found for them, so I had to make my own with my welding torch. By fall, when I completed my work, I knew those machines inside and out, and had learned more about pumps, belts, and gears for heavy equipment than I had learned in all my correspondence courses combined.

I still had a lot to learn the hard way. For my last repair job, I overhauled an irrigation pump and then started it up to fill a reservoir about a quarter of a mile back from the river. Both the six-inch concrete pipe and the reservoir were empty at the time so the water flowed along briskly though I did notice that along toward evening the pump had to work a little harder as the weight of the water in the reservoir built up. I shut it off and returned the next morning, setting the pump at the same speed it had operated at most efficiently the day before.

Right off it began to labor and groan. I couldn't figure that out. I thought maybe the gasoline engine wasn't getting enough gas, so I souped it up a little. That only made the groaning louder. Right then I had a horrible feeling I was doing something very wrong, but the feeling came too late. Before I could shut off the engine a hundred yards of pipe burst, spraying the countryside with mud and water. While that tremendous geyser was still in the air, out of the shattered pipe poured all the water in the reservoir, cutting a gully all the way down to the river and covering me and the pump with mud.

As any irrigation man could have told me if I'd had enough sense to ask, it is one thing to start a flow of water through an empty pipe, and quite something else to start a flow through a full one, especially if there is a reservoir of water standing on top of it. There's a little thing called the inertia of water to be reckoned with. When I started up the pump at high speed that morning the water in the pipe was no longer flowing as it had been the evening before. It was just lying there, and even if it had wanted to move there was all that weight of water in the reservoir holding it back. Thus when I put the pump into high speed, I was building up an enormous pressure at the pump end of the line long before the water at the reservoir end was even getting ready to move.

I ran into a sign on a safety bulletin board one time that went like this: "Where did you get your good judgment?" "From my experience." "And where did you get your experience?" "From my bad judgment."

I didn't have to write that down to remember it. When you are rebuilding a pumping station and replacing a hundred yards of pipe on your own time, the "inertia of water" has a far deeper meaning than you'll ever find attached to it in a classroom. Just to be sure I never made the same mistake again, I took another correspondence course, this one on hydraulic power, and I doubt that my postal professors ever had a more earnest student.

That doesn't mean that I learned it all. I still had to learn that an expert in one field is no expert if one field is all he knows. There are a lot of angles to hydraulics that have nothing to do with liquids. Cement, for instance. Two years after the pipe-burst for Grunaur, I contracted to build a 4,000 foot pipeline for Carlton Case, a prominent Stockton attorney and rancher. I was so anxious to make good for this influential man that I read all there was to be had on concrete pipe. I surveyed the course from river to reservoir myself. I invented a ditcher and dug my own ditch. As a final precaution to insure top quality, I built my own pipe-casting machine and mixed my own cement to meet the highest standards. Then with the assistance of my brother-in-law, Howard Peterson, we started laying pipe.

The pipe was made in two-foot sections, each section having a collar that would tightly enclose the butt end of the next. As fast as the machine turned out the sections, we snugged them into place, it being my idea that if the cement was still a little moist, the joints would be sealed just that much more firmly. I was right as far as I went, but then I had to go ahead and have another idea.

"If we bury the pipe as we go along," I told Howard, one of the requirements being that the pipe be buried two feet below plow level, "we'll be in an awful mess if we have a few leaks and have to do a lot of digging. Let's lay the whole thing, and then test it for leaks before we bury it."

The idea sounded reasonable to him. We built the line, never once thinking of the fact that the bottom half of the pipe lay in the damp, cool soil of the trench while the top half was exposed to the burning California sun. Came the day that I started up the pump, and you can be sure I did it cautiously. I could have spared myself the worry. By the time the water had progressed halfway up the line, the top of every joint along the way was spraying up water as fast as I could pump it in.

Howard did his best. "Maybe we haven't got a pipe line," he said. "But I'll bet we've got the biggest water sprinkler in the world."

I was a long time in figuring out that while the bottom half of my pipe had been curing perfectly on its foundation of moist soil, the sun-baked top half had been shrinking at a furious rate.

In mechanics a nice feature is that once you have found the cause of the trouble, the cure is usually simple—if you have found the right cause. In this case Howard and I had a simple cure. We just got down in that ditch, straddling that twelve-inch pipe with our backs exposed to the sun where not a breath of air could reach us, and plugged the leaks. We had buckets of wet cement with us, and rock drills to punch three-inch holes in the pipe. With the hole punched we'd reach in with a handful of cement and pack it into the leaky joint at the left. Another handful for the leaky joint at the right. One punched hole for every two joints, two sealing operations, and then one cement plug for every hole. Today I fly some 200,000 miles a year at better than 300 mph, but don't think I don't know that 4,000 feet of leaky pipe line is the longest distance in the world. I've measured it.

I have introduced these mistakes of mine to keep things in balance because there is an impression around that I was practically forced into becoming a success. "You were the right man in the right place at the right time," I've been told more than once. If I was the right man, I was a long time finding out about it, but I can't deny that I was in the right place at the right time.

California in 1919 was just ready to start its irrigation projects in earnest, not that irrigation was anything new in the state. The ruins of a Spanish irrigation system are still to be seen behind the Santa Barbara Mission, and I've been told that the Indians were irrigating long before the Spaniards arrived. Nevertheless progress was slow. Only land that was relatively flat and close to water could be worked at all, and even the rancher that lucky stood in annual danger of seeing his laboriously-dug ditches washed out by spring floods.

A big step forward was made by old Benjamin Holt when he built his first tractor in Stockton in 1885. Not long after that old Daniel Best started his tractor factory in nearby San

Leandro. For some 20 years, using first steam and then gasoline engines, the two rivals turned out immense machines resembling short-line locomotives. Mounted on wide steel wheels and wearing big cleats called grousers, one of these monsters could do the work of 100 mules if the going was good. Unfortunately, as any construction man can tell you, the going is rarely good in the earth-moving business. On even mild hillsides let alone on mountain slopes the tractors were not only dangerously top-heavy, but they needed all their power just to move their own weight. After a rain or in soft bottom land they were helpless. Once the drive-wheels started to spin, the big cleats would throw out mud by the bucketful, and down would settle the machine.

The story is that one day Holt was testing one of his machines in a rain-soaked field when his wheels started to spin. He was a good operator, but in 30 seconds he was dug in to the axles. Tromping back through the mud, tired and discouraged, slipping back two feet for every three he advanced, he felt, he said, "like a hoss on a treadmill."

Some inventions do come in flashes, and the treadmill gave Holt all the flash he needed. Back on his old New England farm the horse on the treadmill walked miles going nowhere, but his plodding turned the gears that ground the corn. Now, figured Holt, if a treadmill could power gears, then gears could power a treadmill, and instead of going no place, the wide, endless belt could be made to roll along the ground at a fine rate. Even over mud like that in which his tractor was stuck fast. By the time he reached his shop, Holt already had in mind a tractor that would be mounted on wide, treadmill type tracks. It was a dazzler of an idea all right. No longer would the tons of tractor weight rest on the few square inches of steel wheels that touched the ground. No longer would two drive wheels spin and dig in. All the weight and drive would be spread evenly from front end to rear of the long, wide tracks.

Holt turned out his first track-type tractor in 1905. "Crawls over mud like a caterpillar," he said, and thus the Caterpillar tractor got its name.

For all that he had a revolutionary idea, public acceptance was slow. Contractors still thought mules were cheaper and more dependable than tractors, and there were very few ranchers big enough, and progressive enough to buy an expensive machine. Then one sale to a gold mining company in South Africa changed the course of history. Quite by chance some British military figures touring the mining property saw the machine in action. No ideas sparked then, but a few years later, when World War I bogged down in the mud of trench warfare, the memory of the old Holt crawling through the mud of the gold mine stirred up some ideas in the British Ministry of War. Things happened fast after that. In a matter of months the Holt, covered with armor plating and carrying a gun turret resembling a water tank, was on its way to the Western Front. The tank became the decisive weapon of the war. It wallowed through water-filled shell holes and crashed over sand bags to straddle German trenches. It knocked down stone walls and trees, crushed machine gun nests, and blew up ammunition dumps. By war's end there was no longer any doubt about what a track-type machine could do.

Along with having developed the track-type tractor, the war had developed a tremendous demand for foodstuffs that had been in short supply for years. Thus when at last the tractor factories could return to peacetime production, the real irrigation boom began.

Jobs there were aplenty. Grunaur was loud in his recommendation, selling me as the mechanic who could fix anything with a welding torch. Ira, to, had more work waiting for me than I could handle. The rub was that even if I doubled as cat-skinner, mechanic and welder, I could still only make about $2 an hour. High wages in those days, yes, but ten hours a day on a tractor, and another four or five hours at night as mechanic barely kept me caught up on my debts. Then there was the boat fare I had to return to Sarah, our pledge to the church, food, rent, new welding equipment—the list seemed endless.

Tormenting me was the thought that if I had my own tractor I could get my head above water. The tractor operator who supplied his own machine could get $7.50 an hour for himself and machine, or about twice, according to my figures, what I was making as a hired hand.

Evelyn knew how I felt. "I'm going to get a job, too," she announced. "It's the only way we can get ahead."

I didn't like the idea of her going to work, especially with her father still sore at me and ready to claim I couldn't support his daughter. We took our problem to our Lord, and felt better about it. You know, a lot of people take their problems to the Lord, and get up and walk away, carrying their problems back with them. Like those who pray for rain, and then go out without an umbrella. If that's all the faith there is, there is not much point in praying. The Lord can't help you if you insist on carrying your problems with you. Leave them with Him, and they are no longer yours but His.

Shortly after that I went back to leveling more land at the Whitehall Ranch down in The Islands for Grunaur. At almost the same time the rancher just across the Grand Line Canal found himself in urgent need of a nursemaid to help his ailing wife with the children. Not even Oscar could resent his daughter's answering a call for help like that. Evelyn took the job at $40 a month, and with no rent to pay or groceries to buy in Stockton, that made the difference.

The situation was rough on us, however. We were close enough to see each other daily, and wave, but that canal was a quarter of a mile wide with not a bridge for miles in either direction, and no telephone connections between the ranches. Just to complicate matters, I had put the car up for sale, the time being near for Sarah to return to China. The best we could do was on Sunday when I would go down to the canal, put my rolled-up clothes on a raft made of fence posts, and swim across pushing the raft ahead of me. Then, dressed again in a suit somewhat damp from the crossing, I could call on my wife for a few hours while she did the housework and minded the children.

We will never forget the Christmas of 1919. With the recovery of the rancher's wife, Evelyn's job had ended, but I was still leveling land on the Whitehall Ranch. The main point was that we were together again in our own home, and it was quite a place. It was a portable cook shack mounted on iron wheels, and in its day it had seen the preparation of thousands of meals for migrant sugar beet harvesters. The cook stove was still there, and the kerosene lamps, and a couple of cots, but the walls were cracked and the roof leaked. Every day the hogs would come to scratch themselves on the iron wheels, and then Evelyn would have to rush to catch a falling lamp chimney or save the stove pipe from collapse. When I was leveling land, the December dust would drift across the fields and through the cracks of the shack to pile up in mounds. To keep the dust off the dishes, Evelyn had to turn them face down on the table until the food was served. Water came from a distant pump. Corn cobs fueled the stove. You may not think that was very jolly, but we never felt sorry for ourselves. I do remember one plaintive remark of Evelyn's after a particularly dusty day. "I tried to wash the dust off the floor," she said, "but I guess I only irrigated it."

Yet it was a wonderful Christmas. God let us know then that He was gifting us with a second child. Our heads were above water, our faith was stronger than ever, and we were together in person and in prayer. A shack we might be in, but who could be richer than we were?

You might call that an academic question, but in April, 1942, Evelyn and I were housed in a leaky trailer in the midst of acres of mud, ten miles south of Vicksburg where I was building a new factory. Our annual report, published a few weeks earlier, had revealed that our company's net earning had topped the two million mark for the first time. I had some "construction man's" coffee on the gasoline burner—two spoons of coffee per cup of water on Monday, keep adding

104

coffee and water to match the rate of consumption for the rest of the week, but under no circumstances throw away the grounds until Sunday night—and we sat chewing on that. It does get a little thick. The rain dripped through, and the winds shook the trailer as the hogs had once done.

Were we happier than we had been that Christmas of 1919? More grateful, perhaps, because God had let us help Him do some of the things we wanted to do then. But happier? We had been in the service of the Lord then, and we were in the service of the Lord now, and there is nothing in that kind of happiness that two million net earnings can add to or buy.

10

It is forgotten now, but only 40 years ago an earth-moving contractor might have 500 mules and more working to cut a road through a single hill. A feature of those hills, especially in Southern California, was that they were never, as the saying went, "closer'n 20 miles to feed and water." Contracts were based as much on the feed and water to be hauled for the mules as the dirt to be moved by the mules. Then there were the blacksmith shops, and harness shops, and the infirmary tent where the doctors specialized in the setting of bones and skulls shattered by mule kicks.

When the crawler tractor and the powered scraper went into action after 1918, the day of the horse and mule began to draw to a close. It was fine that the machines were infinitely more efficient, but for most earth-movers it was enough that they had eliminated the ornery mule. They couldn't ask for more.

I did. Maybe I hadn't been kicked enough by mules. I admired the Holt tractor, and I admired the ingenuity of the compressed air and other systems that raised and lowered scraper blades, but I saw a lot of room for improvements, too. The tractor had only one speed—slow. It was slow picking up a load, slow hauling it, and just as slow returning empty. Furthermore, I thought it was capable of doing a lot more work. I've mentioned some of the faults of the powered scraper, but probably my biggest complaint was with the scraper blade itself. It was bigger than man's first scoop shovel, but otherwise little changed.

When I look back at it, I can see that in 1919 the automobile designers were already introducing most of the features of the 1960 car. The same was true in aviation, Henri Coanda having flown the first jet plane in France in 1912. John Hays Hammond, Jr., had launched the first radio-guided missile in 1915, and even television was coming out of the laboratory. And there were we dirt movers, men, we liked to say, who changed the face of the earth. What were we using? Scraper blades invented by a caveman.

As a hired hand working by the hour, the efficiency of the scraper blade was no concern of mine, but I couldn't get it out of my mind. At the same time I found myself fretting again about money problems. The coming baby would take all we had saved through Evelyn's work as nursemaid, and there we would be, back where we started from and another year older.

I was wandering around the house, preoccupied with my problems when Sarah let me have it. "What's the matter with you, Bob? Don't you love our Savior?"

"Of course I do. Naturally. Why?"

"Well, you don't act like it."

I looked at her in astonishment. "How can you say that? I teach the Young Men's Bible Class while Evelyn teaches Sunday School. We go to church every Sunday. I give a tenth of my income to the mission fund. I take my turn at the Peniel Mission. I—"

"Yes, I know, you have a list of good deeds, and as fast as you do them every week you check them off and say, 'Now that that's over I can get back to work.' Bob, that's not loving Jesus. When you love Him, you'll want to serve Him, and you'll hunt for ways to do it."

I mulled that over. I could tell myself that Sarah was a missionary and I was a dirt mover, and so not subject to her rules, but that didn't do any good. In my heart I knew I had been neglecting our Savior just as I had been doing at the time of our great loss when He had dealt with us so sternly.

But what could I do about it? My job was to deal with material things, and not spiritual things. And when I did my job well, it was because I dealt well with material things. I felt trapped, and more than a little lost.

That Sunday Reverend Devol announced a week of nightly revival meetings at our church, and I resolved to borrow the ranch car and attend. If anybody could help me, Reverend Devol could. Originally he had been a Quaker, drawn to California for reasons of health. He was a quiet speaker but intense, often saying more with silences than a lot of men I've heard talk by the hour.

Every night I was in church, striving to dedicate my life to God anew. I was in a strange conflict with myself. I was a spiritual bankrupt finding fresh hope and rich inspiration in Reverend Devol's sermons. At the same time I had the despairing feeling that I would have to give up my material way of life. The moving of earth, the making of fertile land in the desert, the joy of hard work under God's sun, all the things I had come to find so satisfying.

On the last night of the revival I waited until all were gone, and then went forward and knelt at the old wooden altar. Alone with God I prayed, "Lord, if You'll forgive me and help me, I'll do anything You want me to do from this day on." The words were straight from my soul, and God heard me. I know He heard me, because His glory flooded my soul as

I made that prayer. I rose from my knees, knowing that I had really met Him that night.

Hours later I was still unable to sleep. I went out into the ranch yard where the machines stood. I looked at them as though seeing them for the last time. To me service to the Lord, to which I had just dedicated my life, meant the ministry or missionary work. I couldn't see myself as a minister. I couldn't even speak correct English in private, let alone stand up before a congregation. But I had proved my ability to work for the Peniel Mission, and I knew from my talks with Sarah and Marie that there was much-needed work I could do for their mission in China. But was that what He wanted me to do?

With this doubt still with me, I went bright and early in the morning to the home of our pastor. He didn't seem surprised to see me. He just led me into his study and let me talk.

"Brother Devol, the Lord did something for me last night," I began. "He took me out of spiritual bankruptcy, and I promised Him I would do anything He wanted me to do from that moment on. But how can I know what He wants me to do? I know a layman can't serve Him like a preacher can, but tell me, does He want me to serve as a missionary? I need your advice."

Reverend Devol was a man of God and a man of prayer, and he said, "Let's pray, and find your answer there."

We both knelt, and each one of us asked God what He wanted me to do, and as we arose from our knees, God spoke to me through the words of my pastor. "You know, Brother LeTourneau," he said, "God needs businessmen as well as preachers and missionaries."

Those were the words that have guided my life ever since. I repeat them in public at every opportunity because I have discovered that many men have the same mistaken idea I had of what it means to serve the Lord. My idea was that if a man was going all out for God, he would have to be a preacher, or an evangelist, or a missionary, or what we call a full-time

Christian worker. I didn't realize that a layman could serve the Lord as well as a preacher.

I left the parsonage in a sort of daze. If God needed business men, he could certainly find a lot better material than a dirt-mover with a lot of debts piled up by his failure in the garage business. But I said, "All right, if that is what God wants me to be, I'll try to be His businessman." By the time I started up the tractor to begin the day's work, all my doubts were gone. If I didn't amount to much, I felt, it was because I had tried to struggle along too much on my own. Now that I was in business to serve God, in a sort of partnership, as it were, how could I fail?

I would not lightly refer to God as my partner. He is my Lord and Savior, and I am His servant. But by His grace He has made us members of His family, and we can refer to Him as our Father which art in Heaven. More than that, He has let us be "workers, together with Him." The Bible says, "We then, as workers, together with Him, beseech you also that ye receive not the grace of God in vain." *II Corinthians, 6:1.* So it is in that sense that I mean we are partners, remembering always that real partners don't try to see how much one can get from the other. They work for the good of the partnership. They try to help each other.

I remember one of my customers who told me, "I try to shovel out more for God than He can for me, but He always wins. He's got a bigger shovel."

I can testify to that. Early in January of 1920 the sudden demand for cars, new and used, was so great that we sold the Saxon for $1,000, thus getting Sarah off to China and leaving us with a $600 profit. Then a contractor with new equipment dumped an old 1915 Holt tractor on the market cheap, and the $600 went for a down payment. Ira Guy had an old Schmeiser scraper for rent, and would let me pay off the rent in repair jobs for him. I still needed cash. The banker, to whom I had already repaid $1000, was willing to lend it back to me in return for a mortgage on everything but our unborn child. The Islands were loaded with ranchers ready to pay the going price of $7.50 for the man with a tractor and scraper, with the rancher supplying his own man to operate the scraper.

No longer was I a hired hand. I was a land-leveling contractor with my own mortgaged machinery. For a week on my first contract I was one of the happiest men in California. Then I began to fret again. The burr under the saddle was, as usual, the scraper operator. My contract required that he work ten hours a day. With the days getting longer, I wanted to start at dawn, work 14 hours, and break the magic mark of a $100 a day. But could I get that scraper operator to ride another four hours, even with a bonus of a dollar an hour? By the time he had followed me around for ten hours in the thick of the dust, he didn't care if I starved to death, and he probably hoped I would.

Today I do my best thinking in an airplane or in a filled tub of luke-warm water, but I still remember my "thinking seat" on the old Holt with a great deal of nostalgia. Moving along at a mile or two an hour. Dust in your face and the sun on your neck. No traffic, no telephones, no distractions. Enough noise and bumps to prevent real sleep, and enough motor purr and seat spring to prevent full wakefulness. A lot of things rolled through your mind then. Put a belt on the tractor flywheel and let it turn a 10 h.p. D.C. motor. No good would come of that, but there was Mac Maroni, better known as Macaroni, my old foreman at the Mare Island Navy Yard. Showing me how to convert a D.C. motor into an A.C.-D.C. generator with a few slip rings. And there was Hank Rogers and his electric automobile starter. Hank showing me how to take the power off a gasoline engine to run a generator.

I would dump one load and start back for another. You've got the generator and you've got the starter. Now you toss in a couple of reduction gears. A pinion gear goes round and round, but a rack gear goes up and down, or back and forth. Put a rack on the scraper and a pinion on the reduction gears of the starter. Press a button and the pinion gear goes round and round, and the rack goes up and up, raising the scraper blade. Press another and it goes down and down, biting into the earth. Why be cheap? Put two motors on the scraper blade. One on each side. Raise one side and lower the other. A tilting blade. Boy, would that be something. Some switches on the tractor, and one man in the driver's seat. Running both machines at no extra cost. Work both ends of the file as well as the middle.

So ran your thoughts while leveling land in the San Joaquin Valley. Most of them drifted away with the dust, but for me a lot of things were adding up. I knew exactly where a lot of Navy generators and motors were being sold as war surplus at junk prices. They were the same kind of motors and generators I had worked with at Mare Island. When they all came together in my mind, complete with rack and pinion gears for the scraper and a generator belted to the flywheel of the tractor, it was with a jolt that nearly flipped me out of the driver's seat.

Two weeks later, working nights with scant time out for eating or sleeping, I had the tractor rigged to generate electric power, and the scraper rigged to use it. The same flywheel and belt that had turned the air compressor was now ready to turn the generator I had welded to the tractor frame. On the scraper I had welded motors and gears to work the blade up and down.

I'm not bragging when I say the results were astonishing, because I was among those most astonished. I have mentioned that when compressed air pushed the blade into the ground, the blade bounced when it encountered a resistance greater than its air pressure. I had accepted the uneven surface left behind as the normal behavior pattern of scrapers. But my rack and pinion gears just didn't have any bounce built into them. Whatever the blade hit, it cut through. Sometimes I'd have to shift gears and tromp hard on the gas, but we cut through. The result was a path behind me of the required table-top smoothness.

It was something! Not only was one man operating both tractor and scraper, but the job was being done better than could be done by follow-up crews with plows, harrows and shovels. Boy, was I excited. Maybe I was just a dust-coated figure in overalls, but I felt like an inventor fitting in somewhere between Edison, Bell, and Holt. I ran that machine until dark, and then turned in for my first full night's sleep in two weeks.

The next morning when I returned to the tractor, the rancher was already there. "How come the rest of the field isn't as good as this?" he wanted to know, pointing at my latest work.

Proudly I told him, and proudly I pointed out the features of my electrical system. Then I hit him with my next idea. "As long as I can run the machine alone and do a good job," I said, "you won't have to pay your foreman for riding a scraper. I'll be doing the work of two men, so maybe you could give me half the second man's salary, and save the rest."

He backed away from me as though I had gone crazy.

"Not on your life. Right in the contract it says you and your machines for seven-fifty an hour. It doesn't say anything about paying you extra for an electric motor."

I dug up some other arguments to no avail. He couldn't see splitting with me the salary of a man who wasn't there. That was my first encounter with the "man who isn't there" theory, and I'll probably spend the rest of my life not merely encountering it but rushing out to meet it. Man is worth what man produces, and when machines increase his production he is worth more. The reason we have the highest standards of living in the world is because we are the most mechanized country in the world so our production per man is highest.

My pride in my electric scraper might have lasted longer than a week if my next contract hadn't required a long haul from a high "island" to a low quarter that was practically swamp. I was still being paid by the hour at the same $7.50 scale, but at least I was working all the hours I could put in, with no scraper operator howling his rage at me from time to time. So I should have been happy. The more hours the job took, the more money I made.

Somehow I'm not made to think that way. I've heard it called both efficiency and laziness, but when I start a job I instinctively hunt first for the easiest way and then, mindful of Mr. Hill in Portland, the fastest way. "Don't work hard; just fast." So I started shaving the top off the "island" and dragging the dirt down the slope to the swamp 2000 feet away. Now if I could have picked up four yards of dirt at the top of the heap and carried it intact to dump in the lowest part of the swamp, I wouldn't have minded. But the scraper blades we had at the time didn't work that way. The dirt I scraped up at the top spilled out when I reached the downward slope.

In mathematics there is a thing called an asymptote—a curved line approaching a straight line with the curve so gradually reduced that never can they meet in a million miles. That's what I was as an earth-mover. An asymptote. I spread a small knoll across an area 500 feet in diameter. Then I spread that across a lower area 1,000 feet in diameter. On to a lower level and a 1500-foot haul. You can see why, by the time hill and swamp had become one nice flat field, I was becoming pretty discontented with the wasteful duplication of effort.

On the other hand, I was moving more dirt than any one man had ever moved before in history. And because I was doing my job faster and better, I had more contracts offered to me than I could handle, even when I raised my rate to eight bucks an hour. But that still didn't count with me. For a man who likes to start a job and get it over with, moving the same dirt over and over was a pretty frustrating line of work, even when more hours meant more pay.

I sat in my thinking seat on the Holt, waiting for an idea to strike. Nothing happened. As far as I could see, a scraper blade was a scraper blade, always had been, and always would be. That began a restless period for me. When the rainy season struck, turning the lowlands into impassable mud, I got out my welding torch and took on a lot of repair jobs. Then a Mr. Clark came in with a problem. He wanted to raise his now famous Clarkadota figs on some high ground that was fertile enough but baked so hard it was shedding rain like a tile roof. Could I crack it open for him without bringing up the sandy subsoil like a plow would? I invented and welded together a steel blade that would cut about eight inches under the compacted surface, raising and loosening it without turning it under. We called the process subsoiling, and it became a profitable sideline.

Shortly after that I took on the disastrous job, already mentioned, of laying 4,000 feet of cement pipe for Carlton Case. On that I stood to clear $1 a foot, my biggest contract to date. I had yet to encounter the first hard rule of contracting: The more you can make, the more you can lose. By the time Howard and I had repaired all the leaks, I had lost a month's work and $1000 in cash. Another year shot, and still just as much in debt as ever.

In spite of the set-back, we found ourselves rich in the Lord's blessings. Our daughter Louise had been born on April 2, 1920. We had met our pledges to the Christian Missionary Alliance, and enlarged the scope of our work for the church. If we were low on material things, we had our health and our faith in the Lord to see us through.

11

No one knew better than Carlton Case how busted I was in the spring of 1921. From where I was after repairing the leaks in his irrigation line, I had to stand on tiptoe and reach up to touch bottom. Yet it was only a few days after I had finished his line that Mr. Case stopped me in front of the bank where I had stalled off another payment on my note.

"Bob, I know just where there's a house for you," he began. "Solid construction. A pump in the kitchen so Evelyn won't have to go outside for water. An acre of land, a good barn, and only half a mile from the end of the car line. Out on Moss Avenue."

"Mr. Case, I couldn't buy a house if it was nothing down, and cheaper'n rent."

"You've hit the terms on the head," he said. "Nothing down and $30 a month, or $3000 in cash when you get it. I figure anybody who'll make good on a cement pipe for me will make good on his own home."

So that's how, in May, we moved to 122 Moss Avenue. For Evelyn, after nearly four years of married life in rented rooms, tents and cook-shacks, it was her first real home, to become more so when our son Donald was born on September 29th. For me it was the start of R. G. LeTourneau, Inc. The barn became my machine shop, the acre of land my open-air factory, and the dust in the driveway my engineering department where, squatting on my heels, I could draw up my "blueprints" with my finger.

On the other hand, my newly-declared partnership with God was bringing me a great peace of mind while doing little for Him.

The crusher came that fall when I pinned everything on a winter-long contract in dry Southern California involving several hundred acres of land. I pared my bid down to where, as contractors say, "there were hardly beans left for the table," and I lost it. To quote another old saying, I was left so small I couldn't power a treadmill in a flea circus.

I must have looked as small as I felt because just now, 38 years later, I happened to mention the incident to my wife. "Oh, that awful day," she said. "I've never forgotten how down in the dumps you were when you came home and told me you had lost the job. I've never seen you so low before or since."

The next morning, for lack of anything else to do after pinning all my hopes on the contract, I went out to overhaul the tractor. I don't know why. The rains around Stockton had brought earth-moving to a halt. A nearby rancher came up and said, "Say, Bob, if you aren't doing anything, I've got some stumps to pull at my farm. I'll bet with this tractor you could do it in half a day."

After losing a winter's contract, I wasn't much interested in a half day's work, but he was one of those fellows who wouldn't take no for an answer. "You're making a mistake," he said. "I think you could make a few dollars and help me improve my ranch at the same time. At least you could set a price."

He had a point so I quoted the same hourly rate I would have gotten had I won my contract. "Okay, let's do it," he said.

It wasn't much of a job, but before I was through another rancher came along. Seeing how fast I was pulling stumps, and hearing about my rate per hour, he decided he could afford to have some stumps pulled too.

To make a winter's work short, the ranchers kept coming along one after another. It reminds me of the story in the Bible about the widow who had only a handful of meal in the barrel, but because she did what the prophet Elijah told her to do, there was always more meal in the barrel in spite of a famine in the land.

There was a famine of another kind in the earth-moving business. The winter rains around Stockton that made stump-pulling easy in the softened soil spread to Southern California. The contractor who had beaten me out of that job fought heavy mud for four months and lost money. I came out well ahead, teaching me again to say, "Lord, Thy will be done."

With the coming of spring a lot of things happened at once. For one thing, somewhat to my surprise, I found I was an employer. My welding and repair business had grown to the point where I needed a full-time welder to operate my service truck in the field. In the shop I had set up in the barn, my brother-in-law, Ray Peterson, was getting in so much work from garages and shops all over Stockton that he had to have an assistant, and even young Howard was working for him after school, and, I'm afraid, on a lot of days when he should have been in school.

The next was the return of my welder from a two-weeks' job repairing equipment for a road contractor. Right behind him came the contractor, looking, I thought, a little sore. "Bob, I just paid your man more for his repairs than your whole she-bang is worth," he said. "And you still own the equipment."

"Well, you get paid more for repairing a road than your equipment is worth," I said defensively.

"That's the point. I believe in owning my own stuff. How about fixing me up with a welding outfit just like yours, so I can make my own repairs?"

I hated to lose his work, but I could see that if I didn't build the equipment for him, someone else would. Thus, fittingly enough, the first piece of machinery I ever manufactured for sale was the very kind of welding machine that was to build our company. It was an electric welder incorporating a few new ideas of my own. Later I was to build bigger electric arc welders, and I still build my own, the latest being a big Tourna-Melter that joins thick steel plates by flowing a stream of molten metal into the seam.

I had hardly started work on the welder when a big land-leveling contract at Bellota came through. At once I hurried over to the Guy brothers to rent the Holt scraper I had returned while pulling stumps. To my dismay, they had already leased it to Buck Maistretti, one of my competitors. Worse, Buck had gone off with my electrical system still attached to the scraper.

"Well, I'll have to find Buck and get my motors back," I told Ira.

"I got a better idea," Ira said. "You aren't going to be able to get a scraper this year. There are so many ranchers wanting irrigation that Holt, Schmeiser and everybody else are a year behind on orders. Tell you what, instead of taking your motors off the scraper, why don't you hook up your generator to my tractor and give Buck the whole system? I'll meet your price for the job."

I wasn't happy with that idea at all. Not until I'd checked all over and found there was not a scraper to be had in California did I make the best of a bad situation. I built the generator system for Ira's tractor. Such was my first sale of a piece of earth-moving apparatus.

I still find that an odd start for our company. Building a

piece of machinery to set my rival up in business. There I was, back in his dust, watching him drive off with my pride and joy. A big earth-moving contract in my pocket, and nothing to complete it with.

I've been told that an ambitious young fellow today cannot start a business such as mine. I can agree with that. I will also add that an ambitious young fellow couldn't start a business such as mine in 1922. For example, a few years ago I got an idea for an off-shore oil drilling rig. There's so much oil under the ocean that I thought I'd start a business of making sea-going platforms for the oil companies who would be drilling there.

But first comes the development cost before the business can start. In our engineering department we took all we had learned about making heavy-duty equipment, and all we had learned about electric motors, gears of all kinds, and special alloys to resist salt water corrosion. We worked months checking and double-checking our figures on stresses and strains, on hurricane winds and tidal waves, finding surprisingly little information on the latter two. Reported one engineer drily, "When a hurricane threatens an off-shore drilling rig, competent observers have shown more interest in getting ashore than in remaining to measure the disintegrating force."

In the end, after building scale models and loading them to the breaking point, we were not much better off than the little boy who told his father, "I guess I won't go to school today." "Guess again, son," replied the father. "You're way off on that first one."

Maybe we were way off, and maybe we weren't. We sounded out some oil companies drilling off shore and got this answer: "Go ahead and build it. If it works, come see us again." Now it was up to me to decide whether to back our project with the real thing, at a cost of $3,000,000, or drop it with a loss of a quarter of a million in paper work and models. I happened to have the three million, but I wouldn't have it long if I was wrong.

We made a deal that I believe is unique for untested equipment running into so many million dollars. The Zapata Off-Shore Company of Houston, Texas, gave us the order for the platform, later christened in New Orleans as *Scorpion*. They would test it for us under actual operating conditions. If it worked as guaranteed, we were all in business. If it didn't stand up to my guarantee, and that's where I had to be pretty sure of myself, well, I'd be the small boy going back to school on a wrong guess.

It worked. We saw our electric motors lift a 9,000,000 pound platform high above the water on its three legs at the rate of a foot a minute. We saw it as the only off-shore drilling rig on the Gulf Coast to take the full brunt of 1957's Hurricane Audrey and escape undamaged. Since then we've built a dozen more, and seen them towed to as far away as Arabia and Italy, and you can say we've started a business. But quite frankly, under those circumstances I think a young man would have had more difficulty in finding a backer with three million than I found in backing myself.

But, and I can't say this too emphatically, the young man of today is far better trained to start a business such as mine than I was. The point they miss in their impatience is that I didn't start a big business. It may sound like an exaggeration, but I was in my business for five years before I noticed it had started. It was that small.

The way it came about was through sheer force of circumstances. I had this Bellota contract and no scraper. I had my shop and welding equipment and what my wife called "the junkyard" of scrap iron and steel plate that seems to accumulate around a repair shop. Looking that over I said to Ray, "We've got a scraper right here if we just weld it together."

We squatted down in the dust of the driveway and began to draw up some plans. Ray was a natural-born mechanic and designer. He knew by instinct all that I had figured out from my correspondence courses. As our enthusiasm grew, our voices became louder and louder. Young Edna, who was helping Evelyn with the baby and the housework, thought a terrible fight was in progress and came flying out.

"What's all the yelling about?" I remember her asking.

"I dunno," answered Ray, "but if I holler louder'n Bob, and he shuts up, I'm right. If he out-hollers me, he's right."

For more than 30 years, until Ray's untimely death from a heart-attack, we settled many of our technical problems that way. The rules in the book might be telling us we were wrong, but if we found our vocal volume rising, we knew we were on the right track.

The machine that grew out of the dust was a sort of mongrel drag scraper, part Fresno, part conventional scraper, part scoop. It had so many belts and pulleys that I had to go through a check list, like my pilot before take-off, to know which button to press. When everything was going at once, it sounded like a rock crusher, with a few extra groans when a rock lodged in the gears.

Two things came out of my first scraper. First it enabled me to get back into the land-leveling business with a one-man earth-mover as good as any in operation. My contracts were saved. And second, it was such an ugly brute I couldn't look at it without seeing a dozen places where it could be improved. I hired a man to run it, and went back to the dusty driveway to work out my new ideas.

What I wanted this time was a semi-drag scraper. The saying used to be that scrapers, like Napoleon's army, traveled on their stomachs. The full drag, like the Fresno, was skidded along resting entirely on its belly, or, in the improved versions, with some support from wheels. The machine I planned would lift its bucket clear of the ground in front, leaving only the rear to be skidded along while the wheels carried more than half of the weight. The load would be contained within the bucket.

I built a welded steel frame supported in the rear by a couple of big wheels patterned after the bull wheel of a harvester. Between and in front of the wheels I swung from the

The original scraper-type machine, drawn by Holt tractor.

The Moss Avenue plant, Stockton.

The scraper operated by motors from electric automobiles; built in the late 1920s.

An early Tournapull (1937), drawn by Diesel tractor.

"That's what I want for Christmas." A
0 ton capacity earthmover of the 1960s.

A self-propelled, electric-drive, sheepsfoot roller.

Housemover (clearing for the St. Lawrence Seaway).

A Landing Craft Retriever. Note the vessel, in slings, being carried ashore.

Crash pusher. Gigantic bull-dozer-like machines work in pairs to clear crashed bombers from runways during emergency operations. This is "Fantabulous I."

Transporter, for high-speed mobility on big construction projects.

The tracking ability of a rubber-tired train is demonstrated rounding a corner in downtown Longview. Ordinarily, of course, these trains are not for use on public streets and highways.

I needed the boots, gloves, and parka during these Arctic tests of the Snow Train.

The electric, self-propelled, rubber-tired wheel.

An amphibious ship; the rack and pinion leg walks it ashore.

Tree stringer. No tree is too big for it.

Jungle crusher. Clears an acre of forest in fifteen minutes.

A log stacker, medium capacity.

Log transporter for skid trails. This machine has an electric motor geared directly to each wheel and uses no clutches, mechanical drives, or body springs. Its capacity is 30 tons.

Bridge builder; it walks
on land or in water.

Electric saw. The blade, lower left, cuts close to
ground, and the boom governs direction of the fall.

Portable Island for offshore drilling.

Mobile missile launcher.

Disc plow, with six-foot discs for land-clearing operations.

Logging crane tests its delicate bite by lifting an auto.

Panama tow, for pullin[g] ships through canal lock

A talk with Christian ministers in Liberia.

Tournavista, Peru.

The LeTourneau plant, Longview, Texas. Aluminum dome, foreground, is for employee and community meetings; rear dome is used for warehousing. Steel mill is behind it.

The rolling mill in the Longview steel plant.

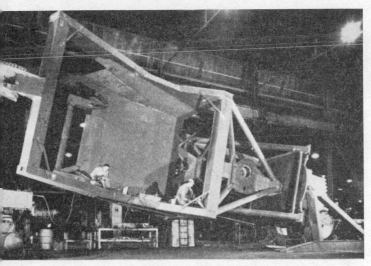

Positioner (right) designed to facilitate welding.

With the plane which takes me on my weekend trips.

Family portrait.

frame a scoop-shaped bucket 12 feet wide by four feet deep and four feet high. Loaded to capacity, it held six cubic yards.

My Italian neighbors across the street and the families of two farmers on either side did not come to appreciate my construction methods. I made the bucket out of quarter-inch steel plate, pounding it into shape with a twelve-pound sledge hammer. With every blow it rang like a gong, and because I worked outside I was noisier than the proverbial boiler factory. The cutting of the scoop to shape, and the welding on of the sides was more silent so I worked out a program of pounding by day and welding by night.

The machine was nearing completion when, one scorchingly hot July day, Mr. Throop, a former designer and maker of scrapers, came out to see what I was doing. I put down my hammer while he walked around the frame, sadly shaking his head. "I'm disappointed in you, Robert," he said. "I'd heard you were building something new. I built one just like this a year ago, and it won't work."

At this belated moment it occurred to me that he could be right. "What kind of power were you using?" I asked sort of weakly.

"Air power, of course," Throop said. "The best there is."

I was relieved. I had something new of my own that Throop didn't know about. What I had was so old that it was obsolete, yet so new it hadn't been touched. Which brings up another point. There must be literally thousands of good ideas in the U.S. Patent Office that never got off the ground. Inventions that died and were buried because they were ten or 50 years ahead of their times, or maybe they were inventions designed to do one job when they could do ten other jobs much better if anyone thought to apply them. What I had was the old electric automobile, killed by a strange set of circumstances just as it was reaching peak performance.

With its quiet battery power, its steering rudder, its high box top and wide glass windows, its vase for artificial flowers, and its non-crank, push-button starting, it had long been the favored vehicle for elderly women and fading spinsters. So much so that it became known as the "Old Maid's Car," and when that reputation spread, it was too much for the old maids. By 1922, with the introduction of reliable self-starters on conventional automobiles, they abandoned their electric cars by the hundreds. You could buy them for a song, even with my voice.

I saw in an electric motor that could push a car up the steepest hills in San Francisco exactly what I needed on my scraper. I bought two, welded them to my scraper, fixed them up with gears and pulleys, and practically cooed when they boosted six tons of dirt out of the ground while whining for more. Air power might be the answer for other earth movers, but that old electric car put me on the path to electric power I've been following ever since.

I thought I had built a pretty good machine, but I didn't know the half of it. Thanks to its all-welded construction, it was freed at last of the massive cast iron frames and braces used on other machines. When loaded, its weight was almost all pay load; when empty the tractor pulling it didn't know it was there. It could careen along at the tractor's top speed of four miles an hour with no bolts or rivets to work loose. Shocks that would shatter cast iron had no effect on my machine's tough steel frame. Rocks that would crimp the regulation scraper blade had no effect on the flame-hardened steel cutting edge of mine.

Its performance was even more gratifying. Even when semi-dragging a six-ton load, my aging tractor could move along just twice as fast as when it was dragging a four-yard mass of tumbling earth. I could carry a third again as much per trip, and make twice as many trips. There remained its greatest advantage of all. There was little spillage. When I picked up dirt I carried most of it directly to the low spot where it would do the most good. Saved were all those countless trips going back to pick up spilled dirt.

For example, my first job by previous estimate would take

a month. I raced through it in ten working days of fourteen hours each. On the next job, estimated at two weeks, I was through in four full days.

This is the machine I named the Gondola. With it, familiar with all its moving parts, I built the Stockton County Horse Track in record time as already mentioned. And as already mentioned, it was as a free exhibitor at the fair that I came in for the deflating comments of Mr. Harris of the Harris Harvester Works.

Mr. Harris was right, of course, but before I could act on his well-meant remarks, I heard some comments that sent me off on another track.

Carlton Case, more than a little impressed by my demonstrations, suggested, "Better protect yourself with some patents on that machine. It might be worth something."

Patents! That was more like it. Patents made me sound like an inventor. At once I turned my attention to all the good points of the Gondola, finding just enough to work on, and managed for a time to overlook its flaws.

12

I've read that Alexander wept because he had no more worlds to conquer. I've heard young engineers in my own shop complain that they've arrived too late to make any major discoveries. That's all nonsense. All inventors stand on the shoulders of the inventors who have gone before them, and the bigger the inventors, the higher the newcomers can stand. We mechanics are particularly blessed because all fields of science are constantly discovering new theories and products that open new worlds for us to conquer. I remember when fiber glass insulation first came out. We thought of it as something more durable than rubber, and therefore better. Then we discovered that with fiber glass insulation we could cut the size of our motors in half and maintain full power. Finally, with contributions from other fields, we could build motors so compact and powerful that we could fit them inside of wheel hubs. Another world was opened for us with a piece of cloth made of nothing newer than spun glass.

Some of the above steps, from the spun glass of the ancient glass blowers to fiber glass insulation, might be called invention, but most of them are a part of the long and costly process of development. I don't know what it cost the other fellows, but I do know that after using every scientific contribution I could lay my hands on, it still cost me 15 million to develop the compact motors and the electric wheel.

Fortunately development costs on that scale were not my problem during the winter of 1922-23. I worked my Gondola on land-leveling jobs around Bellota and Escallon, making money while my competitors with their heavier machines had to wait for the end of the rainy season. As far as I was concerned, that fact alone proved the superiority of my Gondola. It is true that my wiring system shorted out in the rain one time, and I shot out of my seat in a cloud of sparks. I wasted more time maneuvering out of tight corners than I saved on long hauls, and in mud my self-dumping bucket wouldn't dump. These were the flaws Mr. Harris had pointed out, and, exactly as he had warned, I looked at my machine as a perfect baby, and didn't mind when it cried.

If I was pleased with the scraper, I couldn't say the same for the aging tractor. By spring I had repaired it so often that it was more LeTourneau than Holt, and not the best of either of us at that. With what I had made that winter I bought a brand new super-Holt with a fringed canopy on top. Today I build the largest earth-moving equipment in the world, and I've got a few other specialized monsters around that will do for size, but that super-Holt still lingers in my memory as the BIGGEST chunk of machinery I ever owned. I'd walk around it, and pat the radiator higher than my head, and back off 20 feet or so to look at all of it at one time.

At the same time, as the owner of a *Big* machine, I couldn't help but think a little bigger, and on my next land-leveling contract, all the weaknesses of the Gondola, that I had refused to admit before, became starkly apparent. The Gondola was a runt, so puny that even when fully loaded my tractor could pull it while practically coasting. When a man loafs, you can't be sure if he's an idler, a dreamer, or a deep thinker; when a machine loafs you can be sure the inefficiency is not its fault. Quite obviously what I had to do was build a scraper big enough to match the bigness of the tractor. Once again it was a case of using the whole file, and not just the middle.

At this point, I'm afraid, a good technical education might have ruined me. I am reminded of the bumble bee that, according to the laws of aerodynamics, is so bulky and has such little wingspread that it can't fly. Not knowing this, it flies anyway. Not knowing what I was up against, I just went ahead and did it.

In retrospect, I guess my problem was a little unusual. I wanted to double the size of my scraper, and it was already as big as it could get. It was a cumbersome 12 feet wide and carried eight tons. The first couple of tons could be scraped up easily. The next two tons had to force the first two up and back. The last ton had to force seven inert tons aside to make room for itself, but after that the loading could become difficult. It would take as much power to squeeze in one more ton as was needed to load the first eight. In short, I could pick up eight tons with 75 horsepower, but would need 150 horsepower to scrape up nine tons, all of which did not strike me as being very practical.

Curiously enough, while drinking out of one of those old telescoping aluminum cups, I found what I was after. Remember how the sections nested one inside the other when the cup was collapsed? In that condition only the bottom section held water, but when the next section was raised it held twice as much.

I didn't know if it would work or not, but I built two buckets, one nesting inside the other. Because I welded my steel plate together instead of using bolts or rivets, I got a nice, smooth fit. The bottom bucket carried the cutting edge over which the dirt flowed smoothly into the upper bucket. The upper bucket carried the back-plate, four feet high, against which the incoming dirt piled up.

And there was the beauty of it! When the upper bucket was full and presenting an eight-ton resistance to taking on any more dirt, I released a catch. Back it rolled on oiled tracks, easily pushed to the rear by the dirt entering the bottom bucket. In good going, with 16 tons in the buckets, I could still scrape another four tons ahead in the conventional manner, giving me a load of 20 tons with very little spill.

After my first demonstration, somebody said, "That thing will move mountains," so Mountain Mover we named it. It was to live up to its name. For four years it was operated for me by a man named Ephraim Hahn, a natural-born earthmover if I ever met one. He took great pleasure in his artistry, and he told me why. "Y'know, Bob," he drawled, "when I was a mule skinner, I couldn't do a bit better work than the mules they give me. Some runt with better mules could do a better job than me every time, and you just know you can't take no pride in work where only the mules count. But on Mountain Mover here, and knowing how to operate it, and makin' it do more'n anybody, you got pride. Why, even my wife thinks I'm somebody."

When I went into heavier construction work, I sold the Mountain Mover to Eph, and he continued to run it on land-leveling jobs until he retired in 1943. His brother Clarence then took it over and ran it until the end of the war. A few years ago the brothers wrote to me saying the Mountain Mover had outlasted six new tractors bought to pull it, and had moved, according to their best estimates, some 4,200,000 cubic yards of dirt. Add to that the million or so yards it had moved before I sold it to Eph, and you have quite a mountain.

I don't know how many times the machine was rebuilt, but recently my wife was in California and took a picture of the relic. Upon her return, she told me she recognized my original welding in the frame. She would bring that up. At the time we were finishing the Mountain Mover we were so broke again we couldn't buy any more tobin bronze welding rods. But in the house she had some polished bronze curtain rods. Down came the curtains, and it was her rods that went into the welds she recognized.

That particular financial crisis was only one of the many I kept getting into. My ideas for new machines were constantly getting ahead of my income from land-leveling, welding, and repair work. The Mountain Mover, despite the fact that it was mostly scrap steel and second hand motors, had taken all my cash and credit to complete. If I could have sold it—but no. Down in the Modesto Valley, Eph Hahn was using it to move dirt four times as fast as it had ever been moved before, and at half the cost, but do you think its proven success meant anything to earth-movers in those years? They were a bunch of rugged individualists who were dubious of anything new. Even my best-wishers gave me six months for the machine to break down under the weight of the innovations.

The Gondola was out on a good contract, the Mountain Mover was out on a good contract, the shop was loaded with repair work, and the welding truck was seldom idle. I suppose a good businessman would have waited for some of these enterprises to catch up with the bills. I was out on the trail of another hot idea. I couldn't wait.

The Mountain Mover had two telescoping buckets. The drinking cup that had set me off had had five sections, so now I wanted to build the whole cup. I did some figuring in the dust of my driveway, and came up with one answer right away. Five buckets carrying a total of 40 tons would require a frame as long, strong, and heavy as a county bridge. I settled for five buckets to carry four tons each. The big and wonderful idea there was that they would *carry* 20 tons free and clear of the ground.

Right there I was ahead of myself, but I had another jump to make. I made it, and jumped clear off the calendar. My electrical system had made it possible for one man to do the work of two. What I wanted it to do now was make it possible for one machine to do the work of two. I wanted it to electrify the scraper so I could get rid of the tractor.

I had it all figured out. I built four big steel wheels, and into the hub of each wheel I installed a second-hand electric car motor so geared that it would cause the wheel to turn around it. Those were pretty big wheels that would be hard to steer in mud, so I geared another electric car motor to the front wheels to give me electric steering. Two more motors went to power the five telescoping buckets. Seven motors in all. For their supply of electricity, I welded a big Navy surplus generator to the front of the machine, and powered it with a Locomobile auto engine recovered almost intact from a wreck.

No clutches were needed. No transmission system. No brakes. Just some flexible electric cable to carry the power to each motor. Nothing for the operator to do but push buttons, occasionally pouring a little more gas to the Locomobile in hard going.

And it worked. So did the Wright brothers' flying machine. In comparing my self-propelled, electric-wheeled scraper with their flying machine, don't think I'm stacking myself up with them as an inventor. I am only once again pointing up the difference between invention and development. The airplane had a long row to hoe before it got off the ground commercially. My electric wheel had a hard row to hoe before it got into the ground commercially. Both at the start lacked, among other things, the contributions from the other fields of science needed for their development.

My machine moved at the ponderous rate of one mile an hour. It was the dumbest brute of a machine I ever made. No life or responsiveness. It picked up twenty tons of dirt at one mile an hour, and moved away with it at the same speed. Loading, emptying, or hauling, it didn't seem to care. I didn't bother to name it. In later years, when I have something I'm proud of, and willing to back with my reputation, I call it a Tourna-pull or a Tourna-crane, or give it my full name of

LeTourneau Electric Wheel or LeTourneau Log Stacker. That one I called merely a self-propelled scraper. Yet I could never forget it, as I can most of my mistakes. Those electric wheels, the first of their kind, were to haunt me for years until at last electrical engineering had developed to the point where I could make electric wheels perform in the revolutionary manner I thought those first ones should.

The odd thing that came to my rescue in the case of the self-propelled scraper was a feature I had overlooked. I was so disappointed in the slow performance of my electric wheels that I failed to note the efficient way the machine loaded its buckets and racked them up all neatly in a row within the frame. With all five buckets filled and racked, I at last had a scraper that no longer traveled on its stomach. For all its slow speed, it was, as the saying went, "riding high, wide, and handsome."

Ira Guy, watching the thing work, pointed this out to me with an unenvious statement. "Remember when we used to holler at an automobile driver to get a hoss?" he asked. "I think I oughta holler at you, 'Get a tractor.' "

It was a wonderful idea. I yanked the electric wheels off the machine and replaced them with non-powered, track-type treads. I put a tractor and generator out front, and away I went. Now I had something. A self-loading, self-dumping, self-spreading scraper that was freed at last of all the friction, wear, and tear of the drag, or semi-drag scraper. No longer did I have to wrench and twist at a twelve-foot bucket as it dragged its weight through mud or sand on a turn. With all my buckets clear of the ground, I could pull out of a tight corner like the proverbial stage coach that could turn on a dime and leave nine cents change.

That is the machine that opened the way to modern earth-moving methods. Do you think I could sell it to raise the desperately needed cash I had spent on its construction? They thought I was nuts when I built the Mountain Mover. Now I was clear around the bend.

I had the Gondola, the Mountain Mover, and the telescoping scraper in action, on land-leveling contracts. Eventually they would pay for themselves, but right now I had to pay Eph Hahn, Ray Peterson, and about nine others who needed some immediate cash for groceries and rent. A loyal bunch, some of whom had gone six weeks without a payday.

Buck Maistreti came around. He had had such success with my electrical system on the tractor and scraper he had rented from the Guy brothers that now he wanted to buy his own equipment. I tried to sell him the five-bucket machine, but like the rest, he saw no future in something as radical as that. He wanted the Gondola, already work-tested. I snapped him up so quick I forgot to ask if he had any money. He didn't, but he had some credit at the bank, enough to meet my payroll, and once more I was back in business.

I see I'll have to change the above statement. I was back in business, but I didn't know what business I was in. I wanted to build machines, and sell them on the merits of their improved performance. When no one wanted my "newfangled contraptions," my thoughts turned to the other side of the heavy equipment business. We had three types of contractors in those days. The big boys who built railroads, highways and dams; the intermediates who built county roads, canals, and small bridges; and the land-levelers who would do anything from flattening out 20,000 acres of land to filling a city dump. I decided to raise my sights a little. If no one wanted to buy my untested earth-moving machines, I would enter the heavy construction business, and test the machines myself. I would be a contractor to end all contractors, with my superior machines to back me. They say pride goeth before a fall, but that is when your pride is let off easy. Mine didn't just fall. It crashed and burned.

13

Heavy construction, ever since the building of the Pyramids, has been considered a rough game. The contractors who built the Roman roads and aqueducts worked men by the thousands and killed them by the hundreds. On our own early highways, railroads, dams and levees, brute manpower was the only answer, augmented somewhat by brute horse and mule power.

This was still pretty much the state of affairs when I plunged into the game. I'll have to admit I was a pretty queer duck. I had an idea that if my men were inspired to go to church on Sunday, they wouldn't feel like blowing their salary on Saturday night. I had an idea that if my men saved a few hundred on the job, they would stick around to save a few hundred more. I had an idea that if I built my own machines for a job, I wouldn't have to fire my men when it was finished. I could put them to work building new machines and repairing the old ones to get set for the next job.

Idealistic? Of course, and my competitors got many a laugh out of me. Still, there's something in having the last laugh. I didn't then go out of my way to hire good Christian men for my jobs. I haven't since, and I never will. The fact is, if I ever thought my crew was composed of men wholly dedicated to Christ, I would deliberately hire some non-believers for my crew to work on.

What did happen was that with a Christian atmosphere around my jobs, I did attract a good Christian element, and ever since the birth of our Savior, the time hasn't been when a good Christian can't work rings around the toughest roughneck you ever saw. Not only that, but in that kind of atmosphere your toughest roughneck is very apt to find Christ himself, and then you've got something.

There is another point to consider. With my self-loading, self-dumping, self-spreading machinery, I didn't have to hire hundreds of shovelers, barrow pushers, pick-axers, sledge-hammerers and mule skinners. I didn't have to drug their minds with physical exhaustion, and revive them on Saturday night with a quart or so of hootch. My men worked with machines that built up alertness, stimulated their thinking, and increased their self-respect. Where previous contractors employed hundreds of men on work that reduced them to drudges, I employed dozens on work in which they could take pride. Just compare the operator of one of my earth-movers with a wheelbarrow chauffeur of 40 years ago. Instead of a labor gang, I had a tightly-knit work crew. That in itself was as revolutionary as anything the construction business has ever seen.

As usual, my first step in getting started was to borrow some money. This I did on the strength of the machines I had in operation and the prospect of some big land-leveling contracts in the future. Then I called Dad in to build my first factory. It was of American-barn architecture measuring 40 by 60 feet, with wide sliding doors at both ends. It was a proud day when a sign painter proclaimed in letters three feet high: R. G.

LETOURNEAU—GRADING MACHINERY. I was in business, but in a baffling sort of way.

Because no one had built machines like mine before, I couldn't buy any machinery with which to build them. Even the lathes I bought couldn't turn axles 12 feet long, so I had to cut the axles in half, machine them, and weld them back together again. In the end, I was forced to build my own machines to build my own machines, something I still have to do. I had to build cranes and hoists and jigs to hold steel frames up to 50 feet long while they were being assembled and welded. I had to invent rollers to bend heavy steel plate into wheels up to seven feet in diameter, and when spoked wheels of this size began carrying as much mud stuck in the spokes as there was in the buckets, I had to invent my own form of disk wheel and the machine to make disks. Thanks to the California climate, I could do all the big assembly work outside, and use the factory for machining small parts.

I can't pass this phase of the business without mentioning my non-existent stockroom. We didn't have enough money to build up an inventory, so everytime we ran out of an item it was up to Evelyn to take the car down to Higginbotham's or Castle's warehouse to pick up everything from welding rods to 20-foot lengths of angle iron. And unless Edna was around, this meant she had to take Louise and infant Donald along with her, the baby in her lap and Louise belted into a child's seat beside her. Not until the morning she made three trips in a row did she complain.

"Three times I've lighted the wood stove to heat wash water," she said, "and three times it has gone out. Either you get a messenger boy, or I get a gas stove." Since messenger boys who could drive a truck came high, she got the stove.

It was at this time that I got a chance to bid on a job that would put me up with the big boys like W. A. Betchel and Henry Kaiser. The Hetchy-Hetchy pipeline, that largest and longest water pipeline built to date, was in the process of construction to augment San Francisco's water supply. The pipe, six feet in diameter, was being laid in a trench dug eight feet wide by ten to twelve feet deep. The earth dug from the trench was heaped high on one side in what is called a spoil bank. By the time I got wind of the job, sub-contractors had already signed up to replace the spoil bank in the trench and pack it over and around the pipe with the exception of one rugged 12 mile stretch at Redwood City. With my brother Bill, I went to look it over. It was not hard to see why the other contractors didn't want to fill in that stretch. In some of the passes the line went through, there was no room between spoil bank and hillside in which to operate a scraper or any other kind of existing earth-moving machine.

"It looks like a job for hand shovels," said Bill, "or maybe a big drag line."

I shook my head. As a machinery builder, I didn't want a job calling for hand shovels, and as a little guy, I couldn't afford a big drag line.

But I felt the challenge, and when I feel one of those wild challenges, I'm happier than if I had good sense. "Bid on it for me," I told Bill. "I think I can work something out."

"How much?" he asked, surprised.

"Whatever the other fellows bid on the easy part of the job."

That's how contractors can go broke, but this time I didn't. You've all seen overhead cranes in factories. They roll along on tracks under the roof, and the operator can either move his hoist from one end of the factory to the other with the whole crane in motion, or he can stop the crane and run the hoist from one side of the factory to the other on tracks built within the frame. That's what I built for the Redwood City job. A 50 foot traveling crane that would straddle the spoil bank, and operate at ground-level. My tractor supported one end of the crane and generated the electrical power. The other end, on the far side of the spoil bank, was supported by two huge, electric-powered wheels. Traveling back and forth was a bucket that scooped dirt out of the spoil bank and dumped it into the trench. One operator and a few push buttons to control the electric motors, and I was doing a job that other contractors in easy going had had to do with scores of men.

Before saying goodbye to the back-filler, I'll add that a few years later I built a modern factory for Henry Kaiser, the big innovation being a 50 foot overhead traveling crane. It was my old back-filler, modified only to travel on rails instead of on tractor and electric wheels.

That year of 1924 was a good one for our partnership. I was able to raise my contribution to the Christian Missionary Alliance Church to $5,000. I built a truck and 24 foot trailer, with which Evelyn could cruise through Stockton, collecting kids in the trailer for Sunday School, or taking them off to Mt. Herman for summer camp. I helped enlarge the Peniel Mission, and for a reward, our son Richard was born on January 3, 1925.

We had almost more work than we could handle. The Moss Avenue factory was so busy building telescoping scrapers that Ray had to devote his full time to it, meaning close to 24 hours a day. As fast as the machines came out, which was not nearly fast enough, I was running around getting more contracts to keep them busy. By fall I built my first railroad for the Spring Valley line, piling up a roadbed in such record time that other contractors were forced to take notice. I remember that it was Ernie Rider who bought my first telescoping scraper, another one of the boys with whom you could do business with a handshake, and wonder if you were going to get paid later. You always did get paid, though not always on time. We expected that.

In the spring of 1926 I tackled my first big job as a major league contractor. That was the construction of a highway through Crow Canyon and across the Dublin Mountains between Oakland and Stockton. Heretofore I had worked my machines in soft, or relatively soft ground sprinkled with a minimum of rocks. In Crow Canyon I was up against everything from gravel to sticky gumbo to hard shale. Now I had to prove to myself whether my machines could do a man-sized job or were just boys at heart.

I built a heavy, steel-toothed machine we call a rooter that could sink its fangs into everything but solid granite. With that chewing up the loose shale ahead, my telescoping scrapers could scoop up the debris left in its wake as easily as they could scoop up sand. Where I was in real trouble was with all the washes that sliced down through the sides of the canyon. I would cut my way around the shoulder of a ridge to find a wash in front of me 50 to 100 feet deep that had to be filled before the road could bite a chunk out of the next shoulder.

My scrapers simply couldn't do the job. They could cut and carry 20 tons up to the wash, and that was it. Tractor drawn as they were, they had to stop some 30 feet from the edge, dump their loads, and then, with an enormous waste of time in backing, turning, and climbing over the dumped loads, finally get turned around for a return trip. In the meantime I was left with the dumped loads that had to be shoveled or wheel-barrowed into the arroyo.

To fill an arroyo in that primitive manner struck me as ridiculous, and I hunted frantically for a way out. In the early days, when a fill was being extended beyond a cut or across a swamp or lake, the earth was brought up in carts and dumped. Then men with shovels humped themselves to move it on from there, thus earning for themselves the name of "humpers." Their replacement was a mule-drawn scraper blade, so hitched that it was pushed ahead of the mules instead of being drawn behind them. With such an arrangement the mules could buck or "bull" as much as a yard or two ahead of them and over the edge of the hill or fill. So far so good, but when it came to turning around or backing up for a second trip, the mule-skinner was left with a frightful mess. The cart was before the mule, so to speak, and I'll let your imagination back the thing up or turn it around.

I have it on good authority that no one knows where the

name bulldozer comes from, nor who invented it. But that's its name, and I'll put my name in with many others in claiming to have invented it. Up to now, with minor concessions, I've won all my arguments with other claimants to the title. Plowboards, or what we now call dozer blades, were used by the Mormons in the early days of Salt Lake City, and were later used with varying degrees of success with mule power and tractors. All had the same weakness. The blade couldn't be lifted out of the ground for turning or backing.

Stuck up there in Crow Canyon, my contribution was the first practical blade that could be raised or lowered at will, with push-button controls. Remember my first experience with donkey engines and snatch blocks and cables, pulling stumps? I put a steel scraper blade out in front of my new Best tractor, rigged it up with an electric cable winch, and wove the cable through some sheaves. A press of a button would lift the blade out of the ground for easy turning or backing up. Another touch of the button would shut off the power, and the blade would dig into the ground of its own weight. It was to change the course of heavy construction history, but all I knew then was that it was bulldozing me out of a tight spot.

In talking about a contract that involves the movement of thousands of yards of earth and rock, man against Nature, one is apt to forget that Nature is not just Mother Earth. I remember the rattlesnakes, for instance. Blast out a rocky promontory, and you would irritate so many rattlers on the hillside above that they all went on the warpath, hunting for someone to bite. Slightly deafened by a few hours on a noisy tractor chewing rock, I got off one time for a drink of water just as a bulldozer operator shoved a load of rock into a wash. I heard the rattle of rock, thought it was a snake, and took off from there. I'm no athlete, but I think that was more of a flight than a jump.

Then there was one of my cat-skinners who cut his scraper too deep under an overhang of dirt and brought the whole thing down. There he sat, buried up to the neck. "Weren't you scared?" he was asked when we dug him out.

"Naw," he answered. "As long as I had the machine under me, I knew Bob would be around to dig it out pronto. And me being on top, he'd have to save me first."

I wasn't that fanatical about my machines, but it could be that I created that impression.

The Crow Canyon job, what with my rooter, telescoping scrapers and bulldozer, sort of stirred up the construction world. I had a lot of visitors and a lot of offers, both to buy my machinery, or to buy into my factory and put it on a big scale.

I was frankly bewildered. I had accepted Rev. Devol's statement that God needs businessmen, fully aware of the fact that in letting me in as a partner, God was getting a sorry specimen. When it came to making crisp, business-like decisions, I was still a dust-covered country boy trying to get out from behind the plow.

The best offer came from an Oakland engineer who had surveyed the Crow Canyon highway and didn't think it could be built in less than three years. When I showed signs of knocking it off in six months, he made some hasty revisions in his plans and came to me with a suggestion. With his engineering background and my machines, he said, he could interest enough Oakland and San Francisco capital to put our operation on a national basis.

I will say that sounded pretty big to me. I was on the verge of signing a contract when one of my foremen came up to me on the job, real excited, and said, "Henry Kaiser is down there watching your big scraper work."

I knew Kaiser was a big contractor, but I had never met him. I went down and introduced myself. Boom! He was the fastest talking, hardest driving man I had ever met in my life. I remember that out of the first rush of words he said, "That's quite a machine you've got there." I managed to say, "We think so."

"I'll buy three of those machines from you right now, and pay you cash on delivery," he rushed on. "I understand you're going to sell the patents and work out a deal with some engineer. Right?"

I managed to say, "Yes, we've been talking up a deal. In fact, I was going in to see him this afternoon."

"You're crazy if you sell to him," said the blunt Mr. Kaiser. "I'll do better. Now what do you say? Are you one of these men who can recognize a good thing when he sees it, or are you one that needs weeks to make up his mind?"

I didn't know what I was making my mind up to, but I didn't like the idea of waiting weeks to make it up. I've jumped into many deals like that since, most of which I have learned to regret, but not that one. "It's a deal," I said, and so began a remarkable association.

14

The general idea of building big machines is to turn them loose on bigger jobs. The fact is, there are no big jobs; only small machines. The Panama Canal and the Suez were big only because they were measured with a team of mules and a hand shovel, like the small boy who announced to his mother he was six feet tall. He had measured himself accurately enough, but with a small ruler he had made himself. Today we have machines that could dig a canal across Nicaragua or Arabia so fast that they would make of those "big" jobs an exercise in ditch digging. Yet the tendency is still strong to measure future jobs on the basis of past experience instead of modern machinery.

In 1926 that attitude wasn't just strong. It was a set policy. One man who didn't think that way was Henry Kaiser, six years my senior. He had quit school at 13 to go to work in a dry goods store. At various times, working his way across the country from Lake Placid, New York, to Spokane, Washington, he had been a photographer's helper, a hardware store clerk, and structural steel salesman. Steel put him in touch with contractors, and when they began buying more reenforcing rods than structural steel for concrete highways, bridge abutments, and concrete foundations, he quickly jumped into the sand, gravel and cement business. That, in turn, lured him into the street paving business, which in turn lured him into building a 16 mile concrete highway leading into Everett, Washington. There he lost his shirt but not his ambition. He worked his way out of the hole with small road contracts until, in 1921, he was ready to tackle another big one.

The story is that when Kaiser heard bids were about to be opened on a 30 mile highway between Red Bluff and Redding in California, he didn't even wait to telephone. With A. B. Ordway, his construction boss, he jumped on a San Francisco-bound flier only to discover the train didn't stop at the construction station where the bids were to be opened. It did, however, slow down to about 30 miles per hour for the engineer to snatch his orders from a bamboo stick held up to him by the stationmaster. So out jumped Kaiser and Ordway. Kaiser was short and round even then, and he set some sort of record for the long-distance roll through cinders. Ordway, taller and leaner, did more horizontal plowing than rolling. Both came out of it in tatters, the tatters including their skins as well as their clothes. But they won the job, and Kaiser was off.

What sold me on Kaiser up there in Crow Canyon was not the fact that he could talk rings, spirals, and helical turns around me. He was the first contractor I had ever met who didn't look upon my machines as trick instruments to do small jobs faster. He saw them as instruments to make big jobs small.

"There's a big dam job up in the High Sierras near Philbrook," he told me. "I've been figuring on it, but I didn't see how I could tackle it without tying myself up for a couple of years. With those scrapers of yours we can put that thing in like a boy damming a gutter. How about you coming along to see that they work?"

He didn't wait for my answer, but I must have nodded my head. "Have the machines ready by September, huh?" he said, and away he went. He's still a fast man, but you should have seen him then.

The machines were completed in seven weeks. I didn't have to take my hat off to anyone when it came to moving a little fast myself. We shipped them up to the end of the railroad in the Sierras along with a tractor and a few other machines of mine that Kaiser wanted. According to agreement, I went up with the machines, taking with me my key men, now added to Kaiser's payroll.

That was rough country up there. I remember the first night we camped out near the edge of the timber and were invaded by a couple of big bears. We had been assembling some of the machines that had been taken apart for shipment, leaving a lot of small parts and tools around when night caught us. When those bears came, we went right through there, heading for the tall timber, and some of those parts we never did find. Bill Wickman, one of my foremen, saved our beds and grub for us with a bit of quick thinking. He jumped into a Ford truck, and with lights blinking and horn blowing, went to the rescue. By the time he had chased those bears over the rocks and through the underbrush, I am sure they were never the same again. Neither was the Ford.

The Philbrook Dam was a milestone in the engineering business and in my life. It was the first major project in which the new broke entirely away from the old. There was not a mule on the site. We were still using some men with shovels and pick axes for clean-up work, but the heavy labor was done with power shovels, mechanized dump trucks, and, in the starring roll, my scrapers. From the start it was clear that nothing short of an earthquake would stop us from setting an all-time record in dam building.

For my part, I was getting my first lessons from a master organizer. At one time we must have had 1,000 men on the job, with some crews working on digging, and others on hauling, and some on concrete mixing, and others on concrete pouring, and others on 57 varieties of odd jobs. Kaiser had that big job timed to perfection. More, he knew how to get along with men even when the men didn't know how to get along with each other.

One night things didn't go at all well for me. My scrapers were in tough going and the crew that was supposed to break up the hardpan for us hadn't done a good job. The road to the dam site was full of loose rock that was hard on the caterpillar tracks of my scrapers. The electricians hadn't strung the lights in the right places. Kaiser came out, and of course I was full of excuses, blaming the other fellow.

"Well, now, Bob," he said, "when things haven't gone as well as they probably should have, and you start to blame circumstances and other people instead of yourself, you are never going to improve. It's when you start to improve these matters yourself that you improve the matters and yourself both."

I can't say I was completely convinced. Late that night I got into the car with Kaiser and another superintendent named Tom. Tom had had a bad night, too, and he was glowering in silence in his corner. Kaiser stood it for a while, and then he said to me, "Tom, there, is smarter than you are. He isn't giving me any complaints or excuses. He has enough sense to keep his mouth shut."

I got that point all right, and Tom brightened up some. Kaiser wasn't through with us. "The trouble with Tom is that while he isn't blaming anybody or excusing himself out loud, he's sure thinking about it. In that way, he's just as guilty as you are, Bob. He won't improve any, either, until he stops thinking someone else is to blame and starts thinking of what to do about it."

That lesson has been worth a lot to me down through the

years. I continue to preach it to myself and to anyone else who will listen. You will never improve unless you blame yourself for the troubles you have. Then when you realize your troubles are your own, you can take them to the Lord, and He will give you guidance. Just don't make the mistake of asking Him to believe the other fellow was to blame.

The speed with which we completed the Philbrook Dam astonished the construction world. Kaiser was swamped with offers of even bigger jobs. He came to me as we were getting the machines ready to move out. We had that big dam there, and the water was already backing up behind it, and I suppose I was feeling like a graduate student is supposed to feel when he looks back at his college for the last time. "Your machines did the trick, Bob," he said. "I'll be needing a lot more of them. How about selling me the patents?"

Considering that they had been inspired by a ten-cent drinking cup, I was willing. "How about $50,000?" he suggested.

It was about twice what I had figured on, but I didn't object. A few days later he drove over to see me in my shop in Stockton. "A nice lay-out you got here," he approved. "A lot of good machine tools, and I see a lot of jigs you built yourself for turning out those scrapers. Do you want to sell any of it?"

"Sure," I said. "Anything I make is for sale."

"Well, as long as I've bought your patents so I can make your scrapers, I might as well buy your machines to make them with. Why not make a list of what you have, set a price on it, and bring it over to my office in Oakland tomorrow night?"

I drew up a list of my machines, valuing each according to what it was worth to me, and not necessarily according to what it had cost me on the second-hand market or what it had cost me to build. The next evening—we'd never heard of a construction man who kept nine-to-five hours—I drove over to Oakland with the list. I figured there were not more than a dozen key machines he would buy, and if I had set the price a little high, it was not because I didn't know he was a shrewd bargainer.

He had a couple of his buyers with him. They went down the list, asking a few pertinent questions about the condition of the machines, but not saying a word about the price I had put on them. When they reached the bottom of the list, they nodded, and Kaiser turned to his secretary. "All right, add it up, and write out a check to Bob LeTourneau for the works."

He didn't ask me to knock one dime off the price. I took the check, of course, but you might say I was dazed. I drove home asking myself why he did it. "He's driven sharper bargains than that," I kept telling myself, "he must have known that I had set a high price, expecting it to get knocked down. Why did he do it? There must be some method in his madness, something I haven't seen through."

I never did have time to figure it out then. The next day Kaiser arrived with the men who came to remove the machinery he had bought. "Your shop was all right, Bob," he began, and never slowed down after that, "but it was getting crowded. What I'm thinking of is the ideal factory where we can really turn out your scrapers. Cranes, hoists, one of Henry Ford's assembly lines. Things like that. You know how to build the machines so you ought to know how to build the factory to build 'em in. Why don't you come over with me to Oakland and build the factory and see that it gets going right, and—"

"Now wait a minute," I managed to get in.

"What for?"

"I've got my men to think about—"

"Of course. Your men know how to build your machines so they are the very men we'll be needing. We'll move them all over on my payroll instead of yours—"

"Don't forget I've got some good construction men that don't work in the factory. I'll—"

"Yeah, and I'll need them on that big construction job I

just landed in Cuba. Now that that's all straightened out, when can you start?"

I won't say we reached an agreement quite that fast, but that's the way it seemed to me. I do know that within a week Evelyn and I were housed with the children in a big tent in Livermore, and all the men who chose to come along or go to Cuba were more than fully employed. The tent gave an outing flavor to the move, being a lot more luxurious than some of the quarters we've had to occupy from time to time. It had running water, a bathroom, electric stove, washing machine and refrigerator, a full-sized bed for us, two smaller beds for Louise and Donald, and a tiny bed that could be rolled under the big bed when Richard was not sleeping in it.

The next six months were a revelation to me. Kaiser didn't seem to care about how much money I spent on his factory as long as I built him a good one. Thus with plenty of money to spend for the first time in my life, I built the factory I had dreamed about when our shop in Stockton became so crowded we had to move outside under the broiling sun to get needed space. As I mentioned, the steel structure I had built for use as a back-filler became our traveling overhead crane. I lined up the machine tool department for an orderly flow of raw stock and finished parts, did the same with the welding department, and then set up the jigs—in case I haven't defined a jig, it's a shaped frame that, at least in our shop, is used in holding steel parts together for welding into a complete unit —where they could all be served by the overhead crane. Then I built enough jib cranes to eliminate almost all the back-breaking lifting that was the bane of our business.

I had also figured out why Kaiser had bought me out lock, stock, and barrel without haggling over the price. He knew that if he had left me with a few machines in my shop, I would be finding work for them to do. "He knows I could give him an honest day's work, and then hop in my car to keep a night program going in my shop in Stockton," I told myself.

149

"He doesn't want that. He wants me to give all my energies to his job."

In His great Sermon on the Mount, the Lord said, "No man can serve two masters: for either he will hate the one, and love the other; or he will hold to the one and despise the other. Ye cannot serve God and Mammon." *Matthew 6:24.* I couldn't serve two factories and do right by either. I think a lot of people get mixed up that way, too. They have just enough religion to make them miserable, and not enough to make them happy. They can't enjoy serving the pleasures of sin because they know better, and they can't enjoy serving the Lord because they are not willing to serve Him all the way.

I didn't have time to rest once the factory was in full production. "The Southern Pacific wants a big freight yard built in Fresno," said Kaiser. "Why don't you get over there and see what the job will cost? Give me an estimate, and I'll make a bid. If we get the contract, I'll rent you all the machines you need, and turn you loose as a sub-contractor."

It was just the kind of proposition I was ready for. After six months of night-and-day work in the factory, I was eager to get out into the field again.

I sized up the job and gave Kaiser an estimate. He looked at me as though he thought the heat had got me. "You can't do the job for anywhere near that price," he said flatly. "I'm going to raise it 25 per cent, and the price is still too low." He was more convinced than ever when the bids were opened. We were so far below the others that Kaiser saw no hope for us. "Well, it will be a lesson to you," he said in a very gloomy voice.

I thought I might get a lesson out of it, but not the way he meant it. The freight yard was to be nearly two miles long, meaning that I was faced with some long hauls. What made it worse was that much of the dirt to be moved consisted of hardpan that would defy a scraper blade. I knew it was because of the hardpan that the other contractors had bid high, thinking they would have to use tons of dynamite. I had other ideas.

I rented a big power shovel from Kaiser, several tractors, but only a few telescoping scrapers for short-haul work. Then I rushed over to my empty Stockton shop, bought up a lot of second-hand machine tools and welding equipment, and went into production on a couple of ideas that I thought would do the trick. One idea was for an all-welded, self-dumping hopper wagon that would hold up to 15 tons of dirt. It was an ugly thing, high in front, and with a steel bottom sloping sharply to the rear. The big tailgate was held closed by a spring fastener. To empty a load, the operator had but to pull a rope to release the fastener, and the dirt would slide down the bottom and out.

On the job the hoppers were loaded by the power shovel and hauled away by tractor, one tractor being able to tow three or four wagons at a time. That way, on the long hauls I was able to move about 50 tons a trip instead of the 20 the telescoping scraper could pick up, and move them faster.

The other idea was for a big rooter, so designed and weighted that it was about twice as efficient as any ever built before. When I turned that loose in the hardpan, it rooted through the stuff like a hog through turnips. Not one stick of dynamite did I have to use. Between the use of the hopper wagons and the rooter, I came out so far ahead on the job that I decided it was time I take stock of the situation and see where I was going.

I couldn't think of a better way of doing it than in getting closer to the Lord. Evelyn and I had long wanted to know more about the Bible, so taking a leave of absence from Kaiser and leaving the children with my parents, we went to Los Angeles and enrolled in Bible School. For Evelyn it was a highly rewarding experience from which she emerged far more confident of her ability to organize and conduct Sunday Schools and summer Bible camps. She was still shy in large groups, but no longer hesitant if there was work for the Lord to be done. As for me, I did learn more of the depth of wisdom in the Book that has changed history. Yet as a man who had been active in heavy equipment and heavy construction work, I had to fight hard against the confinement of a classroom. As one preacher said in introducing me, "Mr. LeTourneau can tell you about the power of God, but he wouldn't recognize homiletics if he saw it walking through the door."

Frankly, I was relieved when I got a call from Kaiser. "Grab a train," he shouted through the long-distance telephone. "I'm in Salt Lake City. I've got something hot." Long distance phone service was not at its best in late 1927, but I think I could have heard him without the phone.

Whatever he had that was hot when he called me had cooled off by the time I arrived. He was already off on another track. "Those hopper wagons of yours," he began. "I think they'll speed up that levee job I've got in Mississippi. How about a couple of dozen?"

"I don't know about that mud," I said doubtfully. "They're fine in loose soil and rock, but mud—"

"They'll work," he said. He was the boss, and he'd seen the Mississippi mud. I was to see plenty of it in later years, and as the old saying goes, if I'd known then what I know now, I never would have made the deal. That mud, called buckshot for some reason, is half glue and half putty, turning to half concrete when dry.

What made the offer enticing was that Kaiser was giving me a chance to return to the manufacturing business, building the hoppers in my shop instead of his. All told, I was ready to get back into business on my own even though my association with Kaiser had been a happy one through which I had learned a lot. And for once I wasn't worried about credit for the purchase of machinery, new or second hand. I filled up the Moss Avenue factory with so much equipment that we didn't have room to build anything, let alone get it out when it was built. Once more we overflowed into the outdoors, with a few tarpaulins to protect the more delicate machine tools in case of rain.

The hopper wagons were shipped on schedule. Three weeks later came the report on their performance. "You'll have to come out here and do something about them," I was ordered by phone. "They won't dump. The mud sticks and . . ."

It was not my day to listen to complaints. I had a couple of land-leveling contracts hanging fire, a simplified cable control for my bulldozer was proving too complicated to work, I'd had a flat tire that nearly blew the fender off my truck, and I'd been too busy to eat since I didn't know when. "I told Kaiser I doubted those machines would work in mud," I snapped. "You'll just have to figure it out from there yourself."

A perfect example of a fine Christian way to build up customer relations. And my best customer at that. An hour later, realizing what I had done, and considerably subdued, I called Mississippi to announce I was on my way. "Kaiser says don't bother," snapped the voice. "We're figuring it out from here, and where we'll buy our next machines."

I could have walked under a small worm. It wasn't the loss of Kaiser's business that bothered me. It was the way I had lost it. I didn't have a leg to stand on. I didn't know what I could have done about the hoppers if I had gone to Mississippi, but at least I could have built up some good will. If you can't build that up with your fellow men, you most certainly can't build up good will with your Lord and Savior.

To make matters worse, the more I worried about those hoppers, the more I thought I might have done something. And once you start thinking something can be done instead of can't be done, you'd be surprised at how fast the ideas can start to flow.

Here's how it worked out with me. If mud was sticking in the hopper, it needed something to push it out. To me that could only mean an electric motor. Where? Well, there was that tailgate. Put an electric motor on the tailgate to swing it up and over like the paddle wheel of a steam boat. On the downswing it would sweep out the load as clean as a whistle.

Now I had the cure but had lost the patient. Still, the idea of a powered tailgate was too good to drop. From it grew the powered tailgate I use today to ram-dump my big scraper that carries 150 tons and more. I now have a machine on the drawing boards that will carry 200 tons. It has ten wheels eight feet high, all with electric motors in their hubs, to carry two 100 ton side-dumpers. The operator can swing around to the side of the dump at about 15 miles per hour, press a button, and those two side-dumpers will flip over so fast they will actually toss their loads free and clear of the big wheels without even slowing down.

All of that out of one sorry hopper that wouldn't work in mud, and a big mistake in failing to make good with one's friends. "There is a way which seemeth right unto a man, but the end thereof are the ways of death." *Proverbs 14:12*. It had seemed right to me to snap back when my hoppers wouldn't work in mud. Hadn't I warned Kaiser on that point? But it didn't seem right later, and when a man admits his mistakes, and is willing to learn from them with the Lord's help, new worlds can open up.

15

Without knowing it at the time, I was in a remarkable position in 1928, and one that gave me a big advantage over my competitors. As a contractor I was able to see all the weaknesses of the earth-moving machinery then in use, and as a manufacturer I was able to do something about it.

The rooter, the hopper wagons, the bottom-dump carts, the bulldozer, and the semi-drag scrapers were all products of what the contractor in me demanded and got from me, the manufacturer. They were built exclusively to help me get ahead as a contractor, but they were to become the foundation of our company.

I was in no position to recognize that at the time because suddenly my contracting business began booming in all directions. First, I was low bidder on the contract to dig an irrigation canal known as the Patterson Ditch. I've never been told so, but I've always suspected that I got the contract because no one else wanted to bid. It was a strange job, the first of its kind, calling for a canal that would carry a goodly river of water, not through a hill, but up and over it. This meant I had to dig a series of ditches along a difficult hillside, with each ditch being a stage higher than the last, with pumping stations to boost the water up a step at a time.

While I had the Moss Avenue factory on overtime turning out the ditch diggers, and the hoppers to carry away the overburden for the Patterson job, a highway contract at Oroville came through. I had bid high on that one, just to sort of keep my name in front of the contracting public, and when I won it, I began to worry. To be low bidder on two jobs in a row meant that the other fellows, older and wiser than I, had seen some difficulties I didn't know about. I could only guess at that, but of one thing I could be sure—they hadn't deliberately bid high just to throw the work my way.

I talked it over with Ray Peterson and Carlton Case, and we agreed that there were too many uncertainties ahead to risk a costly enlargement of the Moss Avenue factory. At the same time we didn't want to buy machinery from other manufacturers when we could, as we liked to say, "roll our own for half the cost of the tailor-mades." So we improvised our expansion, as we have had to do ever since.

Ray moved our growing engineering department out of the factory and into a construction trailer parked in the front yard. "Everytime an engineer has to use a slide-rule," complained Ray, "he has to step outside for elbow room." Outside was not much better. Pop Cook, my best turret lathe operator, claimed he had to push his two-ton lathe out of the driveway whenever a truck load of steel came in or a new machine went out. Harry Andrews, who was my whole business department, was moved into the parlor of the Italian family across the street, and there he had to fight payrolls, bill collectors, and the smell of garlic sauce and spaghetti. Evelyn always had 2:00 a.m. coffee ready for those of us working through the night, gallantly claiming that as long as she had to heat the baby's bottle, a few gallons of coffee was no extra chore.

In the midst of all this, I got a call from Ordway, Kaiser's top man. "We've snapped the boom on a power-shovel," he said. "Can you weld it together, or do we wait three months for a new boom?"

"I'm on my way," I said. This was the chance to redeem myself for the hopper fiasco that I had been praying for. I loaded a truck with welding equipment and drove 200 miles through the night to the site of the ailing power shovel.

Once on the job, I was able to get in a sincere apology for my arbitrary attitude at the time my hoppers had failed to work in mud. I also made sure that when I finished welding together the snapped boom, I left them with a machine that was stronger than it had been in the first place.

A few days later I got a call from Kaiser. "Nothing important," he said. "I cracked the aluminum head of my motorboat engine that I need here in San Francisco Bay. Think you can fix it?"

He knew how busy I was. I didn't think he was calling me away from my shop and construction business just to repair an engine. I drove to San Francisco, taking with me my own arc-welding system that I had developed to handle aluminum, about as tricky a metal to weld as there is. He sat in the cockpit of the boat, talking while I worked on the motor. As I figured, he had some bigger deals in mind, deals I might never have heard about had I failed to do him a favor. When I finished the job we went for a trial spin. He was a demon driver, always trying to coax 100 miles an hour out of a boat designed to do half that. We looked over the site where work was beginning on the San Francisco Bay Bridge while he rattled off a dozen more projects he had in mind. With the boat bouncing in the chop, I must have nodded my head several times because I found myself with more sub-contracts.

By the time I got back to Stockton late that night, I felt like the little dog that chased freight trains and finally caught one. Now what? In adding the sub-contracts for Kaiser to my own work, I had about four times as much as I could handle. My only out was to design some machines to do four times as much work. Kaiser had the patents on my telescoping scrapers, so I couldn't build them, though I knew he would be glad to let me rent as many as I could use on his sub-contracts. That would help there, but for my own contracts I needed more.

The most serious problem facing me in building a big machine was lack of power. The tractor manufacturers had some notion their machines were as powerful as they could get. Back when I was building Kaiser's factory and he was getting ready for the job at Eureka, we had tried to interest a tractor company in building a machine with Diesel power. The amount of interest we aroused was notable for its absence. "I'll build my own," said Kaiser, and did, installing a Diesel in the frame of an old tractor. I finished the job on this first Diesel tractor by equipping it with my electric generators. For a while up there in Eureka we were really moving dirt, proving we were on the right track. What we had overlooked was that the Diesel as then built was a stationary engine. Its separate cylinder blocks couldn't take the banging and wrenching they got in an uncushioned tractor. We blew out so many pistons we had to scrap the engine. And the tractor people, instead of noting the superior performance of the Diesel while it lasted, pointed to its failure and dropped the subject with relief. Eventually they were forced to accept the Diesel, but not in time to save me then.

Then one night, deeply worried about all the contracts I couldn't fulfill, I got down on my knees and prayed, "Don't let me down now, Lord. I've got all this work, and if You let me down, I'm ruined." Right there I saw my mistake. "Strike that out, Lord," I hastened to say. "I didn't mean that. I'm not asking You not to let me down. I'm asking You to help me not let You down. I'm not asking to use You. I'm asking You to use me."

That had been my trouble all along. All wrapped up in my own petty problems, I had once more begun to think I was working for myself instead of the Lord. I slept well that night, and when I woke up, I had the answer to my problem.

It didn't look like much of an answer at first. It was that old burro engine I had used while pulling stumps for my brother Bill nearly 20 years earlier. It had been weak and erratic, and it had only one cylinder, but when I rigged my cables and sheaves right, it could sure pull stumps 20 times its weight.

With that for a starter, one thought led to another fast. The electric motors I had used on the Gondola were ten times as powerful as that old burro engine. I had used them with rack and pinion gears, but suppose I had geared them to cable winches? And rigged the cable through some sheaves over my buckets? Why, with that kind of an arrangement I'd be able to lift loads with all the efficiency and power of an electric hoist. Instead of using five telescoping buckets to pick up 20 tons, I could pack 20 tons into one bucket, and lift the whole works with the press of a button.

It was a fine idea, but the tractor hadn't been made that could pull a scraper with a 20 ton bite. I had to compromise by building a semi-drag scraper that could carry about eight tons in the bucket while dragging three more tons ahead. While I was at it, mindful of the trouble Kaiser had had in shoving mud out of my hopper wagon, and the remedy I had thought up of a powered tailgate, I added one of those to the scraper. The finished machine had only half the capacity of the telescoping scraper, but because of its compactness, ease of handling, and the speed with which it could be loaded and dumped, it moved twice the tonnage on long hauls, and up to five times the tonnage on short hauls. That one machine made obsolete all the patents I had sold Kaiser.

In designing the cable-controlled scraper, I began a practice of working with my engineers that is still in effect. I drew up a plan for the cable controls, and handed it to them. They

159

got out their slide rules and figured out why it wouldn't work. I got my pencil, figured out why it would, and handed it back. I liken it to a chess game in which my engineers will checkmate my moves with every technical trick at their command, or I'll checkmate them with a few moves that aren't always in the books. Back and forth we go, give a little and take a little. When I've got a good design, I can win in a week. When I've got a poor design, they win, but it takes them longer. That's what makes us unique. We've got the only engineering department in the country where the president of the firm wears out as many erasers in the drafting room as his engineers.

While Ray Peterson put the factory on double shift to turn out cable-controlled scrapers, I started out to catch up on the construction jobs. I didn't have to look very far to see that I had a serious problem. The Oroville job would need every new scraper I could build, while the Patterson Ditch—I just didn't have the machines to swing it. The only bright spots were my sub-contracts for Kaiser where I was leasing his equipment.

At this point my old friend Buck Maistretti came to me in deep trouble. On a big highway job he had lost his well-worn shirt on the same freak circumstances that would later trap me at Boulder. The test holes on which he had based his bid had shown easy digging over most of the route. And where the holes were, he had found the digging easy, but seldom beyond the diameter of the hole. In between he had encountered solid rock, and by the time he had dynamited and power-shoveled his way out of that one, the sheriff was waiting to attach his machines at the other end.

Where this hurt me was that he had a lot of my machines on that job, still unpaid for, plus about 10,000 in cash I had advanced to help him meet his payroll. I'll admit I was no altruist. I had to keep Buck going in the hope he would come out ahead and pay for the machines. That was one of those deals we could all get into in those days before bankers stepped into big contracts and demanded security more substantial than a hand-shake. I wish we could do it today. I still think a hand-shake between Christian men is worth more than all the fine print you can find in 50 pages of contract.

It was to work out that way then. Buck still had the machinery while fighting off the sheriff, and his ability and his machines I could use on the Patterson Ditch. That would let Buck work his way out of the hole, pay for my machines, and still leave me a profit as the prime contractor on the job. Altruism? Charity? An easy way to get my money back? Or just good business? I know that Buck did a whale of a good job on the Patterson Ditch. He pulled me out, I pulled him out, and the people around Patterson got an over-the-hill canal that has paid for itself many times over.

Abruptly I found myself in a different set of circumstances. As is a feature of the construction business, one minute I was frantically trying to complete four jobs at once, and the next I was faced with a lot of men and machines on my hands and nothing to do. The cable-controlled scrapers had proved so efficient at Oroville that they were completing the road three months ahead of schedule, bringing all of my jobs to a close at about the same time.

What I wanted now was something big to prove both myself and my machines, and let my competitors know I was really in business. The only job in sight like that was too big, but I wanted it anyway. The California State Highway Department was getting ready to straighten out some of the old highways that twisted around through the mountains between Los Angeles and Bakersfield. The one section still open for bids was a stretch near Newhall now called the Newhall Cut-off. The old road going north out of the San Fernando Valley had laboriously wound its way over the first range of mountains with a series of dangerous switchbacks. The new road was to cut straight across, slicing through the crest of the ridge with a vertical cut 180 feet deep.

While I was wondering how I could swing it, I ran into a member of our church, likewise a contractor, who was also on the lookout for something to do. I thought this was a wonderful chance to demonstrate how a couple of members of the church could cooperate, so we were not long in drawing up a fifty-fifty partnership which we named the L & L Construction Company. We put in our bid on the job and got it.

From the first day we were in trouble. The clay and shale that had shown itself to be reasonably soft in test holes dried up and hardened like concrete as fast as we exposed it to the fierce sun. Even after my rooters cracked it, the sharp chunks of shale that were left were doing my scrapers no good. We had to buy two power shovels and bring up my big hopper wagons to do the hauling. To get those big machines to the site we had to build our own road, which meant bringing in my bulldozers.

No matter what we did, though, we got further and further behind, our losses mounting rapidly. My partner was a hard-working man, but when he saw his life savings were in danger, he began to go pieces, storming and scolding on the job, and that didn't help a bit.

One day he came up to me in a fine rage. "I'll tell you what's the matter with this job," he snapped. "You've got too many relatives working on it."

Oh-oh. He had me there. On the job were my brother and three brothers-in-law. My wife was assisting my brother Louis in keeping the books, and heading up the construction work were the brothers Jack and Joe Salvador, who counted as members of the family. But I've always been of the opinion that there is no harm in hiring relatives as long as they work twice as hard as anyone else. Another important factor was that in my uncertain progress, with chicken one day and feathers the next, my relatives would go without salary a lot longer than I dared ask of others.

I was deeply troubled by his attitude. I wanted to get along with him, but I wanted to be fair to my relatives, too.

"What do you suggest I do?" I asked as mildly as I could.

"Fire 'em," he said bluntly. "All except your brother Louis. He's the only one who knows the books."

Considering the job they were doing, firing them merely because they were related to me did not seem right. As always, I took my problem to the Lord in prayer. "My partner is a member of the church," I said, "if I fight with him, that would be a fine example of how Christians get along. I'm leaving it in Your hands. Show me what to do, Lord, and I'll do the best I can."

Two days later I got a letter from the Southern Pacific Railroad. They were inviting a select group of contractors in whom they had confidence to bid on building an approach for a new railroad bridge across Suison Bay near Benecia. The old railroad ferry across the Suison arm of San Francisco Bay was to be done away with at last.

Deep in trouble as I was with the Newhall Cut-off, I didn't see how I could bid on another job. Then something reminded me of my prayer, and I thought, "Maybe the Lord is using this to answer me. I will see." The Lord invites us to prove Him. "Bring ye all the tithes into the storehouse, that there may be meat in mine house, and prove me now herewith, saith the Lord of hosts, if I will not open you the windows of heaven, and pour you out a blessing, that there shall not be room enough to receive it." *Malachi 3:10*.

My credit was at low ebb, the word having spread that I was very apt to go broke on the Newhall job. Yet when I asked if I could get credit, just in case I won the S.P. contract, I was told to go ahead and bid. I still didn't think I had a chance. About all the S.P. knew about me was the work I had done on their Fresno freight yard, and they had many big contractors, Kaiser among them, with whom they had worked for years. The bids were not made public, but later I did learn that two big contractors and myself were within a few cents of each other. Whether I was the one who had shaved the extra two-bits off the job is something I don't know. All I know is that I was awarded the contract.

I called a meeting of the relatives. "Boys, I've got a job where we don't have to worry about a partner. Everybody except Louis is going up to Benecia on the new job. We'll settle this business once and for all about whether or not relatives can do the work." I put Howard in charge, and gave each of the others the work he was best qualified to handle.

If we had been in trouble from the start on the Newhall Cut-off, the Suison Bay bridge approach furnished an instance that was the opposite. The railroad approached the bay from the north through a series of hills that sank into salt marshes as they neared the water. It was those salt marshes we were to fill so the bridge could be hung high enough to permit the passage of small vessels. According to the plans of the S.P., we were to get the dirt for this fill from a hill that was on their right-of-way nearly a mile back from the marsh, and it was on that long haul that all bids were based.

While the job was getting organized, I commuted on the night train between Newhall and San Francisco, sleeping in a coach one night going up, and sleeping in a coach the next night going back. Somebody told me later they had berths on the train, but I was too busy to find that out, and too tired to care. I slept all right.

One day after we had been in operation about a month I was watching the hopper wagons go by from the steep, high hill that overlooked the marsh. A couple of men came up who introduced themselves as the owner of the hill and his real estate agent. They were wondering what the railroad bridge and a new highway that was coming through would do to improve property values.

"Not much for a steep hill like this," I said, doing some fast thinking, "but if you'd let me cut it down to size, and terrace it for housing lots, you'd sure have something."

It didn't take them ten minutes to see the light of day. The next day my bulldozers were shoving that hill down to a 50-B power shovel that was loading my hopper wagons as fast as they could be brought up. Instead of having a mile haul we had a haul of only a few hundred yards, and that fill went in there fast. I saved several thousand dollars, and the owner of the hill ended up with a valuable piece of property.

Naturally word of how well things were progressing in Benecia would reach the ears of my partner in Newhall. Now he began to feel that instead of inflicting him with my relatives, I was depriving him of their services. The way things were going in the 180 foot cut, I felt deprived of them myself, but I held my peace. In a series of terraces, we had sliced our way to the bottom of the cut. Now, because it is easier for a power shovel to load a hopper wagon on the terrace below than one on the same level, we had our shovels chewing away one terrace to widen the cut while the hopper wagons hauled away from the step below. It was a slow and painful process, and we saw no way of finishing the job with a loss of less than $100,000.

I put my own confidence in God. If He wants you to make money to serve His purposes, you'll make it. If He doesn't want you to have money, He'll take it away, no matter how much you might have. I couldn't understand why my partner couldn't feel the same way, especially after what God did next.

One of our big power shovels was being moved from the south side of the cut to the north, taking the only route available for such a cumbersome machine. Down through the bottom of the cut, and up on the far side. Except it never made it. It stalled about 2:00 a.m. in the morning, just as it was entering the cut, blocking traffic in both directions. Some 200 men were working on the night shift when the shovel operator got down and posted his red warning lanterns that closed the cut. He was just hanging the last lantern when the bottom terrace bulged outward and the whole west side let go.

I was asleep in a tent when the landslide started. The rumble and shaking of the earth was so great that I started up in terror, thinking I was back in the San Francisco quake. Then the terror became even greater as I came to realize what had happened. All the men of my night shift were out there.

Our lights had been swept away, but even in the dark I could see that the 180-foot cut was now nearly half full of crumbled shale. No one could survive under that. I ran, shouting at some men who were standing there as though stricken numb.

More men appeared, and we began searching over the debris, hoping to find a few who might not have been completely buried. We found no one. I had the roll called from a time sheet. Every man answered to his name. I couldn't believe it. I think we called the roll ten times before I could realize a miracle had taken place.

The timely breakdown of the power shovel that had closed the cut to traffic had saved us from any fatalities. A few minutes earlier the road had been teeming with men.

What had happened, we were to learn, was that in reaching the 180-foot mark, we had cut through a layer of oil shale. No one had ever done such a thing before, so not even the best engineers could anticipate the result, though it's in all the books now. With hundreds upon thousands of tons of overburden bearing down upon that greased shale, it had simply slicked out from under the pressure, and down had come the whole west wall.

No one killed, injured, or even scratched, and for my partner and me it was a complete save. All the rock and shale we had been laboriously dynamiting, rooting, and breaking with power shovels now lay before us in a pulverized heap. In we moved with bulldozers and scrapers, and out went the dirt as fast as the tractors could roll. Instead of the anticipated loss of a hundred thousand, we did a little better than break even.

I thought we had every reason in the world to get down on our knees and thank God. I know I did, nightly, and several times mentally during the course of a day.

My partner actually stunned me with an entirely different approach.

"I hear you made a lot of money on the Southern Pacific job," he said one day.

I admitted that the relatives he had objected to had done a creditable job for the S.P.

"Well, I've talked it over with my lawyer," he said. "You got all the profit on that job, so I think I'm entitled to all the profit on this. You took your crew off our job in the middle of the contract, so that makes the Southern Pacific job an extension of the Newhall job. We didn't dissolve any partnership, so I'm entitled to my share."

I thought he was out of his mind. I talked it over with Carlton Case, leaving him as astounded as I was. "What you did was on your own and within your rights," he said. "Your ex-partner hasn't got a leg to stand on."

"Let him sue?" I asked.

"Let him sue," said Case.

But as I walked away, I couldn't seem to accept the idea of what I knew would be a bitter court battle. Not that I am one to turn away from a fight. Under other circumstances I've defended myself in court, but here I had my church to think about. I had refused to fight with my partner in the dispute over my relatives, and the Lord had approved and shown me the way out. To start another fight would be to jeopardize the unity of our church, the very thing the Lord had wanted me to avoid the first time.

I took my problem to Him. I still didn't want to give up without a fight, but His quiet voice said, "No." I protested that the right was on my side, that my partner had ordered my relatives fired, and that I had hired another crew to replace them. "My lawyer is confident we will win," I argued. "You have confidence in your lawyer," I heard. "How much confidence do you have in Me?"

I was seeing the point, but I had to add, "But how can he call himself a Christian, and serve as the senior member of the church, and still take the money when it's rightfully mine?"

"Going to church doesn't make a Christian," I heard, "unless he goes there with an open heart to seek God." Then He

167

seemed to say, "You may take your choice. You may place the case in the hands of your attorney, or you may leave it in My hands."

In *I Corinthians 13:1* the Bible says that without love or charity we become as sounding brass or a tinkling cymbal. I loved the Lord, and my confidence was in Him. Just the same, I am ashamed to admit, I wasn't feeling very charitable when I went up to my ex-partner and said, "All right, there'll be no lawsuit over this. We'll settle it your way, and leave the rest in the hands of the Lord."

Then I couldn't help but say, "This kind of fifty-fifty partnership reminds me of the cook who made fifty-fifty rabbit stew. One horse, and one rabbit. Sort of one-sided, but no hard feelings." Having got that off my chest, I felt better.

The footnote to the above story is that a year later, after two disastrous contracts on his own, my former partner was wiped out. If the Lord doesn't think you are worthy of having it, He'll find ways of taking it away.

16

For the public in general and the construction world in particular, the big event of 1929 was the crash on Wall Street. Unnoticed, at the same time, one of the biggest events of my life took place. Acting upon the advice of Carlton Case, I became R. G. LeTourneau, Inc. According to the papers drawn up by Case, the corporation was worth one thousand shares at $100 each plus assets of another $27,000 in factory, machine tools, and an inventory that included a score or so of finished machines. On paper, then, I appeared to be worth $127,000, a sum of such overwhelming magnificence that once more I was blinded to the contributions made by my Lord.

Working with us were "the relatives," with Carlton Case to handle our contracts and legal matters. Then there were Jo Johansen, a former city engineer of Glendale, California, who ran the office while I was absent on construction jobs; Vernon Love who managed the machine-tool department of the shop; Warden Webster who kept track of all the equipment sold, leased, or borrowed; Monty Newman who kept an eye on the men and machines on construction jobs; Al Losch, our all-around trouble-shooter; Elmer Isgren in charge of sheepfoot roller development and production; and Harry Andrews, our whole bookkeeping department. On the payroll in the shop were not more than 20 others, mostly welders, with maybe three or four doubling as truck drivers, tool sharpeners, janitors, and hoist operators.

Except for those on the factory payroll, all of us doubled between the work going on in the factory and the work going on in the field. On the jobs, of course, we had an entirely different problem. With each new contract we had to hire between 200 and 500 men; build a construction camp in which to feed and house them; set up all the light, water, telephone, and sanitation facilities of a small town; organize a motor pool and repair yard; buy or lease power shovels, trucks, dynamite, and at least 5000 other items, and then keep the inspectors and the men who had hired you calm and satisfied.

You can see why, with three and four construction jobs going simultaneously, we came to look upon our factory, employing only 20 or so men, as little more than a glorified garage. We built and repaired things there, because there we could get better machines at less cost to keep our construction jobs going, and give us the jump on our competitors.

Then one day my brother Louis came in with a cablegram from Moscow, Russia. Their purchasing office wanted to buy one rooter for immediate shipment. Since it was the policy of our State Department then to help backward Russia, I agreed to the sale, my only comment being to the effect that if we sold them one, we'd never sell another because they would copy it, as the Japanese were already doing with some of our better machines.

Louis saw an entirely different angle. "Bob, you've missed the point," he said. "Don't you see, a sale to Russia makes us international businessmen! We're in world finance now. If we can collect the money."

We were kidding each other, but it did set me up. In fact, I got so proud I began to swell up like a toad. If Russia wanted a rooter, look at all the scores of other backward nations that might need scrapers, bulldozers, sheepfoot rollers, self-dumping hoppers, and a new electric hoist I was working on. The more I thought about it, the more enthusiastic I became.

Up to that point, we had never gone out of our way to sell a machine. We didn't even have a salesman, let alone a sales department. Buyers like the Guy brothers, and Buck Maistretti, and Henry Kaiser had come to us to buy. What would happen if we hired a salesman? Not for around the world, of course. But, say, for Nevada, Arizona, Colorado and New Mexico where the need for new dams and irrigation systems was as great as in California, if not more so?

I had one answer to that question right off. If such a salesman were to sell ten machines, the order would swamp my factory, or as Ray Peterson put it, "We'd have to go on a 48 hour day."

We did a lot of hard thinking then. It didn't occur to us that the manufacturing business would one day become the tail wagging the dog. We still thought of ourselves as construction men with a profitable sideline in selling our machines to other contractors. In a final session lasting from Friday morning until Saturday night, with Evelyn providing the coffee and sandwiches, we drew up plans for a new factory triple the size of our Moss Avenue plant. I will say it was quite a plant. An all-steel, all-welded structure. Once my pencil got going, I couldn't stop it. Not a plant in which the roof and walls would serve to cover an internal framework of steel girders. As I sketched away, it became a plant in which the welded steel roof and walls were in themselves an integral part of the structure's strength. Instead of being supported by the posts and trusses on which I rigged my overhead crane and jib cranes, the walls and roof would serve to support them. All told, I cut in half the cost of structural steel normally

171

needed for a plant of that size while providing, through welding, a method of erecting it at less than half the normal cost of construction. For about $50,000, then, I would get a $100,-000 plant.

Where to build it?

John (better known as Jo) Johansen, held out for Los Angeles. "If we're going to ship machines east of the Rockies, Los Angeles has got the best all-weather railroads and highways. It has a good port at San Pedro for bringing in steel from the east through the Panama Canal, and shipping the finished machines out. Along with that, you've got a better year-round climate than you have here in Stockton."

As a Glendale man, he was a good Chamber of Commerce representative, but his own chamber of commerce wouldn't buy him. We even went so far as to buy the land for a factory site before the Los Angeles city engineers condemned the whole project as one of the most ridiculous propositions they had ever been forced to listen to. "Anyone in his right mind," was their combined opinion, "knows that an all-welded steel building will rust and fall apart after the first rain."

"If that's the way they feel about it, sell the factory site," I told Jo. He did, to another manufacturer who erected a "safe" wooden structure that was promptly eaten by termites. In the meantime Evelyn, covering Stockton regularly with the trailer to pick up her Sunday School kids, had seen some vacant lots for sale over by Roosevelt Avenue and Wilson Way, almost diagonally across town from our Moss Avenue shop. Residentially they were undesirable because the main line of the Southern Pacific cut through the lots and a big highway passed in front of them, but as a factory site—

We welded together our factory during the winter of 1930-31, and had outgrown it before we moved in. I remember our engineering office, with individual electric lights for each draftsman, had to give way to two engine lathes, and only by a stroke of luck was I able to buy an old streetcar from the Stockton transit company in which to house our engineers. The cane seats of the car, set up under an oak tree, gave the men something to sit on during lunchtime, our first step in the direction of our cafeterias that would one day feed 5,000 men.

Now I was a two-factory man as well as a contractor. Then Harry Andrews came around in March with the sales figures for 1930. Total sales, he announced proudly, amounted to $110,808.60, and had brought in a net profit of $34,794.92. Not only had I broken the hundred-thousand-dollar mark, but I had sold more machines in one year than in all my previous years in business. My ego, already dangerously inflated, did not deflate any with this news.

That night I got down on my knees and gave due thanks to God for His bounty, and for sparing us from the business depression that was sweeping the country. "And now that the new factory is finished, we'll really do some business. So instead of giving You Your share now, I'll put it all into expanding the business, and next year You will get a share to be proud of."

To what foolish lengths man will let his pride drive him. God does not do business that way. He keeps His promises. When you ask His help, He doesn't answer that He has a lot of pressing things to attend to, so come back next year. His time is *now*. In the early days the true Christians gave God His share from the first fruits of the crops. They had faith. They didn't wait around to see if the later crops were to be destroyed by locusts or drought. Let God's will be done, and the rewards will be so great there won't be room to store them. But start to hedge, and wait to see how the whole crop turns out before giving God His share, and He knows you as a man of little faith. He sure spotted my false reasoning in a hurry.

17

At the time I failed to share with the Lord, no one ever faced brighter prospects. There was, of course, my new factory, out of which I fully expected a return of at least $100,000 in net profits the first year. And waiting for me were two of the fattest construction jobs a contractor can ever hope to contemplate. Before he starts work, that is. One was a big subcontract with the General Construction Company to build a highway from Boulder City to the site of Boulder Dam, subsequently called Hoover Dam. The construction of the dam itself, one of the world's greatest jobs up to that time, was in the hands of the Six Companies, a group of contractors headed by Kaiser and Betchel who had pooled all their resources in order to swing it. What gave urgency to my contract was the fact that until I built the road, the Six Companies couldn't move in their hundreds of pieces of massive machinery.

The other contract, to be started immediately upon completion of the Boulder highway, was on my own. That called for me to build in Orange County, just south of Los Angeles, the largest earth-filled dam ever attempted. With a little luck and no floods, I stood to clear better than a half-million dollars for a year's work.

With a little luck! What a false goddess that is for a Christian to call upon when he can know with absolute certainty where he stands when he stands right with God. My trouble was that I hadn't done right with our Lord.

First off, as Buck Maistretti had discovered before me, the engineers who drill test holes have an uncanny ability to find soft spots while skipping over the buried layers of solid rock. If you happen to be driving to Boulder after visiting the dam, you will pass through wide cuts where the rock looks loose and crumbly. And you will pass through some other cuts where the rock walls rise almost vertically, so hard, as one of my men once said, that you can dent a fender if you drive within three feet of them.

Those crumbly cuts were where the test holes had been drilled. The vertical cuts are by courtesy of R. G. LeTourneau and his lost shirt.

When my scrapers dug into that black stratum, I couldn't believe rock could get that hard. I turned some men loose with air drills and watched with some satisfaction as the drills sank steadily into the rock. But it wasn't the drill sinking into the rock; it was the rock wearing out the drill. Eventually, after a long and costly process that held up the whole job, the drills bored in deep enough to let me take the next step, known in construction terms as "springing a pocket." You ram a stick of dynamite down to the bottom of the drill hole, about 15 feet in this case, and set off the charge. In rock that is only ordinarily hard, the blast will blow out a hole down there, or "spring a pocket," into which you can pack enough dynamite to really shatter rock.

But it was not to work that way for me. When my drill holes were deep enough, and I set off as much dynamite as I could cram into them, it was like setting off a firecracker in a cannon barrel. I got a loud noise and a burst of flame and smoke, but as far as springing a pocket was concerned, I had no more enlarged the diameter of the hole than a firecracker would increase the bore of a cannon.

Things were looking pretty black for me. I wandered over to the edge of a cliff and looked down into the deep ravine my road was supposed to cross, wondering if I'd ever get there. It was very pretty, I guess, if I had been looking for scenery. The cliff looked like a seven-layer cake, its formation revealed in neat layers of red, yellow, blue, pink and black rock. And right under my hard black rock, like a thin layer of frosting, was a layer of yellow stone I knew to be relatively soft.

Maybe you have noticed how all the tough laboring jobs of my youth—wood-chopping, iron-molding, stump-pulling, lead-burning, and my work as a garage mechanic and Navy Yard electrician—have all served me well as an earth-mover and manufacturer. This time I was saved by my work at No. 5 Gold Mine. There, through a layer of yellow rock much like the one at Boulder, I had dug a long tunnel, packed the rear of it with dynamite, and brought down a substantial part of the hillside with the blast. It had been a good shot, even if it hadn't exposed the veins of gold I had hoped it would.

In dynamiting terms, such a tunnel is called a coyote hole, and to me it looked like my only hope. I ordered a tunnel dug through the yellow rock from the face of the cliff to the site of the cut. Even with power drills it was a long, arduous job through a layer that at times was not more than three feet thick. You have to hand it to construction men. The noise in the tunnel was deafening, the dust-filled air practically unbreathable, and in some places the rock drilled out ahead had to be scooped up by hand, passed under the stomach, and kicked back with the feet to men with buckets who, in turn, had to squirm back to the face of the cliff to dump their loads. But they kept right on punching in two-hour shifts right around the clock. I suffered as much as they did, watching the costs pile up and the days speed by while the tunnel progressed by inches.

When the big day did arrive, I want you to know we didn't skimp on the dynamite. We had nearly a carload in the chamber excavated under the blasting site. I was pretty tense. If I just got a mild whoompf instead of a mighty blast, I might as well resign from the construction business. Came the zero hour. A rock bubble bulged out of the ground, and then the bubble burst. The whole sky was flame, smoke, and rock. We were back in business again.

The big actor for me at Boulder Dam was my cable-winch-controlled bulldozer. Then the bulldozers got going, with Jack and Joe Salvador and Monty Newman discovering tricks you wouldn't believe a machine could do, even if it was your machine.

Loose rock overhead, threatening to tumble into the cut, and no way of reaching it. So they go up to the top of the cut, and push down the overhanging lip. Down they come sliding, their blades socked into the loose rock for brakes, and they scoop up everything in their path. "Just like moving a herd ahead of you," explained ex-cowboy Joe Salvador.

Maybe so, but that is one reason why no manufacturer can make his own proving grounds on which to torture-test his own machinery. No matter how earnestly he tries to find the weak spots, he can never find them with the thoroughness of the men in the field, especially if the men are ex-cowboys trying to round up some rock on the face of a cut. I remember a report I got during World War II, some Sea-Bees couldn't get a couple of my scrapers down a 30 foot cliff so they just pushed them over. End over end they rolled. "No problem," concluded the report. It's nice to know things like that, but I haven't added a 30 foot cliff to my proving grounds in Longview, Texas.

My men had those massive bulldozers running around on steep slopes like so many trained mountain goats. I remember one operator coming down backwards on a slope of sliding shale, riding his own landslide. His track-type treads were churning steadily up the slope as fast as he was sliding backwards, and he had thoughtfully raised his scraper blade over his head like an umbrella to fend off bouncing rock. It was his way of getting the shale down to where my scrapers could pick it up. If I had known his name, I would have had to fire him for recklessness, so I never asked. It's men like that who made the construction business.

What with these impromptu measures, and the arrival of all the scrapers my two factories could turn out, and the calling-in of all the men and machines I should have had doing the preliminary work on the Orange County Dam, I was able to complete the Boulder Dam Highway on schedule. My financial loss was too horrible to contemplate, but at least I had redeemed myself with the Six Companies whose own losses, should I have failed to complete the contract on time, would have made mine look like the proverbial drop in the bucket.

It was July of 1931 before I could move my crews and machines from Boulder to Orange County, and I was what might be called a reasonably desperate contractor. I had to acknowledge that I was at least $50,000 in debt because that was what some of my more impatient suppliers were hounding me for. As long as the Castle Warehouse, suppliers of my steel, and a few others weren't pressing me, I was willing not to inquire into what I owed them, but it must have been another $50,000.

My machines were just arriving at the dam-site when the State Inspector of Dams showed up. "Sorry," he informed me. Inspectors in engineering are vitally essential people, just like doctors and dentists are, as long as they are not your inspectors. "You've been so long getting here, and none of your preliminary work is done, so we'll just have to wait until next year."

I was flabbergasted. "Now what?" I asked.

"You were supposed to have started two months earlier," he

said. "If you start now, you will get this dam about half way up when the fall rains come. Your spillways won't be finished. That means you'll back up a lot of water that might get away from you. No, you will have to wait until next year, and start earlier."

I realized his position. Only recently a half-finished dam had failed, releasing a wall of water that had swept down the valley, taking life and property with it. The state engineers were out to see that it didn't happen again. At the same time, I didn't think the inspector appreciated how fast my machines could move dirt. There was, of course, another reason why I couldn't give up without an argument. If I didn't get this job right now, there would be no R. G. LeTourneau, Inc., to return next year. I'd be wiped out.

I pointed out all the equipment I had and the fact that all of my men were experts. "At least you ought to give us a chance to show what we can do," I urged.

He thought it over. "All right," he said. "There are 400,000 cubic yards to be moved in for the base of the dam. That won't back up much water so I can let you move that in. If you can do that in one month, I'll know you can finish the job on time. If it takes longer, the work stops right there."

That was a pretty big order. The first month of getting organized on a job is always the hardest, and we had not planned on moving much over 200,000 yards a month after we were in full swing.

I returned to my office trailer and went over my work program again. The dirt with which the bulk of the dam would be filled was to come from a number of hillside clay deposits within scraper-hauling distance of the site. Then there was one major deposit on a slope about a mile and a quarter away. To work that I had bought—on credit—a highspeed conveyor belt. Bulldozers were to feed it by shoving dirt down into a loading hopper, and tractor-drawn hopper wagons at the receiving end were to distribute the dirt for the dam where needed. Sheepfoot rollers would then pack it firmly into place.

I called in my key men, and put the figures on the table. "Think we can do it?" I asked. "In one month?" They went into a huddle, sizing up what each one of them would have to do, and what machines would have to be doing what work when. They had to time the job so that no one machine or crew would be held up by another. Finally one turned to me and said, "We don't think it's possible, but we're willing to try." That was good enough for me. I had a mighty loyal bunch of men. If all Christians could unite like that in their loyalty to the Lord, this world wouldn't be in the mess it's in.

I couldn't have tackled that job using old construction methods—I say old, but the methods were still prevalent. I would have had to hire hundreds of men, and train them, and have them quit after the first payday. The labor turnover was enormous because the work was brutal. I know one contractor who hired a hundred men a day for a month, and never had more than 500 men left on the job after payday.

In contrast to the above picture, on the Orange County job, my key men were pretty much my whole construction force. They were skilled operators of machines that could out-produce up to 300 men per man and machine, and instead of going through weeks of chaos, we could tear into the job at near-peak efficiency the first day. In time, what with cable splicers, maintenance men, electricians, oilers, time-keepers and the scores of other jobs that are created by heavy construction, we had maybe 800 men on the payroll, but that was on three shifts that would normally require the training of 5,000 men, two-thirds of whom would make enough mistakes to keep the other third busy correcting them. All of which I call an extravagantly wasteful use of human lives.

We started in, and we worked around the clock, seven days a week. At night, with the flood lights turned on, and the machines milling around, and a sort of clanking roar that you could feel as well as hear—well, there is no sight or music like it. Trenching machines lowered their steel maws into the dirt and spewed out half-ton mouthfuls on the spoil bank.

Hopper wagons dumped clay into the trench, and sheepfoot rollers tamped it to the hardness of fired brick. Up in the hills, rooters broke through the sun-baked clay, and the bulldozers, power shovels, scrapers and conveyor belt began moving in the dirt to cover the core trench as fast as it was dug, filled and tamped. Speed and more speed, and yet we were doing a job the like of which no hand-shovel, hand-tamp, mule-team combination could approach.

It was one genuinely amazed State Dam Inspector who watched us deliver the last ton of his quota, with one day to spare. "Okay," he said. "Finish her up."

I should have been happy, but I wasn't. After the excitement of having won the race, I became uncomfortably aware of a fact that had been nagging me all along. In working around the clock, we had also worked straight through our Sundays, four in a row. "Remember the Sabbath and keep it Holy." That was a command generally ignored in the construction business, but not by me when it can be avoided. I now saw myself in a position to avoid it in the future, and resolved to do so.

I see I have failed to mention the burr under my saddle. Because of my heavy losses on the Boulder highway job, I was in hot water with my surety company in San Francisco. To explain, when a contractor undertakes a job running into hundreds of thousands or millions of dollars—and there he is so broke from the last job that he is lucky to have two nickels to rub together in his pocket—the contracting company, or county, or state, or federal agency wants some assurance that he is financially capable of completing the job. In that case, if his performance record is good, and he has demonstrated a certain amount of integrity, he can get a bonding company to support his financial responsibility for a small percentage of the amount he is to be paid, if and when he completes his contract.

In my case, my surety company, headed by a Mr. Hall, was backing me on the Orange County Dam in the hope of getting back what they stood to lose on me at Boulder. To that end they had put their own man on the job to look over my shoulder and scan every move I made, and every dollar I spent. I don't have to tell you that that didn't sit well with me. I resented that man so much that I never addressed him by name, and wouldn't know his name if I heard it to this day.

He was a firm believer in Sunday work, and was convinced that only by working on Sundays could we stay ahead. I told him that now that we were organized, we could take Sundays off and still increase our output. He blew his stack.

"We got ahead by working on Sundays," he said, "and I intend to stay ahead by working the same way. Either that, or we foreclose and take over the job ourselves."

That was his legal right, and I couldn't argue with it. But I had a lot of catching up with my Lord to do, and I figured that came first. I passed the word around to my men. "We knock off at midnight Saturday, and we start at midnight Monday morning. Tell your crews, but don't let the word get back to the surety man." They knew what I meant. It seems incredible that there wasn't a leak amongst hundreds of men. On that August Sunday morning the only two men present in that whole silent, dirt-heaped valley were the surety man and his assistant. I leave it to you to imagine his frame of mind when he confronted me Monday morning. He started to tell me what he thought of my trick, and I just said, "No profanity, please."

To old-time construction men profanity was as essential to speech as punctuation is to writing, and I can tolerate it as long as I know it is not deliberate. In that case I can usually find an opportune moment, without getting preachy, to point out milder words get through to me without the need of taking the Lord's name in vain. In this case, where I was being deliberately dealt profanity with a shovel, I landed all spraddled out. Left speechless, he turned and ran for his office.

Figuring he was calling San Francisco to report my laxness on Sunday work, I decided I had better stay close to my own phone. Five minutes later the phone rang, with Hall on the San Francisco end of the line. "Bob, did you get my check?" was his first abrupt question.

The check, amounting to some $30,000 if I remember correctly, was to cover two weeks of completed work, and is known in the construction business as a "progress check." You use it, and the ones that follow as you progress, to meet current expenses and the payroll until such a time as you complete the contract and get either the check that gives you a profit, or the bill that shows what you've lost. "I've got it," I said.

"Well, don't cash it. I've chopped it off at the bank and I'm coming down myself."

When he slammed down his receiver in San Francisco my own telephone nearly fell off the wall.

Just the same, I resolved to stand firm on the no-work-on-Sunday rule. I prayed long and earnestly, and Wednesday morning, when Mr. Hall was due to arrive, I awaited him prepared to turn over my company if necessary. I stood up when he entered my trailer. He was a big man, filling the door, and I couldn't see his face against the outside sunshine.

"Bob, you're all right," he said. "Go ahead and cash the check."

"No work on Sunday?"

"Not if that's the way you feel about it."

I've got powerful legs, but they nearly let me down that time. Mr. Hall hadn't come all the way from San Francisco to tell me I was all right. I knew, and he admitted later, that when he had started out, it was to take over the job. Something had happened to him on the way that had caused a change of heart.

I know what caused that change. It was the power of prayer. I didn't ask the Lord to save my company. I was sincerely trying to work with Him as a partner, and it was His company, too, and if He wanted me to lose it He would have His reasons. But I did ask Him to help me observe Sunday, and that is what He did.

The work progressed smoothly after that, more so when Mr. Hall took his overseer back to San Francisco with him. We even got a couple of breaks when clay deposits close to the dam proved large enough to let us shut down and sell the mile-and-a-quarter conveyor belt. But it was not going to be enough to pull us out of the hole. What with all the new machinery I'd had to buy, and all the new machines I had made in my Stockton plants, and all the overtime I'd had to pay for the Sunday work, we would come out slightly ahead on the Orange County Dam, but we still wouldn't be able to pay more than ten cents on the dollars on the long-overdue Boulder bills.

We were just finishing up on the dam in the spring of 1932 when I got a telephone call from Hall. He wasn't threatening me. He was on my side. "But I thought I'd better tell you your creditors are getting impatient, and I can't stall 'em off any longer. They've called a meeting in my office for two weeks from now, so if you've got any ammunition, start getting it ready."

The only ammunition I had they already knew about. The two factories, an excellent record on the Orange County Dam, and a new contract to build a broad highway into Carmel, California. In an ordinary year, they might have been satisfied to wait in the reasonable hope of getting paid in full out of factory production and the Carmel job.

But I knew their thinking in this full depression year of 1932. With factories closing down all over the nation, they thought I would have no factory production. The rocky coastline around Carmel, from their point of view, might lead me into the same financial disaster as had the rocky highway at Boulder. I didn't have to be told that they were ready to quit while the quitting was good, and salvage what they could from the bones of R. G. LeTourneau, Inc. With a whole nation thinking that way, I couldn't blame them.

My men knew the fix I was in. If they hadn't known it, they would have found out when the appraisers came around to see what my earth-moving equipment and machine tools might be worth on the second-hand market. It was then I got the most rewarding show of confidence a boss can get. All of a sudden it made everything worth while.

Vernon Love of the machine tool department came to me. "There's a factory moving out of San Leandro," he said, "and I happen to know we can get about $50,000 worth of machines tools—just what we need—for about five thousand bucks."

I just looked at him. He knew I couldn't buy them if they were $500. "And you know," I added, "in another week we might not have a factory to put 'em in."

"Yeah, we figured that out, too," he said. "So the boys in the shop are going to buy the tools. If you don't own 'em, no one can foreclose on 'em. That way we'll be all tooled up and ready to go if you lose the shop. You lease our tools, hire us to run 'em, and no one gets hurt or fired."

"But no factory—"

"And what's wrong with renting a vacant lot? We've worked in the open air before."

I went to the meeting in Hall's office feeling like a new man. At first glance I saw about five men on my side, oddly enough the men to whom I owed the most money, but the other dozen or so looked all primed to swing the axe. Their combined hostility only served to stiffen my spine and my stubbornness.

"All right, if that's the way it is," I said, "I won't plead with you. I'll give it to you straight. Give me time, and I'll make good every cent. Otherwise I know you can take everything I've got except my wife and family."

They seemed ready to do just that, glad to get it over with so easily.

"But if you do," I said, "I'm going to open my shop tomorrow in a vacant lot, and I'm going to keep right on going, and I can go faster because I won't have all these debts to pay."

Say, there was turmoil then. When the hub-bub got real

185

loud, Hall suggested, "Maybe you can talk this over better if I take LeTourneau outside."

He took me out into the corridor and down to a drinking fountain. "What's this about opening up tomorrow on a vacant lot?"

I told him about what the boys had done, and about the tools already being delivered to a farm south of Stockton. "And there's no law that says I can't start work on a couple of new scrapers and bulldozers I have in mind," I said.

"Boy, I admire your nerve," he said. "Now you just stay out of this, and I'll see what I can do."

I went back to my hotel and waited for Hall. It was after nine p.m. when he arrived, but he looked cheerful. "The execution has been postponed," he said. "You're still almost your own boss."

I began to bristle. Almost was not enough.

"Calm down," he said. "I told them you had some designs for new machines that were going to make a lot of money. And I told them there was no sense in settling for ten cents on the dollar when they could get the whole dollar out of your hide if they waited. They'll wait, but they want, and they're entitled to get, an audit of your books."

That was going to be rough. Harry Andrews, following the bookkeeping system set up by myself and my wife, kept track of every penny spent and every penny that came in, and if more money had come in at the end of the year than had gone out, that was our profit. "It satisfies the income tax people," I said.

"No, no, no," said Hall with something like horror. "You're probably charging too much for some things, and too little for others. You've got to have a cost-accounting system. You're a big boy now. You need some time studies on your machines so you know what they produce per hour, and how much it costs to move a yard of dirt a thousand feet. You've got to have—" and on he went far into the night.

It was dawn when he said, "I'm sending Mr. Frost down

with you in the morning, and you turn over your books to him. He's not going to tell you what to do. He's going to tell you what you have done, and how you can do it better. He's the best accountant I've got, and he'll set up a system that will satisfy your creditors. And I want him back as soon as he has finished."

He didn't get Mr. Frost back for three years, and then only because we moved to Peoria, Illinois. Then, in one of the few jokes I ever heard Frost make, he said, "There's enough frost in Peoria without adding me. I can't stand the stuff myself." He returned to Hall, but by that time my books were at last in order.

We had had our struggles, however. I remember his horror the first week when he discovered I couldn't pay any salaries, including his. I went to church the following Sunday, taking my place in the choir where I filled the bass section with bulk if not melody. I had forgotten it, but this was the Sunday the annual pledges for missionary work were taken up. I listened to the speakers, especially a foreign missionary with a highly stirring plea, and I said to myself, "Lord, I'm sorry, but there just isn't any way I can make a pledge this year. I can't even meet my payroll." Right then I had the thought that I had failed to share with the Lord the year before when I had my first big profit, promising to share with Him this year when my profits would be big pickings. Certainly in dropping me a hundred thousand in debt He had shown me the error of my ways. Was I to fail Him again?

I was almost sold on that reasoning when I had another disturbing thought. I had been pledging $5,000 a year for some years past, and I had the feeling that the Lord wanted me to pledge the same amount again. Our folks didn't read off the names of those who pledged, but it was customary to read off the amounts as the pledges came in, and I knew, and the congregation knew, that there were only a few of us who made a pledge that size. They'd spot me in a minute, and after missing my pledge last year, I could just hear them say, "Why that old hypocrite! He pledges big, but he never pays his bills."

I won't go so far as to say that the Lord is sending me here, or the Lord is sending me there, or telling me to do this and that. I think we need to walk softly before the Lord, and be sure it isn't our own desires that we mistake for the Lord's voice. But I do firmly believe the Lord can lead us when our hearts are right and receptive to His will. I pledged the full amount for His sake, but rather than appear conspicuous before the members of the church, I hedged. I broke the pledge down in small amounts divided amongst the members of my family. It was a subterfuge, and I was wrong, of course. No one has to be afraid of admitting his debt to the Lord. No one has or ever will be able to give as much as He did when He died on the cross to make forgivable the sins of man, past, present, and through all eternity.

I will say Frost was appalled when I insisted upon adding the pledge, plus the same amount for the year I had missed, to our mountain of debts. "There goes the business," he said.

"I don't think so," I said. "We'll add the pledge to the payroll, and whenever we can meet the payroll, we'll meet the pledge."

"I think I'd better get out of here," he said. "The Bible isn't one of the books we use in cold-cash bookkeeping."

"You thinking of quitting?" I asked.

"No," he said slowly. "We can't be any worse off than we are now. I'll stick around to see how the show ends."

Within a month we were meeting the payroll—and the pledge—on time. "We're making it," Frost reported.

"With the help of the Lord," I said.

"If I stick around with you much longer, you'll have this accountant believing that, too." I could see he was on my side, at least partly convinced at last. Now all I had to do was work myself out, and start over from a hundred thousand below scratch.

There's the old success story of the man who said, "Ten

years ago, I owed a hundred thousand dollars. Now I owe millions."

Fourteen years earlier I had wound up my garage business $5,000 in debt. Now I owed $100,000. For a man who, in Reverend Devol's study, had dedicated himself to becoming one of the businessmen God needed, I was doing a remarkable job. It was time I put into effect some of the lessons He had taught me.

18

My worries that summer of 1932 were so great I didn't know which ones to worry about first. Yet now that I had re-established myself with my Lord, my worries were as foolish as those of the spinster who sat weeping beside a well. "What's the matter?" she was asked. "Oh! It's terrible," she moaned. "Someday I might get married, and then I might have a child, and then the child might come down here, and climb up, and fall in the well, and get drowned. Oh, what a cruel, cruel blow."

The first big break, and one that would again revolutionize the industry, came in a back-handed sort of way. Nick Basich of Basich Brothers Construction Company had my biggest cable-controlled scraper down on a road building job near the Salton Sea. He called me up with the bad news. "Your scraper won't work down here in this sand, Bob," he said. "The stuff is so loose the wheels sink down, and we can't budge the load. I've got to go back to using the old belly scraper with no wheels to bog down."

"Now, hold it, Nick," I said. "I've got a standard-sized scraper with wider wheels. I'll send it right down."

"No, I have one of them, and it's too big, too," he said. "I hate to do this, Bob, because I know you've been going through the wringer, but I just can't buy your machine for this job."

When you are in danger of losing a desperately needed sale like that, your mind can turn over real fast. And right then I felt something click. About a year earlier, because a California law forbids the moving of steel-wheeled machinery over concrete roads and oiled highways, I had hit upon substituting the biggest pneumatic-tired truck wheels I could find for my steel wheels, and had saved a lot of freight charges by towing my machines from job to job.

"I've got an idea, Nick, that I want you to try out," I shouted into the phone. "I'm sending you one of my smaller machines, and I want you to give it a real work-out, and if it doesn't work, it won't cost you a cent."

"Well, I can't lose on that," he agreed, "but I think you're wasting your money. Don't count on anything."

"Right, and I'll have it out of the shop today."

I mounted a scraper on rubber-tired wheels, and had one of my men tow it to the Salton Sea by the shortest route. As he was about to leave the shop, he remembered the steel wheels that were supposed to go along as standard equipment. "No, leave them here," I said. "If Nick doesn't have 'em, he can't use 'em."

This was the first time rubber tires were ever used on heavy equipment.

Three days later I got another call from Nick. "Say, that small machine is working like a house afire. Send down the steel wheels that go with it, and I'll buy it."

I tried to tell him on the phone that it was the rubber tires that were making it work so well, but he couldn't believe it. "Listen to me, Nick," I said. "When that scraper is on steel wheels, only a tractor can pull it. Did you notice that when I sent it down there on rubber tires, it was towed by a light truck? Now the same thing is happening on the job."

"No, no, no. I want the whole schmearkase," he shouted. "Rubber tires won't last the week out."

I was pretty slow getting those steel wheels down to him. In the meantime Nick wasn't a man to shut down a high-performance machine just because the steel wheels hadn't arrived. He kept on running it 24 hours a day, noting with some surprise that the rubber tires were holding up as well as those on his trucks.

The next call was brief. "Hey, we'll buy that small machine with the rubber tires. Then we want a full set of tires for the big scraper. And I want another big scraper with rubber tires all the way around.

"Attaboy," I said. "You're talking my language, but Nick, those tires cost money, and the steel, and the salaries. You don't suppose you could put a little down—"

"Stop worrying. I'll pay cash in advance for the whole works."

Cash in advance for unbuilt machinery was an unheard of gesture in the construction business, all the more remarkable because it came in the midst of the depression. A couple of days later my brother Bill dropped by for a short visit. When he discovered the jam I was in, he turned his genius for trading loose, finding a lot of room for it. Up on the Carmel highway job he found a lot of machines I had used in the soft clay of Orange County were not working well in rock. He began swapping around, and in a couple of weeks the Carmel job began booming along in fine style. What with Nick's cash advance, and some increasingly big progress checks from Carmel, I was able to meet the payroll and my missionary pledge. And I've never missed any payrolls or pledges since.

Then Denn Burgess came around. I had known Denn since 1928 when he was a salesman for Schram, Inc., makers of compressed air machinery. In selling compressed air hoists and air hammers and drills, he had come to know just about every contractor, large and small, on the West Coast, and it was his opinion that a lot of those contractors would be interested in LeTourneau equipment if I had a salesman running around calling it to their attention. And Bill had found a bright red paint, only slightly dimmer than fire-engine red, to give my machines "eye-appeal." What with one thing and another, early in 1933 I found myself with a sales department and a full-time sales office in Los Angeles.

Just to give you an idea, the year I failed to share with the Lord, my profits were, as mentioned, $34,474.92. The next year of 1931 I had almost the same figure—$32,507.41—as a loss, and the worst was yet to come. By mid-1932 I had sunk $100,000 below bottom, but had recognized my error and was back in the good graces of my Lord. We ended that year with a net profit of $52,055.61, meaning we had earned that much even if we did owe it all and then some. But with substantial payments on our debts, Frost was able to re-establish our credit rating, and while we were still living hand-to-mouth, we did have beans in the pantry.

I saw the need for two big improvements in my scraper. I could carry more dirt than anybody, but to force a big load of dirt back into the bucket, I had to build up a big wall of dirt to plow into. That was still the old semi-drag system of carrying part of the load and scraping the rest ahead. What I wanted was an upper jaw for my machine.

Let the lower jaw of the bucket scrape through the earth, scooping up a load and piling up the drag load ahead. Then let the upper jaw clamp down over the drag load. When upper and lower jaws met, the load would be fully enclosed. Lift the bucket with cables, and there would be bucket load and drag load all riding free and clear and ready to roll as fast as you could roll it. If it sounds complicated, in action it is about as simple as lowering a broom to scoop up a mound of dust in front of a dustpan.

That was my first Carryall scraper and why I came to build it. But it doesn't explain how I came to build it, which is quite another story. That came about like this: I got the inkling of an idea for the upper jaw, or apron as we called it, one Tuesday afternoon, and it was one of those plaguing ideas that won't let you alone. The answer is always just ahead of you, almost in plain sight, but you can't grab it. Yet I was so close that I didn't want the boys in the shop to go ahead making more standard machines when this improvement could change the whole picture. I went through all Tuesday night and all Wednesday chasing this will-o'-the-wisp idea, feeling every minute that I was getting closer and closer. "Don't start anything until you hear from me in the morning," I told Ray Peterson. "I think I can work this thing out tonight."

I don't remember that I ate anything that evening, but I do remember it was shortly after 7:00 p.m. that Evelyn came into the parlor I had turned into my drafting room. "You haven't forgotten that it's your evening to take charge of the Peniel Mission, have you?" she asked.

Forgotten it? I had forgotten everything except a tangle of sheaves and cables, and a steel apron that wouldn't work.

"Somebody else will have to take it," I said. "Evelyn, I've got to sit right here or the boys won't have any work in the morning. I can't spare a minute."

She didn't say anything, so automatically I knew I was wrong. A half hour went by, and the idea that had been almost within grasp was now clear out of sight. The only thing that came to mind were the words, "And you were the one who promised to put the Kingdom of Heaven first."

I tossed down my pencil. I had learned the folly of putting my own problems ahead of the Lord's work. I went down to the mission, an indoor meeting that night, and it was something. Young voices singing the likes of which you have never heard. I could see it reaching the wine-fogged minds of some of our derelicts, and it must have been acting upon me even more powerfully. My only task that evening was to be there as the supervisor, and introduce the young man who was the speaker of the evening. After that I just had to sit there, and let what was happening to me happen. I didn't know what it was, but I knew it was something that was beyond daily experience.

I returned home shortly before midnight. There didn't seem to be much point in taking up my pencil again. I was tired and drained of strength, but I felt the urge to draw, so I went into my drafting room and turned on the lights. It was an odd sort of a thing I drew. In fact, it was a tangle of sheaves and cables, with the sheaves pivoting every which way, and the cables weaving through them as though they were going to tie themselves into a cable net.

I spent the rest of the night developing the plans in detail, and the boys went to work on them in the morning. Long after the new sheave system was in successful operation, my engineers were still trying to figure out why.

In brief, what had come to me that night was a cable-controlled system by which scraper bucket, scraper apron, and powered tailgate with it could all be operated smoothly regardless of how the tractor with its cable winches might twist or turn tight corners, or wrench itself up one side of a gully while the scraper was still coming down the other side. Swinging and pivoting as the sheaves did, they fed cable to the drum or took it away as smoothly as fishing line is spooled to or from a self-leveling reel.

My brother Bill and Denn Burgess watched the first new Carryall scrape 12 tons of dirt like so much loose snow, and couldn't believe their eyes. They called in Ken Parks. Ken had worked with us as a representative of the U.S. Engineers when we built a Sacramento River levee—I remember he slept in a large culvert pipe screened at both ends because he didn't trust a tent to keep out snakes—and had been the first to make a thorough time study of the performance of my machines. Later he had joined us as a time study engineer, supplying our sales department with figures on what our machines could do when stacked up against others. When Ken got through with his time studies on the Carryall, Bill and Denn had no sales problem. According to their sales talk, anybody in the midst of a depression who didn't use my new machine was an extravagant wastrel throwing away the tax-payer's money.

Personally I thought that was pretty strong talk, but Carlton Case gave me something else to think about. The Carmel highway job was drawing to a close, and I was figuring on a couple of other highway and irrigation jobs. "All right, what are you going to be?" he asked bluntly. "As I see it, you're either going to be a contractor out on the job, wondering what's going on in Stockton, or a manufacturer in Stockton wondering what's going on out at the job. You've said yourself you can't serve two masters, so you had better make up your mind."

Then he added what I considered an unnecessary remark. "Maybe you haven't noticed it, but when you've gone broke on contracts, your factory has always pulled you out."

Well, he was right, and I had to do some hard thinking. In the final analysis, the reason I was ahead as a manufacturer was because I built the kind of machines that would get me ahead as a contractor. If I gave up the heavy construction business and lost contact with the work in the field, would I still be able to develop new machines to meet new situations I didn't know about? And in spite of the licking I had taken at Boulder, I did know construction work, while what I knew about the business world was too little to mention.

My ignorance in that case turned out to be an asset. I still had to meet the still-unsolved vicious circle of big industry. First, no one will buy unproven machinery. Second, even after the machine has proven itself, you can't go into mass production until you get the price down. Third, you can't get the price down until you get into mass production. Fourth, the only thing you can do about it is stick your neck out somewhere. I think if I had known that then, I'd have stayed in something safe and sure, like building highways to Boulder Dam. Instead, I stuck my neck out.

19

My first problem as a full-time manufacturer concerned the performance of the rubber-tired scraper. Joe Salvador went down to Nick's job on the Salton Sea to test the machines himself. The report he brought back was sun-touched, sounding as though he had done his dirt-moving in a desert mirage. He had those loaded machines floating on air, towed along like balloons on a string. When I calmed him down some, he came up with a more realistic figure that was still incredible. He reported that the rubber-tired scraper required only one-third the draw-bar pull of the steel-wheeled machine. "And what's more, using one-third the power, you can roll twice as fast without tearing everything loose."

I couldn't doubt him. Joe was a boy who could tell to the pound what his tractor was pulling. And what a picture that opened up for me! Now I could build a scraper three times as big as my first Carryall!

I began to do some figuring. When a steel wheel is sunk

three inches in sand, it has a three-inch hole to be pulled out of. That's like having the wheel blocked with three-inch chocks. But the starting pull doesn't get it out of the hole. The wheel continues to sink into the sand as it rolls forward, and thus is in a constant state of climbing out of the hole. In short, it has an up-hill climb all the way. The rubber tire, spreading its weight on an air cushion—what we now call flotation—greatly reduced the angle of climb and thus greatly reduced the amount of pull needed.

They had worked fine on Nick's job, where sand was all he encountered. But what about on the average construction job where freshly rooted or blasted rock was the rule? The truck tires I was using, inflated to 80 pounds, just couldn't take it. On the other hand, the automobile industry was turning to balloon tires of lower and lower pressure. If I could get the tire companies to make me some giant, low-pressure tires, then I might have something. A soft tire would enfold sharp rock in tough, yielding rubber, and there would be no blow-out. That thought brought up another big advantage. When a steel wheel encounters unyielding rock, it has to climb over it, be it only an inch high, and every time you have to lift 25 tons an inch, you've wasted more power on lifting than on pulling. A soft, yielding tire would just absorb such obstacles, not raising the load by a tremor.

Of course the above features were not news to the tire companies, but you'd have thought so from the reaction I got. When I presented them with their own theories on low-pressure tires as applied to my business, they gave me the usual verdict. I was crazy.

While I argued it out by mail and long distance telephone with the tire companies, I continued to buy all the big truck tires I could get, and in one instance I was able to pick up some huge, low-pressure airplane tires when a bomber program was discontinued. Their durability and superior performance gave me the confidence I needed to go ahead, especially when I discovered a truly remarkable asset that had nothing to do with my theory. I noticed that when an operator is towing a jolting, banging, spine-wrenching machine, he doesn't care how much abuse it gets. It's his way at getting back at it for the kicking-around it is giving him. But when he has a relatively quiet machine behind him, smooth-rolling and with the shocks reduced to a minimum, he tends to take care of it. And with easier maneuverability he swings around more to find the paths of least resistance, and the result was a pronounced increase in loading efficiency along with an equally pronounced reduction in wear and tear on both scraper and tractor.

Even with these facts, I couldn't get a rubber company to build the tires I asked for. "The point is, LeTourneau," a big company man finally told me, "it would cost us thousands of dollars just to build a tire mold of the size you're asking for. Then you try it out, and go broke, and where does that leave us?"

I thought that one over. As long as I had my neck out, I might just as well put it out full length and give the axman an easy target. "All right, what if I build my own mold? Then will you make my tires for me?"

That is what I had to do. And even now I find the results rather staggering. In 1933 my sales had mounted to $379,-106.53. In 1934 they had shot up to $929,860.67, of which $340,275.49 was net profit, or nearly as much profit as total sales had been the year before. The Stockton plants, what with the machine tools Vernon Love had purchased in case I had gone broke, were filled to overflowing. The scraper assembly line that Elmer Isgren set up was more on the order of a labyrinth than a straight line, with the overhead crane and the jib cranes working overtime to lift the scraper being assembled over intervening machinery, along with a little backing and filling on the way.

We had outgrown ourselves, and the time had come to move. Up to now we had made virtually no effort to invade the huge field east of the Rockies. In the meantime the Holt and Best tractor companies had merged to form Caterpillar, and in the interests of central distribution had set up their plant at Peoria, Illinois. Since we had always worked with them, my scrapers, bulldozers, rooters and dump carts being designed to work primarily with Caterpillar tractors, with special equipment to adapt them to other tractors, Peoria looked like the logical site for my invasion of the East.

To cinch matters, Denn Burgess worked out an arrangement with Caterpillar by which we got sales representation in the many sales centers they had all over the nation. It was not an exclusive deal by any means. Caterpillar, supplying the traction power for contractors all over the world, no more wanted to limit itself to powering LeTourneau equipment than I wanted to refuse sales to owners of Case, Allis-Chalmers, International, and tractors of other makes. I think the best way to put it is that my machines were a selling point for them, and their sales offices were my ready-made selling points.

In Peoria I found that the old circus lot down on the river, covering 23 acres, was for sale. It looked so made-to-order that I didn't even stop to ask about the flood stage of the river, an omission that gave my scrapers and bulldozers many hours of frantic testing, building the levees higher and higher as the floods got worse and worse.

My first trip to Peoria was made in January, 1935. I instructed Carlton Case to buy the property and made some tentative arrangements to have a factory, 60 feet wide by 300, drawn up and completed by fall. But even by the time I returned from that rush trip it was clear that we couldn't wait until fall. The backlog of orders had piled up to the point where either we produced or we lost a lot of sales to customers who would not think kindly of us. On the first of April I loaded a freight train with machine tools, and with about 75 key men started for Peoria, ready or not.

I don't think our neighbors in Peoria will forget our arrival in the midst of a raw spring rain that lasted two weeks without letup. There wasn't even a railroad siding on which to sidetrack our train. Out went the bulldozers and scrapers and sheepfoot rollers, and in went the siding. The factory site was just mud, with some surveyors' stakes sticking up, but off to one side was some slightly higher ground less soggy than the rest. We tied into a power line, got our welding equipment going, and overnight welded a crane around the chassis of a tractor. Maybe the circuses that had once occupied the old lot had set up faster, but in three days the crane had unloaded all the machine tools, carried them to the high ground, and they were in operation turning out the first of the 13 scrapers we built in the rain that month. By the end of that month, too, we had the foundation in for the factory, and as fast as the roof went up, we moved the machine tools under cover, shutting them down only for the length of time it took to move them and bolt them to the floor. Said Pop Cook, "Bob isn't rushing this factory just to get us out of the rain. He just doesn't want to pay for all the tools we're losing in the mud."

Through all this, Evelyn was right with me. I remember the day some industrialists' wives came to call to welcome her to Peoria. She was down at the factory site, using the family Chevrolet to snake steel beams off a flat car so we could clear the track for another trainload of steel. And that reminds me of our house. Case had bought for us a large, old frame house, "Big enough," he wrote, "for all five kids." (Our son Ben had been born on March 21, 1934.) And a good thing it was big. As fast as our homeless crew arrived from California, Evelyn began taking the boys in, until we had 24 of them and seven of us bedded down and fed there on two shifts of day and night workers. It worked out fine during the week, and you only had to be careful about not stepping on anybody in the dark, but on Sunday, when both shifts were home, it got a little crowded.

The confusion didn't end with the completion of the factory in September. When the last weld was finished, we just hauled the welding machinery around to the back and welded on another factory the same size as the first. And when that was done, tired of patching, I sent them around to weld on another section to double the size again, bringing the total length to 1,200 feet. Most of the machine tools which filled it I had invented for my special purposes, and about this time I began to notice I was being called R.G. All my associates from California called me Bob, and I thought the R.G. was just the eastern way of addressing the boss by his initials. "Wal, maybe so, Bob," said Pop Cook, "but the way I heard it the R.G. stands for Rube Goldberg."

All of this was exciting enough, but as far as my partnership with God is concerned, one of the big events of my life occurred on the day I was called upon to address the Peoria Chamber of Commerce. The whole idea of standing up in front of a lot of men terrified me. I still hadn't been able to talk to anything larger than a Young Men's Sunday School class, and not too well there. What could I tell a Chamber of Commerce meeting? I knew also that they thought I was something of a crackpot, with wild ideas about manufacturing with a welding torch, and even wilder ones about being in some kind of partnership with God.

"It's bad enough to have to talk," I told myself, "without being pegged as a looney before you open your mouth."

When the hour arrived, I wasn't calmed any by the fact that the loudspeaker system wasn't working very well. If the experienced speakers ahead of me were having difficulty holding the crowd's attention, what would happen to me? Then I began to wonder how many of those fine businessmen knew the Lord as I did, and had Him to help them over the rough spots. I felt a desire to give a few words of personal testimony. I argued it down, telling myself, "This is a business crowd. They want to hear something about your business." The desire persisted and grew stronger. So I just made a silent prayer. "Lord, if You want me to say a few words along spiritual lines, You will just have to give me the words."

I got my introduction and stood up. I wasn't nervous any more. I didn't need the weak microphone. I discovered the

Lord had given me a good loudspeaker of my own, and suddenly I had the strength to use it. "I'm glad to be in a city with so many fine churches, and so many Christians who love the same Lord I do," I began. "You know our forefathers came to America seeking freedom to worship God. They put on our coins the words, 'In God We Trust,' and God blessed this land above all others. You may wonder what religion has to do with business, and I used to wonder about it myself. Now I know it was our forefathers' faith in God that made our country great. I believe we need to get back to that faith, and when we do, God will lead us out of the depression we've been in."

I was that far, and no one had walked out on me yet. "We know as businessmen that when we have a product that won't work, it won't sell, and we hunt around until we get a product that will work and will sell. Now I ask you, what's the use of having a religion that won't work? If I had a religion that limped along during the week, and maybe worked only on Sunday, or while you're in church, I don't think I'd be very sold on it. I think I'd turn it in on a new model that worked seven days a week, that would work when I was at church, in my home, or out at the plant. And that is what Christianity does."

Then I stated publicly for the first time the theme I'll never stop repeating. "The preachers can tell us that Christianity works. They are God's salesmen, selling salvation and the Christian way of life. But unless we businessmen support them, and testify that Christianity is the driving power of our business, you'll always have doubters claiming that religion is all talk and no production."

I didn't get much of a hand at the conclusion of my first public speech. By the time I got home I was convinced that the only one I had sold was myself. Evelyn and I found a seat on the back stairs that no boarders were occupying at the moment, and figured it out. "We claim to be in partnership with God," I began, "but we aren't really. We have a good year, and we give Him a tithe as his share. In the old days a tithe was forced on people, and they had to give ten per cent of their income to God whether they wanted to or not. Now we aren't compelled to give to God. It's all voluntary. The only thing is, when you consider what God has done for us, we ought to do better for Him out of gratitude than the doubters had to do by law. You get right down to it, and we believers aren't doing a bit more than the doubters had to do in the old days."

"Now what's on your mind, Bob?" asked Evelyn.

"Just this. I think we've got to do more," I said. The idea had been with me a long time, and the talk with Evelyn gave it form. "Let's set up a foundation. A foundation dedicated to God and His works. We give half the stock in the company to the foundation, and keep half for ourselves. Then half of what the company makes goes to the foundation, and half goes to us."

"That sounds fine, Bob," said Evelyn, "but—"

"But what?"

"Well, the company is getting so big, and pretty soon it will be doing all the work. You know what I mean."

I didn't, but I could sense what she was driving at. A hick from Duluth and a small-towner from Stockton, and neither one of us with a high school education. And sales zooming toward a figure that would go over the two million mark for 1935. She was frightened, and now that she brought the subject up, so was I.

"You mean if we just give God half the profits of the company, we won't feel anything personal about it?" I asked.

She nodded. "Your brother Bill tells me we'll have over a half-million profit this year. If we give half of that to the foundation, what can we do with a quarter of a million dollars? The most I ever spent in my life on the house was $5,000, and, well, it's just too much."

"Okay, we'll give half the company profits to the foundation, and then we'll give half of our own income to keep it personal. How does that sound?" I thought that sounded fine, but Evelyn wasn't through.

"That still leaves an awful lot."

But I thought I saw the end of the line. "That goes back into the business for expansion," I said. It wasn't the end of the line. Since then we've been able to increase the holdings of the foundation to 90 per cent of our common stock and 90 per cent of our income. Currently the LeTourneau Foundation is worth some 40 million after distribution of ten million to religious and educational works.

Once more I called in Carlton Case. "I want you to set up a foundation for us," I said. "A foundation to sponsor religious, missionary, and educational work for the greater glory of God. I don't know what the laws are, but I want you to fix it so that the funds of the foundation can never be used for company or personal purposes. If for any reason the foundation is dissolved, its resources are to be turned over to the Christian Missionary Alliance Church."

I clearly remember his answer. "You're out of your mind," he said, "but then, you always were."

Whereupon he became one of the staunchest supporters the foundation ever had.

But even while I was organizing the foundation, another strange thing was happening. Unbeknownst to me, several ministers had been present when I gave my talk before the Chamber of Commerce. I think they came to see what kind of a man it was who claimed to be in partnership with God, and fully expected to find a religious fanatic. When they heard me express the conviction that it was up to the businessmen to support their pastors by testifying to the power of the Lord, they must have decided I was all right after all. The phone started to ring. Would I speak before the congregation of the Baptist Church on Sunday?

"I've made only one speech in my life," I protested, "and you've already heard it."

"And I thought it was fine," replied the pastor. "Just give the same one."

It was with considerable trepidation, and a return of the old panic at the thought of speaking in public, that I agreed. And then, having agreed to speak in one church, I couldn't very well refuse to speak in the others. "Hooked," I thought to myself. "Now how are you going to get out of it, or live through it?"

I had nothing to worry about. Praying to God that night, I received His assurance that my testimony would help His work, not only in man to man and neighbor to neighbor talk, the way I had worked before, but before large congregations. And then, while the prospect filled me with dismay—me, an uneducated man with a vocabulary picked up in the construction business, trying to speak in great churches—I got assurance of another kind. I seem to have heard the words so clearly that I can almost quote them as real.

"When the Lord has a job for you to do, He'll give you the strength and the ability to do it."

20

In this age of specialization I have been asked how I find time to run my business, fly hundreds of thousands of miles to give my testimonies, serve as president of the LeTourneau Foundation and the LeTourneau Technical Institute, write a bi-weekly column for my publication called *Now*, and maintain active supervision of my two missionary projects in Liberia and Peru. Maybe it does sound like a complicated program, but until I was asked the question the first time, I wasn't even aware of it. Everything began on such a small scale that the subsequent growth seems perfectly natural.

Our foundation started out by donating $5,000 to the Christian Missionary Alliance, $1,000 to the Mt. Herman Association, and another $1,000 to my sister Sarah for her mission in China. Then we had to economize because our dividends were running low. Nothing complicated there.

My first training program was begun in Peoria because few men in that city were familiar with the welding technique we used in building our machines. In three months, between classroom instruction and factory experience, the students knew as much about welding as I had picked up in twenty years. That didn't hurt production a bit, so I started some classes in mathematics, mechanical drawing, blueprint reading, and machine tooling. These grew until we were running a regular vocational school, with results so impressive that the Peoria Department of Education took over the program to make it city-wide in its own vocational schools. And having discovered a good thing, it was perfectly natural that I follow it up by founding the LeTourneau Technical Institute.

Our publication, *Now*, got its start in 1935 when a young man came to me asking permission to distribute to my employees a small religious paper by that name. I liked the title, being in line with my own thinking that when it comes to acting for the Lord, the time is *Now*. Also, with more than 400 men on the payroll, I had been feeling the need of a plant paper, the personal communication we had enjoyed in Stockton no longer was possible. Not just a house organ to express my own views and company policy, but one that would also voice the message of the Lord I was trying to serve as a partner. The result was that we set up our own printing plant, and I sat down to write my first column on, naturally, the advantages of welding over nuts, bolts, and rivets. Two more pages were devoted to personal items in the plant, and the last page was reserved for the Lord's messages.

My own recollection is that we ordered a first printing of 500 copies, but when the printer found himself with a thousand sheets by the press, he got carried away and ran off the whole bale. I was a little aghast at that wasting of my own money and the Lord's, but I was forgetting His message was in there, too. So many copies were passed along and mailed to friends that within a few days the request for extra copies exhausted our supply.

Later we added Tom Olson as a contributor. Tom, one of the best known writers of Christian tracts in the world, and incidentally my sister Marie's husband, can find the Lord's message in all the news events of the world, and tie news story and message together in a way that has to be read to be believed. The little publication has been a revelation to me. Thanks to the Lord's messages, its free circulation outside of our organization began to grow from the start, and currently reaches more than 600,000 readers all over the world twice a month.

The growth of the publication has been startling enough, but just as astonishing to me was the reaction to my own column. When I am talking to my engineers, or the men in the plant, or even to an audience of strangers, I can make myself understood, or I can back off and give it a second try. When you're writing a column twice a month for several thousand readers, it's all there in cold type, and you can't even hem, let alone haw. Put down a mistake in grammar, and then read the letters to the editor. "You would think," wrote one, "that a man of Mr. LeTourneau's standing would be able to hire a graduate of kindergarten to edit his column for him." Some of the other comments were less kind.

Well, the readers were justified in their complaints. My columns *were* poorly written. At the same time, they were my columns, expressing to the best of my ability what I had to say. They still haven't captured any prizes in journalism, but there has been a noticeable improvement in the tone of the readers' letters. I can't say what an English professor would have done for me, but I do know that when you are writing for a few hundred thousand critical readers you soon learn to apply yourself to writing correctly.

Another project that began small concerns a more direct approach to getting the people of our company acquainted with God. I suppose it began with my refusal to work on Sunday so my men would have a chance to go to church. Then I began to notice that we had a lot of fine fellows who had heard about the Lord, and thought He was Somebody they would like to get around to meet someday, but they never seemed to get around to doing it. So I decided that every time I could get a good speaker with a spiritual message, I'd bring him out to the shop or job to meet the men. Then I got the uneasy feeling that if I, as the boss, told the men they had to listen to these talks, I'd be doing an injustice to both God and the men. Maybe I'd be giving the Lord a captive audience, which in some cases would be a resentful one, but worse, I'd be giving Him captives when He wanted seekers. "Seek ye first the Kingdom of Heaven."

To solve this problem, I arranged for my "shop-talks" during working hours, and the men could either come to hear the speaker or stay away. An interesting note here is that while some would prefer work to "sermonizing," after listening to their fellow-workers discuss the speaker later, their own curiosity would bring them around to the next meeting or the next.

What I really wanted was a full-time plant chaplain who could devote all his energies to the spiritual welfare of his fellow workers. But when I brought this up at a staff meeting, I was warned of the fate of other companies that had tried to extend their influences into the lives of their employees. Invariably the employees had resented what they considered an "invasion of privacy," and reacted by claiming that what a man does on his own time is his own business. No one can agree with that more thoroughly than I do, so I dropped the program. Once again I was forgetting to consult the Lord. It was His word that an industrial chaplain could spread; not mine. Oh, yes, I've heard, "Your chaplaincy program must help the morale of your company," and I am more than happy to testify that it does, but that is a natural by-product. We are seeking first the Kingdom of God and His righteousness, and He adds all the rest.

Not until 1941, with World War II upon us, and the armed services seeking chaplains for their men, did I realize how foolishly timid I had been. If the men in the armed services needed spiritual advisers and showed no hesitancy about admitting it, why should the men in industry supporting the armed forces be denied the same aid? At once, I found chaplains for my plants in Peoria and Toccoa, and I've been thanking God ever since. We call it "Christianity with its sleeves rolled up," and I am eager to testify that it is a very effective way of bringing peace among men because it begins with their daily work.

In the meantime, the few brief testimonies I had given in Peoria had brought in invitations to speak in adjacent cities. The fact that my own business was growing so fast that I was spending up to 18 hours a day at the shop made it all the more important that I accept the invitations. With the Lord bringing prosperity to my side of the business, certainly I had to do all in my power to carry on His work.

At first, as my speaking engagements took me further and further afield, I traveled by train, lugging my work with me in a big briefcase. To my surprise I found that, freed from phone calls and interruptions, I could do more work while traveling for the Lord than I could in the office. On the other hand, I quickly learned that train schedules and speaking schedules rarely coincide, and either I was meeting myself coming or going, or I was spending more time between trains than I was on them.

Then one Sunday I found myself sharing the platform with Dr. Harold Strathearn, one of the most popular speakers of the day. Together with his wife Dorothy, known and loved all over the country as the Gospel Nightingale, he preached in as many as 30 churches a month. After the meeting I asked him how he managed to keep his engagements and train schedules straight.

"Well, of course we don't have a big factory to run," he said, "but even so we did find ourselves with conflicting engagements now and then. We finally had to set up an association in New York to plan our itineraries and schedule our speaking engagements so we could reach the most people to do the most good."

Oh, boy, was that what I needed! The result of that meeting was a merging of our forces and the formation of the LeTourneau Evangelistic Center, with offices in New York, under auspices of the LeTourneau Foundation. From that time until Dr. Strathearn was summoned to be with God in 1950, we worked so closely that never once did I find myself with two engagements too far apart to reach on schedule. I will say, though, that we had some tight squeaks, not even Dr. Strathearn being able to cope with my pet peeve—our strange time zone lines and odd local ordinances on daylight saving time. And I must also add that as he scheduled more and more speaking engagements for me, I had to buy first automobiles and then airplanes to keep up with them.

Before I took to the air, however, I had to go through what I call my fourth bankruptcy. As I have pointed out, at the age of 16 I was a moral bankrupt. At 32 I was faced with spiritual bankruptcy. Now I was to face stark tragedy and physical bankruptcy.

On May 30, 1937, my wife and I, together with our company quartet, were driving from Bloomington, Illinois, to Greenville, South Carolina, where we were to take part in the commencement exercises at Bob Jones College. Peter Rutschman, a fine driver who had carried us safely over thousands of miles in all kinds of weather, was at the wheel. With him in the front seat were his brother Orin and my wife. I was in the back with Norman Dirks and Bill Itzen. It was a fine day, with very little traffic, and by noon we were looking forward to lunch in Murfreesboro, Tenn., still some 12 miles away. Pete and I both saw the other car approaching us at a high rate of speed, and he eased over to give it plenty of room. There was no hint of danger on that straight, smooth highway, with the visibility perfect. What followed still seems incredible. With the distance between us less than 200 yards, the driver of the speeding car turned his head to speak to the women in the back seat. At the same time, the movement caused him to turn the wheel to bring his car into our lane. Pete pulled off on the shoulder of the road, braking, but it was no use. Seeing too late what was happening, the oncoming driver just threw up his hands. We met head on.

Peter and Orin Rutschman were killed instantly, as were the three occupants of the other car. My wife was thrown under the dashboard. My own body served as a cushion for the other two boys, Bill escaping almost unscratched. Through it all I remained conscious, only partly aware of the extent of my injuries. Because my feet had been braced for the impact, my leg bones had been driven into my body like battering rams, shattering one hip socket, fracturing the pelvis, and turning my abdomen into one vast internal injury. In addition, my chest and one foot were crushed and the bone of one leg broken to splinters.

I instructed Bill in easing me out of the wreckage, realizing then how close to death I was. He put me down at the side of the road, returning a moment later with my wife whom he put down beside me. She was unconscious but breathing faintly. Next Bill came out with Norman Dirks and placed him on my other side.

"Bill," I said, "the Lord is very near right now. I want you to see that our six children all go through for God. Those are my only instructions. See that the children go through for God if Evelyn and I go to be with Jesus."

Then I looked up to Heaven, and my words are still with me. "Lord, this could not have happened if You hadn't permitted it, because I know 'all things work together for good to them that love God.' Lord, it's all right with me. Although I may not understand, I have confidence to know that it will be all right."

The shock was wearing off now and the pain was pressing down. At first I thought I couldn't stand it, and then I remembered. "Lord," I said, "You suffered more than this for me. Why should I complain?" His presence was so very real that once again I could say with Job: "Lord, I have heard of Thee by the hearing of the ear, but now mine eye seeth Thee."

In Murfreesboro where we were taken by ambulance, the doctors treated my wife for cuts and bruises that covered her from head to foot. They set the broken arm and collar bone of Norman Dirks. I waited, wondering why they didn't take me into the operating room next. Finally I discovered that they thought I was so far gone that any surgery would only hasten my finish. Right there I began all over again my feud with doctors. I made them take me in there and start assembling me in the proper order. I am sure they felt they were wasting their time, but I was so mad I forgot all about the seriousness of my injuries, a fact that carried me through the long operation in fine shape. I was determined to get well if only to prove them wrong.

Three days later, encased in plaster from neck to foot, I was taken back to Peoria in an ambulance. Ahead of me was the prospect of being in a cast for six months or more, and no assurance that my shattered hip socket would ever support me again. Well, I could still draw and design machinery. The first machine I designed was a stretcher on which I could be wheeled through the factory on inspection tours.

The second machine was something else again. For a long time I had been bothered by the fact that my machines had a lot more efficiency built into them than was being brought out by the track-type tractors towing them. On their big rubber tires they could carry loads at 20 miles per hour as easily as they could at the four mile per hour that was a tractor's top speed. Not only would that make them four times as efficient, but it would vastly increase their effective working range, 4,000 foot hauls becoming as practical as the 2,000 feet then considered maximum.

I was not considering going into competition with the tractor companies. Those boys were too big for me. But I thought if I designed a rubber-tired machine that would pull a loaded scraper at 20 miles per hour the men at Caterpillar would fall over each other rushing it into production. I began to draw. One glimpse at my first sketches and my own engineers thought it was my head that had been more affected by the accident than my legs. Called crazy again, I knew I was on the right track.

21

The Tournapull that I designed in 1937 was a thing of beauty only when it tore into action. Otherwise it looked so ridiculous that tractor manufacturers could not believe I was serious in suggesting it would one day replace their machines. It had a square, ugly snout housing a Diesel engine, a driver's seat, and two huge, rubber tire wheels. That was all.

"Where's the rest of it?" was a question I was asked so often that I came to admire my own patience in not blowing up. My stock answer was, "What more do you want?" but it didn't seem very satisfactory. Everybody knew that a tractor had to have four wheels, or a whole series of wheels supporting a track-type tread. A machine with no front wheels—or was it a machine with no rear wheels?—just didn't make sense to anybody.

Yet all I had done was obey one of the first principles of engineering. I had eliminated all unnecessary parts, and produced a machine that was stark in its simplicity. Of course it was useless when parked with its nose down in the dirt, but so was a tractor useless if it had no equipment to push or pull. In the earth-moving business the machines that do the pushing and pulling, and maybe generate some electricity to power blades, winches, and hoists, are called prime movers. Like the work horse, they have to be harnessed before they can do anything.

All I had to do was harness my Tournapull to a Carryall scraper and up went its snout. With four big wheels on the scraper, it needed no rear wheels of its own. Now it was all pull or push. Steering was accomplished by powering one wheel while relaxing or braking the other. That feature alone gave it an enormous advantage over the conventional crawler or four-wheeled tractor, but the main feature was that the Tournapull could cruise along with a full load at 15 miles per hour and return empty at 20.

Could I interest anyone? Because of my long association with Caterpillar, I called on them first, but not until I had built a prototype to provide me with some actual performance figures. With people of Caterpillar's background and experience, you've got to get your brains turning over before you put your mouth in high, so I wanted to be prepared. I might just as well saved myself the trouble.

"We don't think you have anything," said President Heacock after hearing me out. "Why don't you put it on ice for a while?"

I'm a poor salesman of my own machines, more apt to argue than sell, and maybe I was that way with Mr. Heacock. All I know with certainty was that I didn't get anywhere with my Tournapull.

I was pretty crushed when I got back to the shop. I thought I ought to have sold harder. Then I remembered the story of the visiting preacher who had primed the empty collection plate with a new dollar bill before going up to the pulpit. At the end of his sermon, he found the usher waiting for him with the collection, still amounting to only one new dollar bill.

"Well, Reverend," said the usher, "if you'd put more into it, you'd have got more out of it."

If I had put more words into my talk with Caterpillar, I might have got more words back, but the answer would have been the same. But now, I thought, there was a difference. Maybe I hadn't sold Caterpillar, but I sold myself.

I still wasn't thinking of going into the manufacture of prime movers in competition with the big tractor manufacturers. Still the time had come to stick my neck out again. Like Eph Hahn when he complained he couldn't do any better work as a muleskinner than the mules they give him, my machines couldn't do any better work than the tractors that powered them. If they were to realize their potential efficiency, I would have to give them the prime mover to produce it.

I'd like to add to that statement. Back in 1934 I was a fair-sized consumer of oxygen for my welding equipment, but I was neither happy with the service I was getting nor the price I had to pay. I squawked, but it was soon apparent that the big sellers of bottled gases thought it was far simpler for one Stockton customer to adjust to their ways than for them to adjust to his. I saw an endless parade of that kind of stuff, with my suppliers telling me to conform with their products. I rebelled. It took a lot of time, but finally, with the aid of a German chemist, I built an oxygen plant that not only supplied my own needs but met the requirements of enough other customers to cause some hasty revisions of policies and prices amongst the big distributors.

I've carried that on ever since. In my business the best is none too good. I know in many instances I can buy mass-produced electric motors, relay switches, gears and even steel plate and steel cable cheaper than I can make it myself, but in every instance I would have to sacrifice something of my machine to make it conform to the limitations of the mass-produced item. To cite just one instance, I bought a highly ingenious control panel and fitted it to one of my big Tourna-pulls at Toccoa. It worked fine, giving the operator greatly improved control over his machine until the steering button he pressed snapped off under his thumb. The machine veered sharply and headed for the embankment of the Southern Railway on the main-line between Atlanta and Washington, D.C. Working desperately to regain control of the machine, the driver snapped off four more buttons. I will say that when he hit the embankment he gouged out quite a chunk before the far rail hung him up.

By the time we had flagged down one express train and block-signalled the rest, we had a lot of explaining to do to the railroad. My operator granted he had been heavy-handed when he snapped the control buttons, but that didn't let me out. Earth-moving is a heavy-handed business, and I couldn't expect an operator to press his control switches with the delicacy of a church organist. Nor could I blame the maker for selling me a control panel that had proved itself capable of handling other people's equipment. My choice was clear. Either I limited the size and scope of my machines to the mass-produced parts I could buy cheaply, in which case we became an assembly plant of other firms' products, or I built my machines the way I wanted them built, and backed them up with component parts built by myself to my own specifications.

That was what I did in 1938 when I put my Tournapulls into production. I was out to provide my own machines with a prime mover that would lift the lid on their present slow pace and let them perform the way I thought they should. And I want to tell you I was the laughing-stock of the trade. But recently I had the last laugh. At the 1958 Road Show held in Chicago, exactly 20 years after my failure to interest anyone in my "monstrosity," eight national manufacturers were represented by eight different versions of the Tournapull. I was flattered, of course, at the laudatory words they had for their models of my machine, but they had caught up to me 20 years too late. My own machine, with every wheel containing an electric power house, could carry as much dirt as three of theirs combined.

The excitement of creating the Tournapull was just what my body needed to knit all my assorted bone fragments together and get me out of the plaster cast months ahead of the doctors' forecast. I've been told that if I had obeyed their orders and stayed in the cast longer, I might have avoided my present limp. My own idea is that they were trying to keep me there until I solidified, and I think I escaped just in time. My limp hasn't slowed me down any for normal business, and for tours of my factory I use a motor scooter that has speeded me up some.

For the record, our sales leaped from two million in 1935 to $6,246,846.05 in 1938, of which $1,412,465.68 was net profit. With this return we were able to put the LeTourneau Foundation on firm footing, and do some constructive work for the Lord. Along with contributing to several churches and missions, we bought beautiful Camp Bethany on Winona Lake, Indiana. It had a large hotel for girls and modern cabins for boys, and there Evelyn was the housemother and supervisor for 200 kids a week during a three-months' season, a practice she kept up for the next ten years when she resigned to take over two homes for boys in need of Christian guidance. My own work for my Partner was equally rewarding.

One day I was on the speaker's platform of an auditorium in Omaha, Nebraska, with Dr. R. A. Forrest, President of Toccoa Falls Institute in Georgia. I had never heard of him or his institute before, but when he spoke I heard a fascinating story. Back in the twenties he had gone into the back hills of northern Georgia on a preaching tour, and had been so impressed by the young people who hungered for the Lord but had no means of advancing themselves that he decided to stay and give them an institute at which they could learn and earn, and come to know the Lord. With his life-savings he had bought the old Haddock Inn of Toccoa Falls for $25,000 and started out with a few students and just enough work to keep them self-supporting. He was in operation only long enough to prove his institute was a vital force in the community when the building burned down. Undaunted, he started over, the students doing most of the work of rebuilding the institute, and often dropping their tools to attend class in the very room they were working on. As you can imagine, his was the kind of educational program that would make a strong impression upon me.

After giving our testimonies, I learned that Dr. Forrest was spending his sabbatical year on a tour of the world visiting the missions headed by graduates of his institute. From Omaha he was on his way to Seattle and thence across to the Orient. Three or four days later it belatedly occurred to me that he probably didn't have much money, so I rushed off a check to him for $1,000 in the name of the foundation, asking him to use it where it would do the most good. I thought that would be the end of it, but a few months later I received a bale of receipts accounting for every dollar and the cause for which it had been spent.

By this time I was using a single-engine Waco airplane to fly to my speaking engagements, so when I found myself in the vicinity of Toccoa Falls, I instructed my pilot to drift over that way. It was rugged, mountainous country, all right, but if it was economically backward, it wasn't with any kind of backwardness that a little modern industry couldn't cure. And maybe do a lot for modern industry while curing itself.

I had a long and revealing talk with Dr. Forrest, in the course of which I agreed to support him with foundation funds. I was so impressed, in fact, by the practical way in which his students earned while learning, and learned by earning, that upon my return home I sold my oldest son Donald on enrolling there in the fall.

Now there was something else bothering me. My Peoria plant was overflowing its 23 acres, and the nearest local site for expansion was ten miles away.

Why not a plant in Toccoa, Georgia, served by the main

line of the Southern Railway? I was told why in no uncertain terms by everyone I consulted. There were no skilled laborers there. If I brought in my own skilled laborers, there was no housing for them. If they lived in tents, there were no dairies, vegetable markets, or any other sources of supply. No churches, no recreation, no nothing, but hills.

It all sounded fine. For several years I had felt the need of plenty of hills on which to test my equipment. As far as skilled labor was concerned, the best men I had were the ones I had trained in my own classes. As for the lack of housing, I had just invented an all-steel, prefabricated house that could be welded together in a jiffy. (Later, because concrete was cooler in summer and warmer in winter, I invented a machine on ten-foot wheels that could be fed concrete and lay family-sized houses like a chicken lays an egg.) As for the lack of schools, churches, recreational centers, dairies, and general supplies, what a benefit and blessing it would be to a community when a modern industry brought all those things in.

My next step was to design a factory. Up to now I had designed some radically new machine tools to build my radically new machines, but even my so-called, ultra-modern glass-and-steel addition at Peoria had pretty much followed conventional factory planning. What I wanted for Toccoa was a factory that would be in itself a sort of super-machine tool, implementing all the machine tools within it. For the walls and flat roof I designed some panels made out of one-eighth-inch steel plate measuring four feet by eight. These panels, welded together, had enough rigidity to make them steel trusses in their own right. Added to that, their brightness so reflected the Georgia sun they were practically heat-resistant. With my walls and roof all but self-supporting, I could use the interior columns that normally supported the roof for jib cranes spaced 50 feet apart. The trusses that normally gave rigidity to the whole now became tracks for overhead cranes and monorail conveyor systems while the roof panels gave rigidity to them.

Most of the key men who had helped build the Peoria plant in the spring rains of 1935 went down with me in November of 1938 to work through the winter rains of Georgia. Our scrapers built railroad sidings, highways, and dumped two mountains into a valley to create an airport. The bulldozers cleared land, and we started a big truck farm. We bought a herd of Jersey cows and built a dairy. The cranes hoisted up the factory, 400 feet by 400, and then turned to lifting twenty prefabricated steel houses and a dozen large dormitories into place. In the meantime we began hiring and training 400 local men, and by July we were a self-supporting community, complete with our own telephone company, radio station, and public utilities.

Reported the July 11, 1939, edition of the *Atlanta Constitution*:

> TOCCOA FACTORY IS DEDICATED TO PRINCIPLES OF CHRISTIANITY—GUIDANCE OF GOD IS IMPLORED FOR A $2,000,000 PLANT
>
> BIG GATHERING OF FRIENDS AND EMPLOYEES CHEER DEDICATION IN REVIVAL-LIKE ATMOSPHERE

Continued the news story:

"The strangest pact was recorded on a hilltop outside this North Georgian mountain city of Toccoa when a multimillionaire builder of road machinery dedicated his new factory to the guidance of God and His Son, the Saviour of Humanity.

"Between four and five thousand men, women and children leaped to their feet again and again to cheer while R. G. LeTourneau, America's foremost creator of road-building machinery, pleaded with them to join with him in helping God to solve the man-made problems of today's world by the simple means of honest work and brotherly love."

It was a long and flowery story, and I appreciated it, but why were they still calling my partnership with God "the strangest pact"? They could see the results with their own eyes. It was a working pact, and the only thing strange about it is that others can't always see it as clearly as I do.

To carry on the Lord's work in Toccoa our foundation was able to add a new dormitory to Toccoa Falls Institute, permitting Dr. Forrest to double the enrollment to 400 students. In return I got the help of fine young Christian students as they earned and learned their way through school. Another example of mutual aid is the Lake Louise Hotel and conference center. It was designed by Evelyn, and has seven wings radiating out from a circular auditorium capable of seating 1,700. It is on the shore of a beautiful lake that, when she began planning, wasn't there. It came into being because I had to test some big machines, and rather than just test them uselessly, I turned them loose to build a highway and dam across a branch of the Tugaloo River. I learned all I needed to know about the machines, and in return we got a 185 acre lake that provides a recreational area and a splendid setting for God's conference center.

There is an odd twist to the story of the tests we ran on those machines. Some time before we had tried roller bearing in our big wheels with highly satisfactory results under testing. In the field, however, the bearings couldn't take it, cracking under the strain and grinding themselves to powder to the vast damage of the wheel, not to mention my reputation. Now we were running friction tests on Timken roller bearings, and they, happily in the nick of time, proved to be the solution. Friction, as I often point out in my talks, is the chief enemy of the mechanic. It destroys more than half a machine's power while at the same time destroying the machine itself. But if friction is bad in a machine, it is worse between man and man. The worst form of all, bar none, is friction between man and God.

In 1940 the world was full of that friction between man

and God. Men in Germany, and Italy, and Japan were setting themselves up as gods in their own right, super-beings who would lead the way with no need for God's guidance. From that stemmed the friction between man and man, and from that came World War II. Historians may provide other causes, but in every instance God's Word would have led the way to peace had not petty men thought their word was bigger than His.

When that happens, and God's Word is defied, I'm one to say His way must be defended. But in 1940, in the peaceful hills of Georgia, I had no idea how useful my little friction tests would be when friction between man and man nearly destroyed the world. Who had ever heard of a scraper or bulldozer as a prime weapon of war?

22

As a dirt-digger, I probably knew less about the tactics of war than any man going. At the same time, not even the masters of military tactics knew the strange turn to earth-moving that the war would take. The turn, in fact, began almost unnoticed with the bombing of Pearl Harbor. When the Japs all but destroyed the fleet in the harbor, they also paid special attention to Hickam Field, turning it into a chaos of bombed runways, wrecked planes, and burning hangars. Yet minutes after the attack, out lumbered a weird assortment of earth-moving machines, neglected by the enemy as a worthless target. While bulldozers and cranes cleared away the wreckage, scrapers powered by Tournapulls filled in the bomb craters on the runways and aprons, packing and spreading the dirt so swiftly that the planes that had gone into the air to challenge the attackers were able to return to their own base. There was nothing spectacular about that. The machines were only doing what they were supposed to do, and always had done.

What *was* spectacular was when the dirt-movers weren't there. When our warplanes returned to find their bases bombed out and no place to go. Then the boys could bail out or try crash-landings, always at a fantastic cost in machines, and too often at the tragic cost of young lives. From air bases all over the world came the call for more earth-moving machines, both to build new bases and to stand by to repair the damages of air raids. To the Sea-Bees, the bulldozer was the prime secret weapon of World War II.

Almost simultaneously came a similar call from the Army. It had retreated as far as it was going to retreat, and now it was going to fight its way back from the ends of the world. The big difference between the logistics of retreat and advance was that they had had roads to retreat on, but now every road, railroad, and bridge once held by the enemy in any part of the world had been destroyed or left heavily mined as he retreated. Suddenly our troops were faced with the need of building their own roads across the width of North Africa. They had to build roads from India across Burma to China, across every major island in the South Pacific, and through the wilderness of northern Canada to Alaska. This was the greatest dirt-moving project the world has ever seen.

At the very onset of the war our family suffered a loss that brought us close to all the other families who were to suffer as we did. On August 19, 1940, our oldest son, Donald, was killed with his companion in the crash of his light plane near Canton, North Carolina. He was rushing some spare parts from our plant in Georgia to a customer in North Carolina. He was an excellent pilot, and except that one weather report placed a local squall in his vicinity, we have nothing to account for the cause of the crash. What added to our hurt was that he had just graduated from Toccoa Falls Institute that spring, combining his graduation with his marriage to Wilma Morris. And after their honeymoon he had gone to work with me on the construction of a one-million-pound press designed by himself for the shaping of equipment parts. It is still in operation.

With that loss in mind, you can be sure I was eager, and at times frantic, to spare as many families as I could a similar loss. Yet I seemed to be thwarted at every turn. No sooner would I train a new batch of men than the draft board would send them overseas "where they are more needed." I was glad I was turning out trained operators for the armed services, but if I couldn't have men to build machines, what would the trained operators have to operate? Then the Navy discovered my rubber-tired cranes were just what the aircraft carriers needed for clearing the decks after crash landings. I had to start another assembly line and boost production again.

Every manufacturer of peacetime products who had to convert for war experienced the same difficulties unless he had a product that could be made by elderly or draft-exempt men. I had jobs for those men, too, but I also had some key jobs that needed young men as strong as bulls, as agile as squirrels, and with the intelligence and coordination of fighter pilots. To further confound matters, my machines required high quality steels that the priority boards thought should be allocated to tanks and weapons. "But nothing can move until earth-moving machines break the way," I pleaded. "Even a tank has to stop if the gasoline and ammunition trucks can't follow with supplies." Finally the men in combat, to whom this fact was obvious, got the word back, and steel began to move my way.

In my battles to get men and supplies, I was just another manufacturer standing in line with other manufacturers fighting the same battle. I heard all their stories, some of which sound pretty funny now, but I still think my own matches any. I was instructed to enlarge my facilities to produce more earth-moving equipment and shells. But under no circumstances could I get any high-priority material with which to build the required addition. For a while I seriously thought of going back to the old days in Stockton and opening up on a vacant lot.

At this point I remembered a supply of thin steel plate I had bought before the war when I was thinking of going into the manufacture of prefabricated steel houses. I asked if it was all right to use that, and was told to go ahead, though no one could understand how I could build a factory with it. They just didn't know what an old welder can do with steel plate.

Now I announced that I was going to use it to build a factory on the Mississippi River. Again some red tape, the argument being that I should build the new factory adjacent to the Toccoa plant for easy interchange of parts. Since the interchange of parts was going to be limited, the new factory being independent of the old, I pressed the advantage of Mississippi River transportation of heavy equipment for overseas shipment. Ten miles south of Vicksburg, at the bend of the river where General Grant had once anchored his fleet, was what I considered an ideal site. Big hills all around for the testing of my machines, and a vast expanse of bottom-land in front.

"But you can't build down there," I was told. "Every time the river floods, that land is ten feet under water."

After my years as an earth-mover, statements like that get tiresome. I turned some scrapers loose, and they hauled a hill down to fill in a factory site ten feet above the highest flood mark, in the meantime leveling enough land to provide space for first a trailer camp and then a colony of prefabricated houses.

While the scrapers were busy building a railroad and highway to the site, we started work with our thin steel plate, described by one welder as "tin plate from a can factory." We didn't have any trouble about deciding how high to build the factory. At our disposal was a new crane I had designed for the Navy still undergoing tests. It had a maximum lift of 32 feet, so 32 feet was the height of the ceiling of our factory. And talk about necessity being the mother of invention. Our steel wall sections were so light in weight that instead of welding them to the steel frame of the factory, I just put electric motors at their tops, and on good days, and always during the hot summer, we had but to press a button to swing the wall sections up like garage doors and let the fresh air sweep away the heat and smoke.

Our one serious lack was of enough steel for an overhead crane. That also meant I had no steel for trusses to give the factory the necessary strength to hold it together. This I solved by welding strips of scrap metal to cross members made of welded tubing, producing a truss that exceeded my expectations. For half the weight, I got twice the support. Some years later, when I had more time, this led me to believe that if half the weight of a normal truss gave me twice the strength, then no truss at all would give me four times the strength. Toying around with that idea, I invented an aluminum semisphere 350 feet in diameter and 85 feet high that is supported only by itself, at a cost, I might add, of two dollars a square foot of floor space as opposed to the conventional ten to $20 cost.

Long before the Vicksburg factory was finished, we were turning out 155-mm. shells at full capacity, rain or shine. So far, so good, but when we got our machine tools and electric welders going to turn out scrapers, bulldozers and cranes, we so overtaxed the local power supply that industries up and down the river went into a brown-out every time we got everything rolling at once. And even with a high priority we couldn't get a generator that would power our plant. Finally we uncovered an old gas-powered generator discarded as obsolete when a small town had modernized its electric power plant before the war. With that installed we were in action again, but only temporarily. It was a vindictive creature. When overloaded, it didn't just heat up and quit. It would fill the smoke stack with unfired gas, and then blow off the stack and half the powerhouse roof. Joe Marsicano who ran the thing didn't mind the explosions now and then, but he hated patching the roof. We finally solved the problem by synchronizing the motors of eight Caterpillar tractors to run my largest generators, a trick we were going to have to resort to again when I opened my factory in Longview, Texas.

From the start we had one advantage over most manufacturers. While others had to stand in line to get the component parts they needed for their whole, we had become so accustomed to making our own that we had no difficulty worth mentioning. And thanks to our reliance on welding, we could even design and build our own giant presses by machining and welding together chunks of scrap metal.

We had no time to rest after getting Vicksburg in operation. The quickest way to get earth-moving equipment to our island-hopping troops moving north from Australia was to build our machines in Australia. As early as 1938 Jo Johansen had surveyed possible factory sites around Sydney with the invaluable assistance of George E. Bryant, a manufacturer located in Rydalmere, New South Wales, some 13 miles up-river from Sydney. Australian restrictions on the import of American machinery had made expansion in that direction impractical at the time, but the needs of war had eliminated those restrictions. Now, with Bryant as managing director, we organized LeTourneau (Australia) Pty., Ltd., with our company supplying 75 per cent of the capital and Bryant the rest. Down to Australia went Al Losch and Jack Fremon, men who had been with me since my early days in construction work, and up went a factory covering 12,000 square feet. As usual, factory construction and factory production went on simultaneously. In 18 months the plant had grown to 81,000 square feet, with production climbing to some $3,200,000 for the year. All machines, of course, were destined for the U.S. and Australian forces.

In the midst of this growth I designed some improvements we wanted built into the Australian machines at once. With a spy scare on, however, I was advised not to send down any blueprints that might be valuable to the enemy if stolen. Our answer to that was to make up a batch of blueprints filled with misleading lines and false figures, and then send my son Richard down to straighten things out on arrival. That job done, Rich went to work training the U.S. Engineers in the use of our equipment, a job he liked so well that the next I heard from him, he had joined the 3013th Engineers. As a tech-sergeant in maintenance, he accompanied the machines from island to island under combat conditions all the way to Japan.

Back home we had to get our satisfaction at second-hand from reports brought to us by speakers returned from the front lines. Like the shop speech made by Col. H. A. Montgomery in 1943, after the African campaign. Our seaport of Bone, most easterly of our North African ports, was being bombed daily by the Germans. "It was a pay-target," he said, "so much so that a decision had been made to close the port unless air protection could be provided against constant bombing."

What they had to have, he went on to relate, was a fighter base from which planes could rise to meet the enemy at a moment's notice, but, "The only area near Bone that could by any stretch of the imagination be called flat was the delta of the Seybouse River, pure mud 18 feet deep. We knew the mud was that deep because thousand-pound bombs dropped by the Germans had dug enough craters to do our surveying for us. But we had one possibility. On one side of the delta, piled against a rocky slope, was a huge dune of beach sand. If we could get that across the river and pack it into the mud, we'd have a foundation on which to lay a steel-mat runway a mile long."

He paused, and boy did I wish I had been there. When the engineers got in the bulldozers and scrapers, they didn't even bother about the river. They just filled it full of sand and made a causeway to the mudflats. Then they went to work. Said Col. Montgomery, "In nine more days we moved 66,000 cubic yards of sand to form a thick blanket 150 feet wide over the runway length. As fast as the sand was dumped and spread, we laid on a surface of steel mat. On the last day a B-26 bomber, driven far off course by a storm, was coming up on the coast, so low on fuel that all the pilot was hoping for was to get over land before ordering his crew to bail out. Then below him he saw what he later described as the longest runway he had ever seen in Africa, and by far the most welcome. When the pilot got the ship down, he didn't have enough gas to taxi off the runway."

You can imagine what a story like that did for our morale.

Then there was General Carl Spaatz telling us about five airports built in three days at Kasserine Pass. From there he sent the crews on ahead to build six more bases. Five days later he ordered his air squadrons forward, confident the bases would be ready. They were, though they had been under constant bombardment from the start. Said General Spaatz to our plant audience, "The engineers are building bases faster than we can occupy them."

On D-Day in Europe, as on islands in the Pacific, the bulldozers wallowed ashore to push aside the tank traps and barbed wire, and then rush, with upraised blades fending off machine gun bullets, to storm pill boxes, burying the fire slits under tons of dirt and smothering the gun crews that refused to flee or surrender. They sliced through the hedgerows of Normandy, cut new approaches to bombed-out bridges, plowed through the debris of bombed cities, and had a field day tearing up the dragon's teeth, gun emplacements, and concrete pill boxes of the "impregnable" Siegfried Line. One bulldozer, we were told, did the work 1,000 men did with shovels in World War I.

Then the atomic bombs on Hiroshima and Nagasaki ended the war in two flashes.

Every manufacturer of war equipment had to revise his production schedule overnight. We had it a little rougher. From Pearl Harbor to V-J Day we had turned out for the armed services some 10,000 Carryalls, 14,000 bulldozers, 1,600 sheepfoot rollers, 1,200 rooters, and 1,800 Tournapulls. It was a figure we were proud of, but now we could look at it ruefully. Most of those machines, including scores that had never been uncrated, were war-surplus items, ready to work for peace as hard as they had for war.

As a businessman, I had some other figures to look at. In 1940, on a sales volume of $10,740,846, we had realized net earnings of $1,858,229, or 17 per cent of sales. Because we did not want to profit on what was a world catastrophe in human lives and misery, we had so pared down our earnings that in 1944, the last full year of the war, we showed a sales volume of $42,209,624 and net earnings of $2,151,739, or 5.1 per cent of sales. In the amount of time it took the auditors to add it up, those earnings were lost in the cost of changing back to peacetime production, and we faced a market already saturated with our own machines.

23

Across the river from our Vicksburg plant, behind the Louisiana levee, we had a 5,000 acre proving grounds that offered us a little bit of everything except hills and rock. Such parts of it as weren't covered by scrub pine, sycamore and gum were covered by live oak on the high spots, and swamp on the low. As a veteran land-leveler with machines to test, I thought first of clearing it to see what it could do in the way of cotton, with a couple of thousand acres more by way of grassland for beef cattle.

But when I turned some four-wheeled, rubber-tired bulldozers loose against the scrub pine, toppling the trees over at the rate of four miles an hour for later burning, I was taken by another thought. I was combining the ancient art of felling trees with the equally ancient task of stump-pulling. Why not add to that a means of stripping the trees of bark and branches, and turning out peeled pulp-wood by the carload?

With that, I started looking around. If the earth-moving side of our business was to be faced with a glutted market of war-surplus machines, we needed to diversify, preferably in a heavy-duty field that could use the kind of big machines I liked to build. Right off I hit pay dirt. According to the latest figures available, in 1944 the United States had turned out 15,000,000 cords of pulpwood, and Canada had supplied 8,000,000 cords. Since that was the year of the great paper shortage, with newspapers drastically reduced in size, it was obvious that the future was going to require the movement of tremendous mountains of wood. And moving mountains was our business.

Further investigation was even more encouraging. Timber cutting methods, whether in pulp or the giant redwoods, were little changed since Paul Bunyan put his blue ox to work. In fact, the lumbering business stood in 1946 about where the earth-moving business had stood in 1919 when I moved into it.

If the war had taught us nothing else, it had taught us how to design machines overnight to meet special purposes. One such machine had been a high-speed truck for off-road duty, the main requirement being that it be capable of carrying 75 tons. That machine, on tires three feet wide, I now redesigned as an off-road pulp wood transporter, figuring that if it could carry a carload of wood out of those Louisiana swamps, it would work anywhere. It breezed away with its load so fast that I designed another to carry two carloads. And once you get on the track of something good like that, there is no point in stopping if there is bigger work to be done. From that transporter grew machines with electric wheels up to ten feet high. One wades out into ocean surf to straddle and pick up crippled landing craft for the Army, its submerged motors breathing through schnorkels. A Sno-Freighter on 24 giant electric wheels, designed for Alaska Freight Lines, Inc., carries 150-ton loads through ten-foot drifts at temperatures 50 degrees below zero. Another—but we'll come to that.

Now that I was thinking in terms of lumber, I saw several

more machines in need of an inventor. Why leave stumps to impede the movement of logs and machines? I designed a tree saw with a blade ten feet in diameter to cut trees flush with the ground. The diamond-hard teeth, spinning at 170 mph, could cut through root buttresses, trunk and dirt at the rate of one, four-feet-in-diameter tree a minute while an overhead boom directed the fall of the tree with lumberjack accuracy. The same boom could push the trees over, roots and all, if there was no objection to root holes, and the same saw, pivoted to vertical position, could cut the fallen trunks into logs.

To pick up the logs I didn't have to invent anything the elephant hadn't already invented for me. With his two tusks and trunk, he had long been used in jungle countries for picking up and carrying logs. My mechanized elephant, with two trunks instead of one, could pick up one log or a truck load. Today, on electric wheels, the log stacker can pick up a whole carload of wood in one bite. With the logging train emptied in a minimum of time, it then sorts and decks the logs according to size and kind, and in the meantime keeps the sawmill supplied with the requirements of the day. In short, it has become what one lumberman described as a one-man mill pond. Now the mill can go to where the logs are instead of being tied to where the water is.

Next I saw a need for a logging arch to do what Babe, the blue-ox, did for Paul Bunyan. Something big and powerful to skid the logs out of hitherto unreachable places. But why one log? Why not a whole truck-load of logs? So I invented an electric logging arch to bunch up logs as much as 48 feet long, lift their front ends off the ground with cable winches, and skid them out of roadless valleys or down mountain sides like you could drag a half-dozen fence posts behind your car.

While I was in the midst of designing machines that would prove of value to the lumbering industry, our sales department discovered we were still in the earth-moving business. We knew, of course, that during the war years our highways, rail-roads, airports, docks, waterways, irrigation systems, and city water reservoirs had deteriorated sadly, but at most we figured on a giant repair job, with our war-produced machines fairly capable of taking care of it.

I don't think any industry was prepared for what the repressions of five years had done to the American public. And all of those repressions suddenly were concentrated on the earth-moving business. It wasn't enough to patch the chuck-holes in a highway and take up where we left off. And our commercial airports. There was no point in repairing runways built for twin-engined aircraft if they were too short for the four-engined aircraft developed during the war. The "Big-Inch" pipeline that had been the pride of the oil industry before the war was now looked upon as something on par with a garden hose. The reservoirs around big cities, once regarded as magnificent engineering achievements, were now considered to be small-town mill ponds, and city lawns could be sprinkled on alternate days, or weeks, or not at all. Then there were the navigable waterways, the irrigation ditches, the rural electrification systems, the docks and jetties, the open-pit mining of iron, copper, and coal—the list seemed endless, and all were in urgent need of up-dating. And all of these required the movement of dirt.

Abruptly we were faced, not with the job of repairing the nation, but of remaking it.

There was another factor that caught the earth-moving industry by surprise. Contractors had always been conservatives, leaning heavily on the old tried-and-true ways while dabbling cautiously with the new. But after seeing or participating in what the armed services had done in the way of moving dirt, they were ready to take off from there, their traditional ways forgotten. What was more, they had thousands of service-trained engineers, like the boy who looked over one of my new machines and said, "Yeah, we had to put up with that during the war because we couldn't get anything bigger. Is that all you've got?"

With that, I want to tell you, one R. G. LeTourneau went

back to the drawing board and into action. My biggest scraper, from Tournapull nose to tailgate, was 75 feet long by 22 feet wide, and weighed 40 tons empty. With its 165 horsepower Diesel motor it could pick up 50 cubic yards of dirt, roll away with it at 15 miles per hour and dump and spread it like a housewife spreads soft butter. I decided it would do for my medium-sized scraper and settled down to see what I could make in the way of a big one.

You will recall that among the first machines I ever built was a self-propelled scraper with an electric automobile motor in each wheel. It had moved at the ponderous rate of one mile an hour, but it had moved, and I had never forgotten it. From time to time, as my electric motors increased in power while being reduced in size, I had tried fitting them into wheels, but had always been disappointed. Now, with the tremendous advances we had made in motor design during the war, I thought it was time to try again.

I was deep into my plans for the electric wheel when I was brought face to face with an even more urgent problem. First, last, and always I am a designer of machines, and details like finance, advertising, and sales I prefer to leave in the hands of specialists in those fields. Every now and then, however, I am reminded that I am the president of the company as well as the designer, and then I have to back off, straighten my necktie, and size up the situation. This time the urgency was pleasant. Thanks to the thousands of men who had been trained on LeTourneau equipment during the war, and wanted more of the same in peace, we had to have another factory.

I had a lot to consider, and time to consider it in. In building a plant in Peoria, I had wanted central distribution along with closer association with Caterpillar whose sales offices represented me around the world. The latter motive was no longer valid. The "ridiculous" Tournapull that Caterpillar had told me to put on ice, having proved itself during the war, was no longer ridiculous. Caterpillar was working on its own version of a two-wheeled prime mover, and under the circumstances saw no need of using their sales offices to place my machines in competition with their own. And just to warm matters up a little, as long as I was making prime movers, Caterpillar saw no need of refraining from making a scraper that bore an uncanny resemblance to mine. I couldn't blame Caterpillar for at last seeing the light any more than I could blame my other competitors who were doing the same thing, but it did put me on a spot. Without sales representation around the country and the world, I had to start from scratch setting up my own sales and service centers.

Then there was my factory in Toccoa. There I had learned that a big factory could carry the Word of God and testify to His power in an area hitherto neglected, and not lose one ounce of efficiency. Vicksburg had proved the same thing while at the same time providing a deep-water port. Rydalmere, born of the necessities of war, was carrying both the Gospel and American industrial methods to Australia in gratifying fashion. From my experience in setting up all these new factories, what did I want next?

You see? There it was again. After all these years I was still asking what I wanted next without asking the Lord what He wanted.

More than anything else, I wanted my own steel mill. For one thing, I was through with castings. From now on I wanted to forge the heavy-duty parts of my machines, replacing with forged strength the inherent brittleness of castings. Since these parts came in scores of shapes and sizes, I needed my own mill in which to prepare the billets for forging, one very good reason being that even if I could get a steel company to prepare these special billets for me at enormous cost, I didn't want to wait six weeks for a rush order to be filled. I am one of those who, if he gets an idea for a 100 ton capacity crane hook, wants to see it lift 100 tons first thing in the morning.

For another thing, my machines required all thicknesses of steel plate, from bulldozer blades to roof panels, and all kinds of alloys from the hard steel in saw teeth to the tough steel in rooter teeth. And then there were the big items such as no one else made, like the huge elephant trunks on my log stacker, and the five-feet-in-diameter pinion gears, and rack gears up to 30 feet long. All told and everything considered, I needed two or three electric arc steel furnaces where I could cook up special alloys like a housewife cooks up a three-course dinner, and I needed a rolling mill that could turn out steel plate a foot thick or as thin as roofing. The question was where to locate.

The congested steel centers were out. I needed several thousand acres just for my machines to roam around on while they proved themselves. And right at this point the Lone Star Steel Company of Daingerfield, Texas, built during the war, was beginning to prove that some of the rusty soil of East Texas was loaded with iron if you scratched deep enough. And Texas was a state with a lot of room. I dropped some inquiries and got some replies so fast I thought they had been shot at me. Carl Estes, publisher of the Longview *News and Journal* and a lifetime exponent of East Texas as one of the few places in the world fit for human habitation, was inviting my wife and me over for a personally conducted tour of inspection. If we located next door to a going steel mill, then I wouldn't have to build my own.

We flew over. Immediately Longview made a favorable impression on me because it had a good airport. Then we took off with Mr. Estes for the flight to Daingerfield. The wheels were scarcely up, and we were still circling to get on course when we flew over an array of white buildings covering nearly a section of pine-studded land.

"Harmon Hospital," explained Carl. "During the war it held nearly three thousand convalescent patients. Now it's closed, and the government has it up for sale. Of course it isn't anything you could use for a steel mill."

Evelyn and I looked at each other. Those white buildings amongst the tall pine. A small lake in one corner. The large administration building. I picked up the airplane phone and instructed the pilot to circle the hospital grounds again. Then we went on to Daingerfield, finding there a steel mill ready to supply me with almost anything I could want. I'm afraid I wasn't very enthusiastic. Evelyn and I were both thinking of those white buildings in the beautiful setting.

"What a place for a school," said Evelyn when we were at last back in our hill-top home in Vicksburg. "You're always talking about a technical institute to carry on where your shop classes leave off. Don't you think——?"

I was thinking. Our own children, as they progressed, were going to Toccoa Falls or Wheaton College in Illinois, both of which stressed the Christian way of life along with higher learning in the humanities. But what was there for the boys who were mechanically inclined? There were several wonderful schools, including all the state universities, where a boy could get a fine technical education if he and his parents could afford it. But there were no technical schools founded on the earn-while-you-learn plan. Put all this in a good Christian environment——

As Evelyn and I talked about it, the whole plan seemed pre-arranged. Maybe I had gone out hunting for a plant-site adjacent to a steel mill, but the Lord had something else in mind. He wanted a school in which to train Christian engineers, and let me build my steel mill adjacent to it.

After that things moved fast. Through the cooperation of Mr. Estes, a program was presented in Washington for converting Harmon Hospital into LeTourneau Technical Institute, with specific attention being paid to veterans desiring a technical education under the G.I. Bill of Rights. It would be a nonprofit organization under the direction and support of the LeTourneau Foundation. So enthusiastic was the approval of this program that buildings and grounds, valued at some $870,000, were turned over to the foundation for the token payment of one dollar down, the only provision being that in the event of need within ten years, the whole was to be returned to the government for its original use as a hospital.

Fortunately, that need never arose, and the Institute, grown to an enrollment of more than 400 students, is now fully accredited, with four-year courses leading to degrees in a wide variety of technical subjects. As I have mentioned, several industries, as well as our own, cooperate in providing the students with practical experience and earning power to accompany their classroom work. Of interest here is the number of married students we have, earnest students who might otherwise have had to sacrifice their educations in order to support their families.

The factory site, located on the southern edge of Longview, provided us with 12,000 acres of proving grounds, much of it heavily wooded bottom land between the factory and the Sabine River. The factory itself, because we no longer had to cope with war shortages, is so arranged that there is scarcely a foot of floor space that cannot be serviced by overhead cranes or jib cranes. Lathes, milling machines, flame-cutters, and assembly departments are all so laid out that no alterations are necessary, whether scrapers, transporters, log stackers, bulldozers, jungle crushers, or even electric mules are progressing through the assembly line. If some special item, like a 200 ton side-dump truck or a 250 ton crane boom, has to be rushed through, the same machines, torches, and men just railroad it through without batting an eye. When occasionally a few machine tools do have to be moved, cranes sensitive enough "to thread a needle," meaning they can raise, lower, or move tons with one-thousandth of an inch accuracy, just shuffle them around as a housewife moves furniture for sweeping.

The 88,000 square-foot steel mill that I still slip out to watch whenever I get the chance, is just a couple of hundred yards behind the main plant. For it I designed three electric arc furnaces, each of which can produce 25 tons of molten steel every three to four hours, depending on the kind of steel being cooked up. A special feature of their welded construction is that when a heat is ready for pouring, electric motors pick up a whole furnace, raise it above a 30 ton ladle, and then tilt it forward to pour out its molten contents like pouring coffee into a cup. Then it settles back in its saddle, opens its big mouth, and an electric-powered bucket rams in the next 25 ton charge.

Right beside the furnaces is a 144 inch plate mill that can take the heat-soaked ingots and roll them into heavy slab, or into steel plate 12 feet wide by 40 feet long. If some special alloy is necessary, we can pick the assorted steels out of the scrap pile in the morning, cook it up, and have it served red-hot over in the main factory in about the time it would take an outside supplier to inform us that we'd have to wait three weeks for the order.

Through all this, neither Evelyn nor I was neglecting our Lord's side of the business. During the winter months, where somehow she picked up the name of "Mom," Evelyn served as house mother for the boys at the institute, one special problem being the young wives who thought their husbands were neglecting them when they studied to all hours of the night. During the summers she ran Camp Bethany at Winona Lake while in the meantime devoting full attention to our own five children. I must explain that in undertaking the establishment of the Institute, we moved from Vicksburg to Longview. There, in what had once been a warehouse back by the pond, Evelyn had made a completely modern home which she refused to let me see until the last wall was papered and the last curtain hung. There we still live, and though our grandchildren now number seventeen, the time hasn't been when we didn't have room for everybody.

My own activities in behalf of the Lord, with the release of war-time restrictions on travel, has also increased. In 1947 I was able to buy, through war-surplus, a Douglas A-26 bomber that, when converted for private use, was capable of cruising at 320 miles per hour. At the same time I was able to secure the services of Royce Barnwell, an Air Force pilot of Longview with several thousand hours of bomber time to his credit. With Barney at the controls of the twin-engined A-26, no place in the United States was more than five hours away, and Europe, Africa, and South America were just sleeper hops. On a Monday night I could give my testimony before a Christian Business Men's dinner in El Paso, a scant hour from Longview. Back home by 11 p.m. after two hours of air time uninterrupted by phone calls or personal visits. Wednesday night in Oklahoma City to give my testimony before a youth rally. Saturday in Lethbridge, Alberta, Canada, for a city-wide revival meeting, and Sunday in Calgary to speak before the congregations of three churches of three denominations. Total flying time, ten hours, or what I once spent in a day coach or in an automobile to reach one meeting. Ten hours with my own drawing table in front of me, a light over my shoulder, the stimulating purr of fine motors, a wonderful sense of floating, and no phone calls. There is nothing like it for perking up your thinking machine. I was doing the Lord's work, and He was giving me the perfect environment in which to be His businessman.

I've been told that in continuing to fly on my rounds, I am inviting the same fate that overtook my son Donald, that if God had meant man to fly, He would have given him wings like the birds. That's ridiculous. In the three million or so miles that I've flown, I've been able to carry the Lord's message to more people than I could have met in three lifetimes of land and sea travel. God didn't have to give us wings to fly. He gave us the mechanical genius to fly further and faster than any winged creature in His realm, and as a mechanic, that is good enough for me. I always say, with the conviction based on the bones I have broken in automobile crashes, that the most dangerous parts of my travels are between airport and hotel, and hotel and church. The air is God's, too, as well as the land and the sea, and His Will will be done no matter where you are. It's a nice thing to know. You are never out of His reach.

24

One day, speaking at the 1951 World Trade Conference, I got going on my favorite subject of production. I said men can have what men produce, and they can't have what they don't produce. Then I went on to say that if you paid every man that labors $1,000 an hour, he couldn't buy a bit more than he is getting now, because he has to produce it before he can buy it. God gave us the raw materials to work with for nothing, and there is plenty to be had if we go to work and produce the things we want.

In terms of world trade, I pointed out, the raw materials cost less than 1 per cent of the finished product. All of the rest of the cost is in wages, sales, and distribution. Some of the richest countries in the world in terms of raw materials, like the jungle areas of Asia, Africa, and South America, are the poorest economically because they don't produce enough of their raw materials to live on.

"Now my suggestion is that those of us in world trade, like

me and General Motors," I said, raising my size a little, "should buy finished products from these countries. I'm not saying I can set up a factory in the jungles of Africa and start turning out scrapers and electric motors right away. But with some of our machines and our know-how, we could set up a plant where we could teach the local people how to wind an armature, or machine a few parts, or perform any number of jobs easily learned. In that way they would be worth what they produced, and not just what they took from their resources. We manufacturers would then collect the finished parts and ship them in our machines. We would make a profit on the deal, and the backward nations would be encouraged to build up their economies by learning how to produce more and more. It's a sure vaccination against the smallpox of Communism, and a practical demonstration of the power of Christianity."

I hoped some good would come of my talk. In my own right, I was already looking around for an opportunity to start such a project. I had, in fact, already encountered some resistance among missionaries I had talked to, who thought my program was much too commercial to be Christian. However, through the missionary work of my sisters, and the Joneses, and many other friends of the Christian Missionary Alliance, I was long familiar with the difference between a rice Christian—one who hung around the mission professing his love of God for the free rice and clothing being handed out—and the working Christians. And through my own work at Peniel Mission in Stockton, I knew the difference between a professional mission stiff who sang psalms for his supper and the working Christian in need of a helping hand.

A few days after my talk, some Point Four men who had heard it invited me to Washington to repeat it before representatives of several tropical nations. I was only too glad to do so, adding this time, "If we can teach the local people to use machines, they can help themselves. One machine in action, producing goods, will show them more in a minute than they can get from books or lectures, or motion pictures in years."

In talking like that, I was only repeating what I had heard first-hand from missionaries and from my own men who had accompanied my machines to various corners of the world. I didn't know how abruptly I was to be plunged personally into the whole project, head over heels.

Among the men who had heard my repeat performance were the Washington representatives of the Republic of Liberia. They called on me in a body the next day. They had, they said, an undeveloped jungle country that corresponded exactly to what I had described in my talk. Had I had Liberia in mind? Well, when you are stuck, you had better admit it rather than try to bluff it out with people who know better. I didn't even know where Liberia was.

I was enlightened immediately. Liberia, on the western bulge of Africa just north of the equator, was a republic put together more than 100 years ago largely for the purpose of providing a homeland for hundreds of freed American slaves. In spite of the fact that the original colonists were of African descent, they had faced the hardships of colonists everywhere. The native tribesmen resented them as English speaking turn-coats, and refused to accept them or their Christian way of life. The result was that the Liberians of American ancestry banded together in such coastal cities as Monrovia and Cape Palmas while the interior remained the domain of savage tribes, some of which practiced cannibalism.

Not until the 20th century did Christian missionaries get into the interior in strength enough to produce lasting results. And the results they did produce were pitifully small. They were doing good for the natives, in itself such a full-time job that only rarely could they teach the natives to do good for themselves.

"Won't you come over and see for yourself?" one of the delegates asked.

"I sure will," I said before I had time to think it over.

247

From a practical point of view there was no way in the world I could take time out to go to Liberia. Several urgent deals were hanging fire. What was more, gnawing at my mind was the idea that as an earth-moving man I had neglected the oceans that covered most of the globe. I was continually finding my thoughts straying to marine structures and deep sea vessels, all of which I had come to consider as obsolete as earth-moving and logging machines before I moved in.

But when I got down on my knees in Washington that night, praying for guidance, there was no question about what my Lord wanted done. That wonderful and familiar voice, like something heard through earphones on a clear night high above the ocean, said, "Of course you will go. This is the challenge of your life. This is what our partnership is all about."

When my Lord says, "Go," I am not one to dally. With Barney at the controls, we flew over to Africa. In Monrovia, after several conferences with the progressive-minded President Tubman, recently reelected by what amounted to a unanimous vote, we began a tour of the Texas-sized nation. All told, from seacoast to the mineral-loaded mountains of the interior, we touched down at nine missions and every other place of consequence. The picture was both dismaying and encouraging. On the one hand was the inertia of centuries where the semi-savage natives had never done productive work and saw no need to start now. In one village I found babies starving while nourishing bananas grew all around. Why? Because the devil-doctor there said they were poisonous, and don't ask me why devil-doctors say what they do. I was so indignant that I started out to smash all the ju-ju signs in the vicinity, and above all I was going to plant my 200 pounds in the devil's chair and crush it.

That's what you can do when you're impulsive and don't know any better. It took the missionary and about eight of his best converts to dissuade me, and even then I was stopped just short of sitting down in the devil's chair. I know now that had I sat there without any advance preparation, my life and the fate of the whole mission would have been brought to an abrupt conclusion that night. Before you can substitute a new way of life for the old, you have to prove that the new way of life is better.

How best to employ my machines and my know-how in a country like Liberia? Firestone was in there successfully proving the country could produce rubber. Several European countries were in there to develop the mineral resources, especially the iron ore back in the hill country. The big need was for roads and railroads through the "impassable" jungle, and for cleared land on which to raise crops. What struck me as odd was that in a jungle-covered land, lumber had to be imported, and on soil as rich as any in the world the natives couldn't raise enough rice to feed themselves. With my earth-moving and logging machines, road-building and land-clearing looked as though they were jobs made to order for me.

There were several experts ready to discourage me on the idea of setting up a sawmill and lumbering off the jungle. "For every tree worth cutting for lumber," I was told, "you've got 100 that are valueless. You might have an ironwood here, and a quarter-of-a-mile away you might find a valuable white mahogany, and still further off an ebony, but by the time you've smashed a road through to them and hauled them out, they'll cost ten times what they're worth. No, Mr. LeTourneau, unless a commercial tree grows on the bank of a river, you can't afford to go after it. You just don't know our jungle."

Maybe I didn't know the jungle, but they didn't know my machines.

I asked another question. "Why, on this rich soil, can't the natives raise enough food to live on?" Again they told me that I didn't know the jungle. As fast as a native could clear land, they explained, the jungle would spring up behind him. At best he could keep cleared only a small plot for his rice and cassava, and even that would be taken over by the jungle between planting seasons. Then, instead of enlarging his field, he would have to start his endless battle over. Of course he didn't work very hard, but again the jungle was to blame. After a long "hungry-time" between crops, he was too mal-nourished to put out much physical effort. That was the way it had always been. That was the way it would always be.

Again they didn't know my machines. "But you can't use your machines," I was told by men who should have known better. "One of your bulldozers costs $5 an hour, or $50 a day. For that amount you can hire 100 natives at 50 cents a day each."

From what work I'd seen the natives produce, I knew my bulldozer could do the work of 500 of them, and do it better.

On the strength of my survey, an arrangement was worked out with the Liberian government whereby I could lease a half-million acres of land fronting on Baffu Bay and extending inland along the Sangwin River to the foothills, and pay a reasonable rent on the land as fast as it was developed. Since no outsiders can own land in Liberia, the lease was made out for 80 years, a term, as President Tubman told me, "ought to be long enough for both of us."

The program I outlined was four-pointed. *One:* By supply-ing the natives with machinery and training them in its use and maintenance, we would help them help themselves.

Two: We would establish a model village to be called Tournata, complete with electric lights, short-wave radio, air-port, anchorage facilities, hospital, school, and non-sectarian church, to serve as a guide to higher living standards.

Three: We would engage in a land-clearing for the ultimate production of crops and livestock shown by experiment to be best suited to the locality.

Four: By word and example we would teach the Christian way of life, and through the training of local pastors extend God's Word to the villages of the interior.

If I seem to have put teaching the word of God last, it is not because it is not at the top of the program. It is because, as a practical businessman, I wanted the natives to see the power of God at work in their own lives. Once they had seen

His power in better housing, food, and medical care, the spiritual rewards of knowing Christ would be eagerly sought. Maybe a lot of heathens have been converted to Christianity while slowly starving to death, but my own idea is that God, as the great Creator and Producer, would like to have that side of Him shown, too. If our missionaries since the time of Christ had to suffer and starve with their converts, I am sure it was not from choice. If they had had the machines to improve living standards, they would have welcomed them. It would have been un-Christian to keep their converts starving when there was a better way out, and now that we have the machines, it would be un-Christian not to use them for the betterment of humanity.

That brings up again the question of commercialism that I still hear from time to time. I'll let you judge for yourself. On July 19, 1952, the first shipload of material was sent to Tournata from Vicksburg. Billy Graham gave the address and dedicatory prayer. On board were my son-in-law, Gus Dick, and daughter Louise to head up the project, along with their three children. With them were a crew of engineers and technical assistants, missionaries, and Janice Hoffer, R.N. For equipment they had a tree saw, Tournadozer, Tournapull with Carryall, a portable sawmill, crates of prefabricated jungle houses, electrical generators, short-wave radio, water purifiers, freezers, and all the rest of the items needed to establish a small town.

In the seven years since then, we've learned a lot. For one thing, while the bulldozer and Tournapull are powerful, the jungle is more so. There are some trees in there five to eight feet in diameter and 200 feet high that just will not fall over when a bulldozer pecks at their roots. When confronted with a situation like that, established thinking would have you believe the trees are too big. My own thinking was that the machines were too small, and once the problem becomes as simple as that, you build a bigger machine. I built what we call a jungle crusher.

In its current version the jungle crusher looks like a giant steam roller, with its front and rear rollers studded with ax blades. It is 74 feet long, 22 feet wide, 19 feet high, and it weighs 280,000 pounds. Two big Diesels generate the electricity for my motors mounted inside the rollers and for the motor steering. But let me tell you about it, because as a means of opening up the jungles of the world, I think this machine is as important as any I've ever built.

It rolls up against the jungle wall, a horizontal guide bar catching the tree trunks 19 feet above the ground. You think it will have to stop, but suddenly, in your steel and mesh-enclosed cab, you see the wall collapsing ahead of you. The noise of tree trunks cracking is like the scattered reports of rifle fire. Overhead the ripping and snapping of vines and branches almost drowns out the roar of your Diesels. The guide bar relentlessly forces the trees to fall straight ahead. But, and this is an important point, just as the roots are about to be wrenched out of the ground, the ax-bladed roller reaches the base of the trunk, shattering it and forcing the severed, splintered roots back into the earth for mulch. Now the jungle crusher, rolling like a tugboat in surf, mounts the fallen trunks, and its overwhelming weight and ax blades crush them to pulp. So vast is its power that against a jungle of trees four feet thick and 150 feet high, it crushes them like corn stalks at the rate of four acres an hour.

But every now and then you come up against one of those jungle giants so big that what you can see of the trunk looks like a solid wall. Now, you think, you've got to stop. But the guide bar crushes through the thick, spongy bark, and begins to slide up the slippery trunk. The ax-blades of the roller reach the base of the tree and start chewing their way upward. The whole machine just rears up like a dinosaur, the back roller pushing and the front roller pressing forward with all its power and weight. Something has to give, and so far it has always been the tree. Slowly and grudgingly, and with a terrific crashing noise, but down it comes. Inside the cab, the shock when the giant hits the ground is about like that inside the wheelhouse when high surf drops a landing craft on the beach.

During the dry season, where the crushed matting left behind by the machine is thick, it can be burned off as a blanket. Where it is sparse, it can be bunched in windrows with a bulldozer. By the time the rainy season comes around the land is ready for planting with no plowing necessary. After that it is only a matter of deep disking—I've got a beauty of a machine with disks six feet in diameter—until the dead and buried roots have turned to soft mulch, and your conquest of the jungle is complete. For tree crops like citrus fruits, coffee and rubber, our experimental acreage has shown that not even that much work is necessary. Our one problem has been that Texas oranges and grapefruit over there grow so big that they break down the trees before they can ripen.

Now it so happens a jungle crusher like that costs in the neighborhood of $200,000, a price that all the Liberians in my neighborhood could never meet in a lifetime of working at 50 cents a day. The bulldozers, sawmill, earth-movers and modern living facilities add up to much more, but it is not my purpose to act as a Santa Claus and keep supplying one lucky area with new machines as fast as the old ones wear out.

As my jungle crusher cleared land, it spared all the timber of commercial value. On either side of the clearing, it smashed trails through to make accessible other valuable trees. The sawmill went into action, and I had to invent a shallow-draft, three-keeled, twin-propellered freighter to haul lumber to various Liberian ports. In the meantime the cleared land is not only producing food for our own rapidly growing colony, but is producing a surplus to help the economy of the country. Our model poultry farm will open up an entirely new source of eggs and meat, and we are now going to experiment with disease and tse-tse fly-resistant cattle. We are also looking to the sea, wealthy in fish, that the natives in their dug-out canoes have scarcely touched.

Of course it is commercial, and the faster our colony can pay its own way, the quicker it will be able to help other colonies do likewise. With three or four colonies flourishing, the rate of modernization will be tripled, and my feelings will not be hurt a bit if the new colonists want to buy my machines to step up their progress.

"Oh, you dreamer you," I've been told. They don't understand. My faith is not in dreams but in God. You should see some of the boys who come to us straight from their thatched-hut villages in the jungles where their ancestors have lived for centuries. They see what we have and they are awed. They are told that God created it and they want to know God. Within a year they have shed the inertia of centuries. Their bodies have filled out on good food. They are healthy, alert, and eager to learn more of the Lord and His mercy that made it possible. Maybe they are only working as sawmill helpers between classes in school, but they see others from their village only a year or so ahead of them already driving bulldozers. They see others still more advanced doing semi-technical jobs on electric motors and Diesel engines. Ambition replaces lethargy, and they want to do likewise. No one has ever measured the inventiveness that Christ awakens in a man's soul because it is beyond measurement. You may say I am wishing for miracles. That may be so, but if you could come with me to Tournata, you would see the miraculous taking place before your eyes.

25

From time to time as I neared my 65th birthday, I had been approached by several big companies who seemed to think I was ready for retirement at the conventional age. All made enticing offers to buy me out, and I was willing to listen. I am in the business of selling machines, and to me a factory is just a complete machine to turn out finished products like a turret lathe is a complete machine to turn out finished parts. What the bidding companies had in mind, all of them being diversification conscious, was to add a going earth-moving business to their industrial set-ups. What I had in mind I left up to my Lord. If He wanted me to sell and devote the capital—through the foundation He owned 90 per cent of the business—and all my time to His work, I was ready. If He wanted me to build a new factory and continue representing Him as a businessman, I was ready for that, too.

The best offer came from Westinghouse Air Brake Co. A nice round 50 million for everything, with not one of my men to lose his job. It sounded fine until the efficiency experts and market analysts, and production flow engineers got going. Then it turned out that with its existing facilities, Westinghouse Air Brake could do without my Vicksburg and Longview plants and steel mill. The offer was reduced to 31 million.

As a welder who had to buy his first torch second-hand, that still sounded pretty big to me. "But if you are going to leave me with the Vicksburg and Longview properties," I said, "you've got to leave me something to build. I just can't close up the plants and fire all my men there."

Well, the one thing they didn't want me building was earthmoving equipment, so at the end of negotiations that fill a large book with small print, we reached a deal. They would buy my plants in Peoria, Toccoa, and Rydalmere, Australia, along with the rights to all of my earth-moving machines from bulldozers to dump-trucks. In turn, I could use my remaining factories to manufacture any and all kinds of machines that did not move dirt. The restriction on my building of earthmoving equipment was limited to five years. I am sure they thought that at 70 I would have long retired from the battle, whereas what actually happened was that my five years of retirement from the earth-moving business were just what my mind needed to get rid of some rutted thinking and come up with some fresh ideas. Whatever their thinking was, the five years were up in 1958, and my 150 ton scrapers mounted on electric wheels are clear evidence that I have not retired from moving earth.

I will say I never spent a more instructive five years. I know we septuagenarians are supposed to look back at our youth as our formative years, and I did form our company when I was a youth of 41. But actually my first 65 years gave me just the background and training I needed to start rolling. In 1953, with the launching of my Four-point program in Liberia, and faced with the need of inventing new machines to keep my factories operating, everything I had done in life began to add up. My formative years were just beginning.

Liberia and its jungle was a challenge that stimulated a whole line of new land-clearing and logging machines, from the jungle crusher to a self-loading sawmill for handling logs that were just too big to be handled previously. In fact some of those logs were so thick I had to build a double-decked sawmill, with the bottom blade slicing out the lower four feet of a plank, and the synchronized upper blade slicing out the rest.

Then there was my deep water port adjacent to my Vicksburg plant. Being temporarily out of the dirt-moving business, I had time to think about that. Naturally I thought in terms of welded structures—steel barges, floating docks and drydocks, off-shore oil drilling rigs, floating cranes, and shallow-draft vessels. The more I looked into it, the more room I saw for my welding methods and Diesel-powered electrical systems.

And there was my electric wheel that could be adapted to any form of heavy-duty, off-road transportation. Recently I read in a technical journal that: "Accurately predicting the relationships of soil and vehicle on a deformable terrain—of the type encountered in cross-country locomotion—is a complex matter, due largely to the non-homogeneous structure of the soil and the random variation of elevation with forward motion. The problems involved in accurately predicting those relationships have successfully evaded analytical solution for many years." (Daniel Clark in *Research Trends,* Vol. VII, No. 1.) I'm glad I didn't know that when I began concentrating on the production of transporters, log stackers, logging arches, and electric land and snow trains. I'm afraid that non-homogeneous soil structure might have scared me out if I had known what it was, and I know I would have been discouraged by something that has "evaded analytical solution for many years."

In 1953, too, I began my second big Four-point program at the headwaters of the Amazon in Peru. It came about through a meeting with Cam Townsend, head of an unusual organization known as the Wycliff Bible Translators. For many years at considerable peril, as often from headhunters as bushmasters, jaguars, and poisonous insects, this dedicated group has been working in the jungles of Central and South America to translate in writing and preserve on phonograph records and tape all the various Indian languages. Then they translate the Bible into these languages, and so carry the Bible to the natives in their own tongues.

Cam had heard of my Liberian project, and was convinced the same program would work in the jungles of the Amazon on a broader basis. "We still have to carry Christ to the jungle Indians," he said, "but we have another job, too. The eastern foothills of the Andes Mountains are being colonized by several hundred Peruvians. They have brought with them small schools and churches, and law and order, but they need help. They need your machines and your program. Mr. LeTourneau, it will take them 50 years with hoes and axes to do what you can do for them in a year."

It was an enticing picture. Barney flew me down to Lima, and in a series of conferences with President Manuel Odria, a colonization program was outlined and approved. For the government I would complete 31 miles of the Trans-Andean Highway, linking the Amazonian slopes with the Pacific. For its part, the government would grant me 400,000 hectares of land—about a million acres—on the Pachitea River near the town of Pucallpa. The Pachitea, flowing into the Ucayali River, which in turn flows into the Amazon, is considered the head of navigation, though I will say that until I designed my own shallow-draft vessels river traffic was extremely light.

When I first flew over Tournavista, as our colony is named, it was just a part of the solid jungle that stretches from the Andes to the mouth of the Amazon. Its gently rolling hills, at an elevation of 800 feet above sea level, looked like long rollers on a green sea, and the thought of tackling it even with my biggest machines was awesome. My jungle crusher could just roll in there and disappear without a trace.

And the thought of getting my roller there in the first place was equally awesome. Our supply route was 4,650 miles long, from Vicksburg to the mouth of the Amazon and then up river across almost the width of South America, with the upper reaches filled with uncharted sandbars.

Well, there are no big jobs, only small machines, so I designed some bigger machines. Like my tree stinger for felling 150 foot trees in 20 seconds, roots and all. These trees, too thick to be felled with a tree saw, and too valuable as timber to be smashed under the jungle crusher, were a problem until I designed my fast, electric-wheeled stinger with an electrically-powered pusher boom. After that all an operator had to do was roll up to the selected tree, elevate the boom to a good leverage point 30 or 40 feet up the trunk, and push a button. Electric motors would then start forcing an extension of the boom forward with a pressure of a quarter of a million pounds, and that was it. Except that some of those Peruvian monsters seemed rooted in China, and then my stinger would be the one pushed back with all electric wheels churning. I soon found an answer to that. I attached a huge steel blade to the rear of the stinger, and with that blade socked deep into the ground, the stinger was anchored and the tree had to go.

The stinger is winning a lot of friends among contractors who must clear out trees and roots for new highways, and among land-clearers not faced with dense growths requiring a jungle crusher. Another unique machine born of Peruvian necessity was my walking ship, the *Lizzie Lorimer*. This ship has four keels and four propellers for stability on the high seas, with the same four keels providing a wide distribution of weight to operate in water, as one skipper put it, "no deeper than the dew." The fact that I'm proudest of is that it really doesn't need the dew for beaching or crossing sand bars. On each side, amidship, I placed two long steel rams with broad steel feet at both ends. To go forward on dry land, the rear ends of the rams are lowered and they heave and push forward exactly as would a man poling a boat. To back off a beach or sand bar, the front end of the rams, or kickers, are lowered, and a reverse action takes place, even the propellers being reversed, not only to produce a reverse thrust but to send a flow of water gushing forward to flush out the sand or mud in which the bow is grounded.

Today both projects in Liberia and Peru are flourishing. As a businessman I can report that they have required some three million in support from the foundation, and more will be needed. At the same time, as a businessman familiar with development costs, I have never seen any projects more promising. In the short span of six years we have proved that the jungle, unconquered for centuries, can be put to work, and its extravagant wastefulness turned into extravagant production. Yams, potatoes, rice, string beans, eggplant, black-eyed peas, cabbages, tomatoes, citrus fruits, rubber, coffee, cocoa, sugar cane, cotton—all grow to prodigal size. And to my wife's great pride, the Charbray cattle she selected for breeding on our Texas ranch have proved to be great beef producers in Peru.

Today on the banks of the Pachitea River where my son Roy and a dozen assistants landed their machines at the jungle's edge in 1954, there is now a model village with electric power, running water, sanitation facilities, school, clinic, church, airport, commissary, and nearly 5,000 acres under cultivation or in pasturage. The permanent population has grown to more than 500, with other colonists standing by to take up land as fast as it is cleared. North American colonists as well as Peruvians are welcome if they are, in the terms of the contract, "acceptable to LeTourneau and the Peruvian government." To me that means anyone willing to work and anxious to raise the physical and spiritual standards of himself and his fellow-colonists.

In describing the colony to the International Development Advisory Board in Washington, D.C., I said it was pump-priming by private enterprise to the mutual advantages of the nation, the colonists, and the developer. "Sending shiploads of food, livestock and machinery is not the answer," I pointed out. "They have plenty of land on which they can raise more food than we can on ours, so we are providing them with the machines and the training that will help them help themselves. That's what we call priming the pump. But once the well starts to flow, we see no need of more priming. The colonists will become self-supporting, and next they will be buying more machines to continue their progress. Already we've had representatives from many tropical countries who have flown in to study our program, and they, too, have expressed an interest in the machines that made it possible. And since I build those machines, you can see where I come in."

They could see that, all right, but I had to add, "You get right down to it, and that's a hard way to sell machinery. A businessman could not afford to tie up millions of dollars for many years on a missionary project that might or might not work. But God can, and as His helper I try to do His Will, confident that He will help me be His businessman."

It's that simple. And that simply is it working out, though I can't say we haven't been challenged every inch of the way. But where would be the fun of working and designing machines if it was all wrapped up for you in some master-plan that could not fail?

I've never had to face such a monotonous fate. Like the time I designed a sugar cane harvester for Hawaii, the only good of which came when Evelyn and I went to the islands and for once had time to enjoy a honeymoon. Nothing on that machine worked until I got there and straightened out some details. Then it worked fine, but it wouldn't harvest cane. I think it got the idea it was a sugar mill instead of a cane cutter, because it turned out more juice than stalks.

And there was my factory in England, aptly located on Stockton-on-the-Tees, after which Stockton, California was named. I went to England at the suggestion of Dr. Strathearn to dedicate the new factory and join him in speaking before several church and businessmen's groups. To our complete astonishment, the simple tour he had outlined grew into a series of mass meetings at which the overflow audience, reached by loudspeakers, jammed traffic for blocks around. Whether in England or the more staid Scotland, the spiritual hunger was the same, and I was able to give my testimony of the Lord's power to thousands at a time.

But in this case my tour of Great Britain was exclusively on my Lord's side. The factory, built from scratch according to my latest ideas, and equipped with the most modern machine tools and welding outfits, just couldn't seem to get into production. My methods, apparently, were too unorthodox. They had worked in Australia, but manager after manager, including a couple of my best men from the States, could only report disappointment. In the end I had to sell everything and chalk up a half-million loss to that expensive item called experience.

Of course costly experience, if it doesn't wipe you out, turns around and becomes invaluable. For instance, the more experience we got with electric wheels, the more uses we found for them. The Army needed a special vehicle to pick up the huge Corporal missile and transport it from storage areas to launching sites, whether the launching sites be across deserts, the Arctic or battlefield terrain. Right off the electric wheels provided high-speed ground mobility for the giant guided missile. Our experience in building equipment to handle heavy logs made it a simple matter for us to design a loading device that would pick up the missile and carry it piggy-back, softly cushioned by the big tires. Our experience with cranes, hoists, folding spar trees, and all kinds of rack and pinion gears enabled us to engineer a sensitive device that would grasp the missile securely, erect it over the launcher and lower it into position for immediate firing. The same Diesel motors that powered the generator for the wheels powered the generator for all of the other motors needed for loading and for the preparations for launching.

The Army wanted a mobile 150 foot revolving crane for extra-heavy duty work on beaches and off-road terrain, and again the electric wheels and AC-DC electrical systems, powered by Diesel motors, were the answer. It wanted a landing craft retriever to roll out into surf to pick up capsized landing craft and right them, or pick up stranded craft and carry them into deep water. Ten-foot electric wheels were the answer, with schnorkels to let the motors breathe in deep water, along with a complicated array of my old electric cable winches. It wanted a snow train for work on the icecap of Greenland, and while that one was more complicated because of its unusual task, it was not beyond our combined experiences.

Recently, I was notified that the Joint Chiefs of Staff had picked me to receive the tenth annual award of the National Defense Transportation Association as the person whose "achievement contributed most to the effectiveness of the transportation industry in support of national security."

I was pretty flabbergasted, especially after I read the list of previous award winners. William Faircy for his strengthening of transportation defense during his leadership of the Association of American Railroads; Donald Russell for his contributions to the solution of emergency transportation problems; Donald Douglas for his continuing contribution to military and civil air transportation; Charles Weaver for the design and construction of the nuclear power plant for the submarine *Nautilus;* L. B. DeLong for the DeLong Dock which made possible off-shore radar islands; W. F. Gibbs, designer of the *S.S. United States;* and Igor Sikorsky for his pioneering work in helicopter design. The electric wheel has revealed even more power than I thought it had when it can roll me into company like that. I only hope Pinky, who fired me as the least promising newsboy in Duluth, finds out about it.

During all this time I could not forget about the earth-moving business from which I had withdrawn for five years. They tell me time flies, and that the older you get, the faster it flies. Well, I have the answer to that. My five years of withdrawal from the earth-moving business on which I built my career were the longest five years of my life, which maybe explains why I had time to get so much done.

Not that I am not a great believer in the power of youth. I'm so sold on the vitality of youth that all of my children have been moved into positions of responsibility as fast as they are ready. Louise and her husband Gus Dick were in charge of the Liberian project for six years. Roy and his wife Shirley have been in charge of the Peruvian project since its start. Son Richard and nephew Richard are vice presidents of the company. Ben heads the Vicksburg plant. Ted works in engineering with me in Longview. To those not familiar with our organization, such a family arrangement may look like nepotism, but there is a difference that I believe has considerable merit. Through my partnership with God, and with 90 per cent of the business owned by the foundation that is dedicated to His work, I will not be leaving wealth and power as an inheritance. I will be leaving something better than that—a big job to do as businessmen for His greater glory. Evelyn and I find our greatest reward in the fact that our sons and daughter are carrying on that principle with our grandchildren.

In 1958 my five years of exile from the earth-moving business dragged to a close, and I was like a kid looking forward to Christmas. I could hardly wait to plunge back in. I was seething with ideas. I wanted to see that dirt move. True to my word, I hadn't built any earth-movers, but all the restrictions in the world cannot stop a man from thinking, and I had had some mighty big thoughts.

Any one of my competitors' big scrapers, based on my laughed-at Tournapull and Carryall, could pick up a 40 ton load without trouble, and a 50 ton load if it had a tractor pushing from behind. Now it was my idea to replace the free-rolling but lifeless wheels under the scraper with hard-driving electric wheels, all sharing the same power as the two front wheels carrying the diesel-electric system. Boy, with that arrangement, with the front wheels pulling and the back wheels pushing, I'd be able to pick up 75 tons without slowing down.

The day came when we were free to go into production. The steel mill began rolling out steel plate of various thicknesses and of various alloys. Torches began cutting the still-hot plate into all shapes and sizes. As fast as it was cut, cranes and trucks rushed the parts to the factory where welders began pouring whole streams of molten metal into the jigged-up seams. Other flamecutters were turning out thick rack gears 30 feet long, and still others were turning out pinion gears ten feet in diameter. Reported Plant Superintendent, Jim Molpus, "I feel like a kid gluing together a model from pre-cut parts."

We almost did work that fast. We had our first prototype ready for the national mining exposition in San Francisco, and we stole the show. The machine had some bugs in it, but there was one big one for which I alone was responsible. I had only built half the machine. It should pick up 150 tons of dirt. Not a piddling 75.

I went back to Longview and built the other half. That was not hard to do. Just add another bucket and bolt on more electric wheels. You see, with my first 75 ton prototype, the six drive wheels were just getting enough weight aboard to provide a comfortable amount of traction when the bucket was full and they had to quit pulling. By adding another 75 ton capacity bucket, they could use that traction to load the second bucket faster than they had loaded the first while getting an additional boost as the rear wheels of the second bucket settled down to work under the weight of the incoming load.

There was only one thing lacking in the newspaper reports and articles in the technical journals after the writers and photographers had covered my first public demonstration of the new 150 ton earth-mover. No one called me crazy. I was even treated with respect, sometimes overwhelmingly so. Some called me a genius without once qualifying it by adding the adjective "eccentric." Things like that can be upsetting, and they became more so a few months later when the technical journals began announcing the plans of other companies to produce their own versions of the electric wheel.

Always before my competitors had been from ten to 20 years in picking up my "revolutionary" innovations. Now, all of a sudden, they were closing in fast on my electric wheel. Of course I had built my first one a quarter of a century earlier, but with the introduction of my big earth-mover, the scramble was on. Was the new crop of engineers thinking faster? Or was I slowing down? Not liking that idea at all, I thought up a *Big* one.

26

Frequently interviewers ask me what wonders the earth-moving and heavy-equipment industry will produce, and I have a tried-and-true answer. "I don't know what the future holds," I say, "but I know Who holds the future."

That doesn't mean that I am trying to avoid the question, or that I don't try to make some long-range plans to project my business into the future. It means, simply, that in terms of the everlasting life that is God's reward for His children, our plans to prepare ourselves for the next ten, 50, or 100 years are but an infinitesimal part of the future we should really be preparing ourselves for. All too often we are so busy scrambling around to make our worldly future secure that we fight for minutes when we should be preparing ourselves to earn eternity. Only God holds the future, and when you have found Him, you might not know what your future holds, but you will have the blessed security of knowing Who holds you, now and forever.

Some of my machines have been ahead of their times, or at least ahead of my competitors' machines, and I was once introduced as the engineer "who thinks in the future." That's all nonsense. I think I've already mentioned I do my best thinking in a bathtub, and very much in the present. When I was awarded the Frank P. Brown medal of the Franklin Institute, it was for "revolutionary improvements in earth-moving equipment." I like that better. When I get an idea for a new machine, it may be revolutionary in terms of rutted thinking, but it's all right now, and the instant my pencil starts sketching, that machine is of the present even though its road tests may be years in the future.

Like the "overland train" I am currently working on for the Army. This is my *Big* one, nearly 500 feet long, with 13 cars and 52 electric wheels, each wheel being ten feet high by four feet wide. It has several unusual features. The "locomotive" housing the power plants is also the "caboose," being coupled to the rear of the train. Of course, with all my electric wheels being drivers, it doesn't matter to them where the power comes from. The front car, from which the engineer does the steering, has an auxiliary power plant of its own, and what makes it interesting is that only a few years ago I had to hook up two "giant" 300-horsepower Diesels to get 600 horses while this "little" auxiliary whips up 1,000 all by itself. What is more, when the front car is detached from the train, it doubles as an earth mover, snow plow, crane, or any number of machines for which the accessories are provided. All told, the train will carry more than 150 tons of freight in areas such as the polar and desert regions where the supply routes are long, fuel supplies scarce, and roads non-existent.

To develop the power needed for this train I had to break with tradition again, this time discarding the long-popular Diesel in favor of gas turbine engines much like those used in turbo-jet aircraft. Three of these, capable of turning out 1,000 horsepower each, will be in the "locomotive," and the fourth will be in the lead car, serving as an auxiliary when the train is in motion, and as an independent source of power when the lead car is detached for other duties. But the use of gas turbines is only a small part of it. They are but a stop-gap to power the train through its primary testing state. After that it will be powered by atomic energy, probably the first land vehicle to be so equipped. I find a lot of satisfaction in that. From the boy who powered a hand shovel in a foundry to atomic energy in one generation. Maybe others can take for granted the advances of the last 50 years, but I find them staggering. And instead of feeling that recent developments leave little more to be invented, I can see them only as that much more to work with. Truly God moves in mysterious ways His wonders to perform.

Another break with tradition that is opening new fields grew out of my off-shore oil drilling platforms. These platforms, a little more than a half-acre in area, are triangular in shape, and they come equipped with steel legs 175 feet long and longer. When fully outfitted with crew quarters, galley, powerhouse, drilling rig, and helicopter port, one weighs about 9,000,000 pounds. Wherein it differs from other rigs, which must be built at the drilling site, is that the platform also doubles as a barge, easily towed by a tug from one location to the next even though one location be in the Gulf of Mexico and the other in the Persian Gulf. Once at the drilling site, electric motors lower the steel legs to the ocean bottom—about a hundred feet in current instances—and there they plant themselves firmly on broad feet. The electric motors keep right on turning, and since the legs cannot go down any further, the platform goes up, hoisting its 9,000,000 pounds out of the water at the rate of a foot a minute. An hour later, raised above the reach of the highest waves, it is ready to go to work.

The first few platforms I built, I saw as highly specialized machines designed exclusively for the oil industry. But then came the question too often left unasked. If a machine is doing one job well, what else can it do? Once that seemingly obvious question is asked, all sorts of answers come to mind. What about the floating pile drivers and dredges, and cranes that served most of the big harbors in the country and the world? When the waves ran high, often for stormy days at a time, they had to suspend work. But one of my platforms, its legs resting on solid bottom, would provide dry-land stability to all such operations in spite of waves. Press a button and the raised platform would lower itself to become a floating barge in the same time it would take a conventional barge to raise its anchors for the next move.

The net result of such thinking is a platform-mounted crane we are now testing preparatory to shipping it to Venezuela. It's quite a piece of machinery. The boom of that crane can reach out 65 feet, pick up a half-million pounds, lift it to the heights of a 20 story building, and lower the load with split-inch accuracy. Its job—to wade across Lake Maracaibo on its steel legs, planting bridge piers in front of it and hanging prefabricated bridge sections behind as fast as barges can bring up the materials.

We are now preparing for the next step—a bigger platform and bigger crane to operate in fast-flowing water and tidal rips where treacherous currents could undermine the feet of the platform. In that event, the platform would lose its stability as first one leg shifted and then the other, and gone would be the crane's accuracy in spotting its load. It was such a serious problem that we spent weeks in hunting for a complicated answer. When we found it, we could hardly believe it. It is little more than a carpenter's plumb bob suspended beneath the platform. If one leg settles as its footing is washed away, the plumb bob detects the list, be it as little as a hundredth of an inch, and instantly activates the electric motors governing that leg. Be the rate of settlement fast or slow, the motors will match it, and the platform will remain level and stable at all times.

Now let's venture out into water 500 or 600 feet deep. I could say 1000 feet, and eventually platforms will be raised above water that deep, but as a practical businessman, I know we have to develop the 500-footers first. As the first problem, we are confronted with the fact that an acre-sized platform cannot stand on vertical legs 600 feet long. The legs must spread out like a photographer's tripod to be firmly braced against the action of currents, surface waves, and winds, no two of which may be exerting forces in the same direction. We've already got the motors that can pivot the legs out to any desired angle, but we can't move and install those giant legs on a rolling sea. So we're going to build them in sections, and as the legs go down we'll just keep adding more sections to the top, welding them together in minutes. And when the time comes to move the platform, we'll just use our torches to cut the sections apart as fast as the motors can bring them up.

Earth-moving machines will get bigger for many reasons. First they will reduce big jobs to small ones, and change the face of the earth with the canals, waterways, irrigation ditches, highways, and railroads they will make possible. A big machine is more substantial than a small one, and therefore has a longer life, which means the movement of more tons with less depreciation. Then, of course, the cost of your labor goes down because one good man on a big machine can do more than a good man on a little machine. That also means that one big machine causes no congestion on the work site, while ten small machines, not to mention the hundreds of mules I used to see on a job in my youth, are constantly subject to traffic delays. And too, in remote areas like the Sahara, which must be made to bloom, or the jungle areas of the world, which must be made productive, or the polar regions where much remains to be discovered, the big machine is the only answer. In those regions the big cost is not wages but the care and feeding of the men, and with bigger machines fewer men will be needed because one man can produce so much more. I remember when I started in this business two men on a tractor and scraper could move about three tons of dirt at two miles an hour. My new machine rolls away with 150 tons at 20 mph., making its current operator 1000 times more productive than I was. I feel perfectly safe in saying that by the end of this century you will see earth-movers picking up and running away with 1000 ton loads.

But just to prove that my earth-moving thinking is not entirely restricted to scrapers, bulldozers and their relatives, I've got another idea I think may be "revolutionary" one of these days. Back when I was building the Orange County dam and was faced with the problem of moving 400,000 tons of dirt in a month, I used one of the first long-belt conveyors. It was efficient, and it moved dirt in an unending stream from one place to another. What I didn't like about it was that it wasn't mobile, and that it had to be fed dirt by machines at one end, and machines had to carry the dirt away at the other. I saved myself a long haul, but I was sure using a lot of machines as feeders and carriers, plus the steam shovel that dug up the dirt in the first place.

What I have in mind now is a belt conveyor system to move 100 tons of dirt a minute. It will be built in 500 foot sections, and these sections will be mounted on my electric wheels, with each self-powered and independent of the others. The front section will also carry its own digger to chew into the dirt and gulp back its load, to the belt. In a continuous stream the earth will flow from one section to the next. The last section, on wheels that will make it as flexible and as easy to direct as a fireman's hose, will deposit the flow where needed over a radius of 500 feet. No extra machines needed to feed the front end, and none needed for hauling at the rear—just one long self-feeding, self-carrying, self-distributing, snake-like machine to do the whole job. Such a machine would be able to roll across a desert digging a canal and leveling the dirt behind it almost as fast as the water could follow. It could strip mines and transport useless overburden to where it could become useful fill. It could then roll back to deliver the exposed ores, coal, or oil sands to the processing plant so cheaply that it will open up deposits hitherto considered inaccessible, and revive mines no longer profitable to work by existing methods.

The ideas continue to flow. Since my electric wheels don't care where the electricity comes from, we are now producing an ore truck that operates from trolley wires in an underground mine. Brought loaded to the surface, where exhaust fumes no longer matter, it starts up its own Diesel-electric system and roars away, no longer restricted by trolley wires. Not only does this eliminate the transfer of cargo from mine car to hoist to surface truck, but one machine and one operator, doubling in below and above ground transportation, have eliminated all the single-purpose machines in between, and once more made man worth more because he produces more.

If there's one thing I've learned about engineering, it is that if ever you are ready to rest on your laurels, you sit down in a chair that isn't there. You can't, as I was told to do, "put your idea on ice." If it is that good, and you don't develop it first, you can be sure someone else will thaw it out and develop it before you.

I like my plans for an independently-sectioned conveyor belt so much that already I am working on another version that will require no sections at all. There are a lot of currently difficult jobs that call for the movement of a lot of dirt across relatively short distances. I'm just itching to build a shovel with a 25 yard dipper on it that will roll across dry land or swim rivers, the idea being that such a machine can reclaim millions of acres of rich land that are now nothing but marsh or tidal flats. Prosperous Holland is such a country reclaimed from the water, and my machine, traveling through swamps and digging a drainage canal on the one hand, and piling up dikes that will also serve as highways on the other, can do in months what Holland has been centuries in accomplishing. That kind of thinking is often called wishful, but you need it for a starter. Give me a little more time, and see what I come up with.

So now for the final question I am asked most often. "When

you're designing a new machine, Mr. LeTourneau, how do you know you've got a good idea?" The first answer to that is that I don't always know, as I have been frank to admit. But I will say I have learned this about my successful ideas. Every one worth its salt has enabled man to be worth more through producing more.

I can approve of research that leads to rockets to the moon, and men in space, and I'm sure we'll get some good out of cosmic rays, but when the race between our scientists and those of other nations comes up in the course of a conversation, I have a couple of basic questions of my own to ask. "How much have they got to eat? How comfortably are they housed? What assurance have they got of a life eternal?"

I want our abstract scientists to uncover all of God's truths as fast as He is ready to reveal them, but as a mechanic whom the Lord has blessed, I see a limitless need of translating those truths into just plain food, shelter, and the spiritual rewards of knowing Him Who made it possible. I know that in the jungles of Africa and South America the advancements of science make fine reading, but good food, shelter, and the immediate presence of Christ give life its full richness, now and hereafter. I think that is true everywhere.

As I write this, I'm within a month of my 71st birthday. I feel no more like slowing down now than I did 30 years ago when I was just starting to roll. I need seven hours for sleep, and the rest of the time I want to be busy. In the designing, building, and developing of machinery, there's never a dull moment, and that is only a part of it. In the carrying of the word of God to as many people as you can reach by the fastest means available, there are no dull moments either.

Everything considered, I've had my share of ups and downs, but thus far my life has been a miracle of God's grace all the way through. I remember when a man said to me, "I know you claim the Lord does it for you, but I figure you were just smart enough to make machines that would work, and that's all there is to it." I agreed with him that it was that simple, and then said, "But you have to give the Lord the credit for giving me the brains to figure out the machines." Not long after that one of my engineers brought up the same point in another way. "You say the Lord gives you these inspirations," he said, "but I don't think you put the credit where it ought to be." I knew what he was driving at. All of us in the engineering department had been working day and night to whip a difficult problem in leverages, and the boys had crashed through in magnificent style. "Oh, yes, I know where to give the credit," I said. "I fully realize I've got a bunch of men doing the job for me, and I give them the credit for doing it. But I never forget to thank the Lord for sending those good men around to me."

I have learned that God is love, and love wants to be loved. That is why He made us with His attributes, and so gave us the power to love and to hate, the power to choose between good and evil and say "I will" or "I will not." God loves the sinner, but He hates sin. He made the universe, and all living things in it, and pronounced it good, but He wasn't satisfied yet. He said, "Let us make man in Our own image and in Our own likeness." So He breathed into man the breath of life, and man became a living soul. I believe with all the living soul that He gave me that God wanted a creature so like Himself that He could always be in fellowship with him.

That privilege of fellowship with Him is a reward beyond comprehension, but He does not stop there. When you come to love Him and serve Him, then all else is yours, now and forevermore. I believe that when I have done what I can for Him down here, He will change this body of mine "that it may be fashioned like unto His glorious body." *Philippians 3:21.* Not because I was so good, but because the Lord Jesus Christ was good enough to die for me, and I accepted His offer of salvation and have been born again into the family of God. *John 3:16.* That same offer is open to all. No greater can ever be made. Try it. And as I always end my testimonies, "God bless you. Amen."

Epilogue to 1967 Edition

by

Nels E. Stjernstrom*

In 1959, Mr. LeTourneau completed the preceding chapter, and it was with eager anticipation of the future, although he had reached the age of 71. Seven years have passed, bringing him to 78 years of age.

You have read of his machines. His expectation in 1959 of building a machine that could move 150 tons has grown to a machine that moves twice that amount—300 tons. The offshore platform which drills for oil at sea has grown from a measurement of 100-plus feet across the deck to more than 200 feet. No longer are the giant legs 100 feet long, but they are nearly 500 feet in length. No longer are there fifteen hundred employees at Longview and Vicksburg, but nearly four thousand. The school which Mr. and Mrs. LeTourneau founded in 1946 as an institute of technology for men has become a coeducational college of engineering, technology and the arts and sciences, with an enrollment of 700. New dormitories, library, science building, gymnasium, five laboratories, and thirty-six apartments have been completed on the campus.

---

*Assistant to the President, LeTourneau College; Editor of NOW.

One evening in the summer of 1966, Mr. R. G. showed me a large portfolio from which he took a paper and, with enthusiasm that can't be described, began to review the inventions that were begging to be placed on the drawing board. His words, "I want to get them built," are characteristic of him. He has said, "When I visualize a 150-ton crane, I want to see it lift 150 ton the next morning."

I've been impressed with his delight in the very moment in which he is living. He is always less concerned about the particular stage of life in which he is living than with the life being lived in that stage. The past is never viewed as the "good old days" with a wish that they could be relived, but rather with thankfulness for lessons learned and with eager anticipation of tomorrow. As a result, he views time, work, money and contacts with people in a unique way.

Time is precious to him. I've heard him say, "If you waste dollars for me, it's not too serious—I can make that up. But don't waste my time—it can't be recalled." I saw him jotting some things on a small piece of paper one day, so I asked him about it. He told me that he had jotted down what he wanted to get done that day. It was his assurance that things would be done in the order of their importance and that no time would be wasted.

Arriving at an appointment with only two minutes to spare, I remarked about the perfect timing, whereupon he said: "If we'd been here sooner, it would have been too early." He has put into practice the scriptural advice: "So teach us to number our days, that we may apply our hearts unto wisdom" (Psalm 90:12).

When traveling, his brief case is ever with him because it contains work that demands his attention. There is no time for small talk; there is never any time for gossip. His yea is yea, and his nay is nay. But to talk about the solution of a problem, a new idea for an improved machine or operation, the source, course or interesting history of a river or mountain formation over which the plane may be passing, or a

278

lesson learned through some experience of life—for such conversation there is always time.

Time to him is a gift—a precious gift from God—to be treated respectfully and gratefully.

His reaction to work is rather unique. When, after dinner, his wife asks if he is going back to work, he replies, "No, just going back to play with my big toys for awhile." Few of us find our work so captivating. However, he has not allowed this devotion to work to so captivate him that he has left everything else undone. You can count on his being at church for the prayer meeting and on Sundays, or out giving his testimony whenever the opportunity presents itself; but work, as we call it, holds special charms for him. He gives God credit for his special talent, and no doubt this makes him more concerned to be a good steward of both time and talent. He often says he doesn't want his men to work hard—just fast. A bit of humor is involved in that statement, but even the term "fast" has special meaning when used by Mr. R. G.—"fast" in the sense that there is eager anticipation of the outcome, the "joy of accomplishment." He wants to finish the job not just to have it over with, but to rejoice in its completion and to be ready to tackle the next one.

His attitude toward money is also unique. He does not view money as something to be accumulated for the satisfaction of looking at it, counting it each day to check its increase, nor as a measure of a man's worth. He sees it only as a means to produce the machine his mind has conceived or as a means to bring men to God. A suit of clothes, to him, is simply a garment for proper dress; his car, a means to bring him to his destination; his plane, a conserver of time; his office (unbelievably unpretentious), a place necessary to carry out the duties of the day. There are no status symbols in his life; he is too busy to have such concerns. He declares very freely that he does not plan to accumulate wealth to leave behind. He wants to create as much money as possible to build the machines his mind produces and to carry on his Christian work. Although he has made and spent millions, he is remarkably detached from money as such; he is only concerned about what it can accomplish. He often says, "The question is not how much of my money I give to God, but rather how much of God's money I keep for myself."

An unusual example of his attitude toward money was demonstrated when at age 65 he sold two of his factories for 31 million dollars. He held a check for 25 million in his hand—cold cash. He asked himself, "Just how much is twenty-five million?" Did he say, "I guess I really made it; now I can simply take my ease"? No, he did not. He viewed it as the means to perfect his electric wheel and his offshore oil drilling platform. So he spent, as we say, "the whole works." In fact, he almost went broke. Twenty-five million to him was not just *accumulated* wealth, but the means to another "joy of accomplishment." He saw more than his machines. He saw primitive, undeveloped areas of South America and Africa which he wanted to enter, so a sizable sum of money—several million dollars—was invested at Tournata in Liberia, West Africa, and at Tournavista in Peru, South America. There is no way to calculate the spiritual returns on those investments. The story of South America and Africa has also been told in previous chapters.

What of the future in South America? We must wait to see. There are signs of an enlarged ministry. Some of the workers from the States have been there since the work began in the early 1950's. They feel they are a part of Tournavista.

In Liberia, West Africa, the commercial development has been less successful due to high costs of operation, but there is no reason for discouragement, because the original purpose was not wealth but missions for Christ. This past year—1966—after careful study, the commercial work has ceased and all efforts conserved for pure missions. Upon hearing that recommendation, Mr. R. G. said, "Do what seems best. My only concern is that the mission work not be injured." In

1966 I saw the representative of the nearly thirty churches in the jungle which the Reverend Walter Knowles has been supervising on behalf of Mr. LeTourneau, and I was overwhelmed at the results of the work that had been done in training the nationals to do the work of pastors and evangelists. Some of you who read these lines have been partners in the work. Pause now and thank God that you have a part in the salvation of souls in South America and Africa because of that participation.

If you could read the letters received from far and near telling of salvation, encouragement and conviction folk have experienced by reading the monthly publication, *NOW*, and the books Mr. LeTourneau has written about his life with God, you would agree that the dollars spent to produce the books and to send *NOW* free of charge to over 600,000 every month are well invested. Or we might consider the thousands upon thousands who have heard him in his personal testimony. He begins, "I'm just a mechanic that God has blessed, and He has blessed me—a sinner saved by grace."

You will also be pleased to know that the four sons and one daughter of Mr. and Mrs. LeTourneau all love and serve the Lord. This can also be said of their 19 grandchildren. Their daughter, Louise (Mrs. Gus Dick), lives in Moline, Illinois. Her husband is Director of Marketing and Engineering Services for Deere and Company. They are members of Bethany Baptist Church. Louise and her husband pioneered the work in Liberia. Richard, the oldest son, has served as President of LeTourneau College since 1961 and, as of August 25, 1966, became president of the corporation also, when Mr. R. G. stepped from the presidency to the position of Chairman of the Board. Ben, Ted and Roy live in Longview, Texas. They are all involved in the company operation, each in a management position. All the sons are following in their father's footsteps in being not only businessmen but Christian businessmen active in their church responsibilities and frequently traveling to witness for the Lord.

Mr. and Mrs. R. G. celebrated their 49th wedding anniversary August 29, 1966. She has stood with him in all the ups and downs through the years. When he is complimented because all the children are with them in faith, he gives the credit to her. She was faithful as a mother through all his busy years. She has "logged" thousands upon thousands of miles to be with him as he has traveled in his ministry of witnessing for the Lord. She finds ways to combine a bit of rest with a busy weekend. Bringing her own coffee maker, some rolls and other goodies, she "buys time" for him to rest between speaking engagements.

His testimony is always the same, whether he is speaking to a class of men in a small church or before an audience of many thousands. He is thankful that God saved him at the age of 16, led him to fuller commitment at the age of 30, and has prospered him; yet, there have been hard places also, and they have been related lest someone might believe there has been only success and pleasant experiences without discipline and testing.

In December of 1966, a letter came from a *NOW* reader expressing a problem. When reading Mr. R. G.'s testimony of how God had blessed him, he wondered if God was partial by not blessing, in the same way, all who profess Christ. This is a common problem. Mr. LeTourneau told him in a letter that since the day, at the age of thirty, when his little son had passed away and he had dedicated himself to God, never had he questioned God's love. Through all circumstances (even the difficult ones), the thought of questioning God's love had not occurred to him. In that letter, he emphasized that we must *believe*—not just accept the *words*—that "all things work together for good to them that love God, to them who are the called according to his purpose" (Romans 8:28). And Mrs. R. G. shares this commitment to God and understanding of His ways.

Mr. R. G. LeTourneau's message to all who read this is still the same—the words from the Bible which he has repeated to audiences thousands of times around the world: "Seek ye first the kingdom of God, and his righteousness; and all these things shall be added unto you" (Matthew 6:33).

In Memoriam

by Nels E. Stjernstrom

Mover of Men and Mountains was a good title for the autobiography of a man like R. G. LeTourneau. Only eternity will tell how many men and women have been *moved* to accept Christ as their personal Savior—and how many have been *moved* to fuller dedication for service to God.

The year of the original publication of *Mover of Men and Mountains,* in a hardback edition, was 1959. In 1967 it was printed in paperback. The preceding epilogue was added, and thousands of copies have been sold. It is time to reprint and also time to bring it up to date.

When, during the life of Mr. LeTourneau, his book was announced as "the story of his life," he could be counted on to remark, "Not yet." He did not live in the past. Yesterday's experiences were viewed as preparation for what today demanded of him. While looking to the future he always lived in the *now.* He was excited about present opportunities and optimistic about the future.

Of every man it must finally be said, *he was born and he died.* Of some, there is not much more to be said. Of this man, the intervening years were so filled with accomplishments that volumes would be filled if the full story should be told.

Thoughout his life, as he traveled, witnessing for the Lord and conducting his large manufacturing business, he was usually introduced as "God's Businessman." That, in fact, was his commitment when as a young businessman, thirty years of age, he realized that every person, regardless of vocation, was called first of all to full-time service as a Christian.

It was not until his seventy-ninth year that it became evident that traveling and speaking must be left behind. That was a difficult day. His only consolation was that his sons could carry on where he would leave off.

Finally on March 17, 1969, while visiting in California with Mrs. LeTourneau's sister and brothers, he suffered a stroke from which he never recovered.

It was on June 1, 1969, on a Sunday evening at 6:55 P.M., that he concluded his earthly ministry. Surrounded by his loved ones, he bade farewell to them until that day when all whose trust is in the Lord Jesus Christ shall be reunited.

How well I remember those months from March 17 to the first of June. After three weeks in the hospital he came home. There he was happy—he could move about the house and was comfortable among loved ones in familiar surroundings.

As the days passed, we realized that strength was ebbing and memory fading. While he still had strength, he came to the piano; and his spirit was lifted as we sang the old hymns of faith. "Wonderful Grace of Jesus" was one favorite hymn which he sang out as lustily as his condition allowed him. He had another favorite "Until Then," that expressed his love for the Christian life; and even though memory was fading, he would join in to sing the chorus. He would also sing, "There is sunshine in my soul today" and "Let a little sunshine in," plus other favorites. And it seemed that, instead of growing weary, his spirit was lifted; it was good medicine to him.

The book *Mover of Men and Mountains* has certainly indicated his love for his big machines, but when he spoke of this, he always added, "But I must prove to my Lord that I love him more"; and so it must have been, because his last days gave strong evidence that it was the *things of God that endured*.

I remember so well that day when I took him for a ride, hoping to lighten and brighten his day. It was only a few weeks before he left us. Wondering what reaction he would have to his factory and machines, I drove to the factory. Across the front of the building in huge letters is the name "R. G. LeTourneau, Inc." I stopped; we looked around. But there was no reaction—not a word. I continued and drove about twenty miles to a neighboring city, where one of his mighty log stackers was at work lifting entire loads of logs from trucks, moving them to a sorting area, and then stacking them in huge piles. I expected a response, a look of delight, a smile—but again, no response at all. I turned the car and started home, concluding that memory had faded, that a response could no longer be expected. A surprise was in store for me. As we drove along, he turned toward me and softly said, "Window, window." I thought he wanted me to open a window of the car. So, although the air conditioner was operating, I asked if he wanted me to open the window. His reply: "No! No! Window, window!" Suddenly I realized what he was trying to tell me, so I began to sing:

"Let a little sunshine in, let a little sunshine in;
Clear the darkened window, open wide the door;
Let a little sunshine in."*

Upon hearing that, he smiled—a smile of satisfaction. Memory was *not* gone, not his memory of "things that endure." When I concluded, he prompted me in a rather weak, hesitant, soft voice, "Sunshine, sunshine." I knew him well enough to know what he wanted to hear:

"There is sunshine in my soul today,
More glorious and bright
Than glows in any earthly sky,
For Jesus is my light.
O there's sunshine, blessed sunshine,

---

* Charles H. Gabriel, "Let the Sunshine In," in *Simple Songs for Toddlers* (Grand Rapids: Zondervan, 1959). Used by permission.

When the peaceful happy moments roll;
When Jesus shows His smiling face,
There is sunshine in my soul."

While I sang, he tapped rhythmically on the armrest of the car and tried hard to follow. I noted that, though the sound was weak, his lips were repeating those words which represented to this man (who did love his machines dearly) that which endures.

Oh, that we all might adopt his life's verse as our own: "But seek ye *first* the kingdom of God and his righteousness and all these things shall be added unto you" (Mt. 6:33).

His memorial service, held in the gymnasium of Le-Tourneau College, was a triumphant service. The congregation sang with strength, "How Great Thou Art." Reference was made to his unusual contributions to the world, yet each person who participated honored the testimony of his life by giving the glory to God. They kept in mind that he had always begun his testimony by saying, "I'm only a mechanic that God has blessed." Days after the memorial service, people on the streets were remarking, "That was an unusual service! Why aren't more memorial services like that?" Maybe the answer is nearer at hand than we want to admit. As human beings, we tend to neglect balance in life. Young people are sometimes warned against becoming too enamored by success. That is a warning which, if properly understood, is valid. Such an ambition may so imprison a person that all other concerns suffer. On the other hand, lack of discipline, aggressiveness, creativity, or motivation—with the resultant absence of accomplishment—are often excused on the basis of dedication to what is falsely termed spirituality. Those who have read this book, heard Mr. LeTourneau speak, or worked with him, know that through the effective utilization of time, he accomplished in his business what may well be termed phenomenal; yet many men who are classified as full-time servants of the Lord may not reach the level of Christian service which he attained.

Caution must be exercised in this writing lest he should be exalted when that was not his desire. His word to men, especially as he spoke, was, "You will never know what you can accomplish until you say a great big yes to the Lord."

An expression often heard is that the bigger a man's head is, the easier it is to fill his shoes. That being true, it is difficult to fill the shoes of Mr. LeTourneau. It will take many people to step into that place. It sets one to thinking, however, that God may have a plan to honor his dedication. A few months before his death, Mrs. LeTourneau was named Texas Mother of the Year; and just one month before his death, she was selected from all of the state Mothers as American Mother of the Year. This launched her into a ministry of her own, which from 1969 to this writing in early 1972, has seen her appear at various meetings in nearly every state. This speaking ministry was completely new to her. For more than thirty years she had traveled with her husband, mainly to support and care for him, always in the background. At the present time, 1972, serving as president of the American Mothers Committee, Inc., she continues to appear before various groups, with much time devoted to the encouragement of young mothers to dedication of themselves and their homes to God in order to bring up their children to love and serve the Lord.

Every person who has lived a life of devotion to Christ leaves, we believe, a heritage to the generation which follows him. That heritage may vary, depending upon the gifts and resources of the individual. It is sad to realize that perhaps many of us fail through thoughtlessness or negligence to utilize more fully our opportunities and our means. There is no doubt that LeTourneau's vision extended far beyond his days. One evidence of his vision is the college he and his wife founded, where the varied talents in the young people are recognized in the educational program.

His life is extended through this four-year, accredited college. Since he was most at home in the field of mechanics and engineering, it is obvious that engineering would receive great emphasis. Students are fully trained technically but also introduced during their college days to the "touch" of engineering. Think what vision he had for the coming day of increased technology, such as we see now! And he lived to see the college expand beyond engineering and technology to include both a two- and a four-year program for technicians, Bible majors, and persons involved in flight training, the liberal arts, and missionary technology. Thousands of students will go out to witness to the fact that every vocation is sacred when Christ lives in the life of the worker.

Millions will continue to be exposed to the message of the cross through his publication NOW as it circles the world.

His wife, to whom the doors of opportunity for witness were flung open so miraculously almost simultaneously with his death; his daughter Louise and her husband Gustav Dick and their family; his four sons, Richard, Roy, Ted, and Ben, and their families—all are dedicated to the propagation of the gospel he had proclaimed, the gospel of the love and salvation of God to all who believe and accept Christ as Savior and Lord.

Thousands of times to thousands of people, R. G. LeTourneau said, "If you're not serving the Lord, it proves you don't love him; if you don't love him, it proves you don't know him. Because to *know* him is to *love* him, and to *love* him is to *serve* him."

To anyone who has read this testimony of God's grace in the life of a man who recognized his dependence upon the Savior and was so blessed in his fellowship with Christ, this invitation is extended: let Jesus come into your life.

Index

292

293

294